CU00540045

Real
Dorset

To Helen, and for my parents

Real
Dorset

Jon Woolcott

SERIES EDITOR: PETER FINCH

Seren is the book imprint of
Poetry Wales Press Ltd.
Suite 6, 4 Derwen Road, Bridgend,
Wales, CF31 1LH

www.serenbooks.com
facebook.com/SerenBooks
Twitter: @SerenBooks

© Jon Woolcott, 2023
Photographs © Jon Woolcott, 2023
Map of Dorset © Catherine Speakman, 2023

The right of Jon Woolcott to be identified
as the Author of this Work has been asserted
in accordance with the Copyright, Designs
and Patents Act, 1988.

ISBN 978-1-78172-717-1

A CIP record for this title is available from
the British Library

All rights reserved. No part of this publication
may be reproduced, stored in a retrieval system,
or transmitted at any time or by any means
electronic, mechanical, photocopying, recording
or otherwise without the prior permission
of the copyright holders.

The publisher works with the financial assistance
of the Welsh Books Council

Cover photography: Hambledon Hill, by Alamy

Printed by Bell & Bain Ltd, Glasgow.

CONTENTS

WEST

CENTRAL

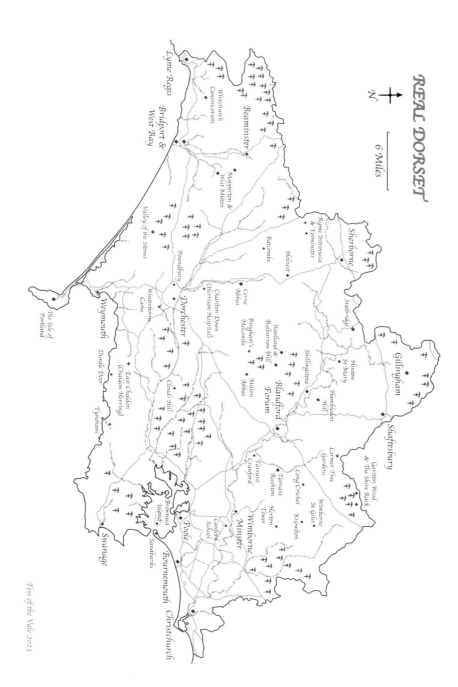

REAL DORSET

N

6 Miles

Lyme Regis
Bridport &
West Bay
Whitchurch
Canonicorum
Beaminster
Mapperton &
West Milton
Valley of the Stones
The Isle of
Portland
Weymouth
Durdle Door
Tyneham
Winterborne
Came
Poundbury
Dorchester
Batcombe
Hilfield
Cerne
Abbas
Charlton Down
(Herrison Hospital)
Bingham's
Melcombe
Ryme Intrinseca
& Yetminster
Sherborne
Stalbridge
Woodland &
Bulbarrow Hill
Shillingstone
Milton
Abbas
Blandford
Forum
Hinton
St Mary
Hambledon
Hill
Gillingham
Shaftesbury
Garston Wood
& The Shire Rack
East Chaldon
(Chaldon Herring)
Clouds Hill
Larmer Tree
Gardens
Long Crichel
St Giles
Tarrant
Rushton
Tarrant
Crawford
Wimborne
Knowlton
Horton
Tower
Swanage
Brownsea
Island
Sandbanks
Poole
Canford
School
Wimborne
Minster
Bournemouth
Christchurch

Tess of the Vale 2023

SERIES EDITOR'S INTRODUCTION

When it comes to county size Dorset sits around halfway between tiny Rutland and giant Yorkshire. At just over a thousand square miles it should be coverable in a few days. But then I arrive and reality kicks in. This county may be only fifty miles wide and forty north to south but doing justice to its maze-like charm is going to take a book.

I'm heading down the A37 to meet Jon Woolcott, place writer, publisher, booktrade navigator, and this Real's author. We've selected Maiden Castle as a site to walk round while discussing how a Real book gets put together. It helps to know your patch and luckily for us Jon has Dorset in his soul. He helps run a bookshop in the county (Little Toller at Beaminster), and knows the byways backwards. "Everything takes an hour to get to" he tells me, and he's right. It's about that in the car from the northern border to the Maiden Castle car park. When I arrive I discover there's just us here amid the dusty earth. The rolling green ramparts of this majestic structure enclose more vacant space than any other hillfort in Britain. The walk round is a launch into emptiness to dispel emptiness as W.G. Sebald might have had it. Neolithic wind ruffles neolithic spaces. Jon talks about the power of borders and the intricacies of the Dorset he's going to write about. It's going to be a good book. After the Iron Age there were Romans here. We pass the place where their temple stood, a stone scratch amid the evergreen turf. With its ley lines and rituals this place has incredible power.

Dorset has a fair share of extant ancientness. The Winterbourne Abbas Nine Stones Circle, the Grey Mare long barrow, Hambledon and Hod Hills, the Cerne Abbas Giant. This latter piece of early Viagra advertising in chalk looked a little faded when I visited but there are plans for refurbishment. It's easy to imagine alternative lifestyles at work in this county. Diggers, hippies, druids, celebrators of the solstices. At Weymouth a steampunk rally is in full swing. Victorian polonaise dresses, brass goggles and pith helmets fill the streets.

There are no motorways in Dorset and dual carriageways are few. Dorchester, the county town, has a ring road and feels twenty-first century but that sensation doesn't last. Along the coast resorts – Bridport, Swanage, Lyme Regis – have barely shifted from their Victorian heydays. Poole and Weymouth are exceptions simply because of their size, while interloper Bournemouth (annexed from Hampshire in 1972) is a stretched-out classic of the English Riviera.

Generally, though, Dorset is a fog of green: slow-paced, labyrinthine, undulating. "The Dorset hills rolled and billowed, like a shaken-out blanket settling on to a bed" is how Bill Bryson describes his visit. He's one of many of the famous who've been here. Most significant is Thomas Hardy who was born here. His "partly real, partly dream country of Wessex" novels name the empty land west of Dorchester as 'Egdon Heath'. His invention, but Egdon Heath this 'uncultivated waste' has by now become.

Dorchester – Hardy's Casterbridge – has as much history hanging round it as Rome. Rome might be an exaggeration, but you get the idea. The town was occupied by the Romans who have left their marks in the form of walls and aqueducts and an amphitheatre they made from the local Neolithic henge at Maumbury. Post Roman this space was used for gun emplacements and later for executions. In the town itself there is Georgian architecture, medieval walls, a Tudor almshouse and the prison where the Tolpuddle Martyrs were held. There is also a recreation of the tomb of Tutankhamun on High Street West. With a population barely topping 20,000 the town can be walked round in about an hour. Dorset tradition.

Hardy is buried in Westminster Abbey but his heart is here, where he wanted it to be, buried at St Michael's Churchyard, Stinsford. Nearby is the grave of the poet C. Day-Lewis whose work was so greatly influenced by Hardy that he wanted to rest near him.

In *The Kingdom by the Sea* travel writer Paul Theroux, who lived for a time in a cottage at Marshwood Vale in Dorset's lost far west, declared Bournemouth to be "a country town that became a city too quickly". "People sat silently in cars, eating bananas, chewing sandwiches and reading the gutter press," he writes. It was somewhat livelier when I went through.

Walker Raynor Winn's life-affirming story of traversing the 630 miles of the South West Coast Path in the company of her terminally ill husband Moth is told in *The Salt Path*. Their walk finishes just outside Poole Harbour. There's a marking sculpture on the edge of the Studland sands. Both Bill Bryson and Paul Theroux tracked through this same piece of coastline. They took the 'floating bridge' of the chain ferry at Sandbanks west from Poole towards Swanage. Both describe the same flat stretch of windblown sand and scrub that forms Dorset's still extant truck with nudism. Beyond are the white chalk sides of gleaming Old Harry Rocks, stared at by lines of tourists, clothed this time.

Nicholas Crane, of the seemingly endless TV travelogue *Coast*, walked the line of longitude known as the Central Meridian over the length of Britain. He describes the adventure in his book *Two Degrees West – An English Journey*. He started at Berwick-on-Tweed and finished at Dancing Ledge on Dorset's Jurassic Coast in the Isle of Purbeck. I visit, just to say I've done it.

Literary works and litterateurs with Dorset origins abound. From dialect poet William Barnes' "windblown heäir, an' zunbrowned feäces" to Elisabeth Bletsoe's linguistically innovative late modernism via John Cowper Powys, Sylvia Townsend Warner, Enid Blyton, T.E. Lawrence, Jane Austen, Julian Fellowes, Ian McEwan. The list runs right on through to Mike Leigh's hilarious Dorset-set 1970s play *Nuts In May*.

I stay overnight in a room on the outskirts of Swanage. This was the place from which Edgar 'Taff' Evans departed in 1910 bound for Scott's Antarctic adventure and death. It's on High Street. There's a plaque. From my bedroom window I can see the harbour, the pier, the whole minor-key Victorian seafront. A newsagents is within walking distance as well as a chip shop. In the town itself, five minutes further, stands a bookshop. I've yet to see a sun parlour, a tattoo shop or a new generation barbers but they'll no doubt be in place by the time you read this.

Round at the arts centre they run record fairs upstairs. There's also a railway station. This, on the revived Swanage Railway heritage line, offers genuine Battle-of-Britain class steam-giant-hauled period rail trips through to Corfe Castle and beyond. It's fun but proceeds at period speed. You could almost walk the distance faster. The whistle blows, the amazingly-wrecked castle ramparts fill with streaming lines of smoke. Down at the tea shop there are still spaces and they serve toast with the butter melted in.

The Isle of Purbeck, this non-island peninsula, lies an hour's drive to the east of another Dorset island that isn't quite – Portland. Here a prison and a Young Offenders Institution sit in a surreal and treeless drift of chalk and sea. The eighteen-mile-long shingle barrier of Chesil Beach that began back at West Bay finishes here[1]. The atmosphere is unworldly. Chesil's pebbles vary uniformly in size as the beach heads south. Smallest at West Bay, largest at Chiswell at Portland's top edge. En route to look at the lighthouse, which everyone does, is the free to access Tout Quarry. Here space has been given to dozens of sculptors who have left their works emerging from the stone including the hard to find but certainly there 'Still Falling' by Antony Gormley.

I'm wearing a Covid mask today, on my own in the car, heading east. Who am I afraid of? Infecting myself? At Melcombe Regis, once a village now a suburb of Weymouth, the Black Death landed in 1348. Sailors are reputed to have brought the plague ashore returning from the Hundred Years War. The country went from slow progression to depopulated devastation. At Melcombe's Custom House Quay they've put up a celebratory plaque. The first Viking raids on Britain happened near here too when the Wessex Saxons under Alfred were the ones who had to cope. Dorset down the centuries has buzzed.

Seren's Real books, of which this Jon Woolcott volume is an excellent example, are not supposed to be guides in the traditional sense. In them you won't habitually find systematic tour routes, walk instructions or details of accommodation, prices and the availability of food. What you will find is a new take on an often over-written place. In 2018 when I tried to buy myself a Dorset handbook at a shop in Dorchester there was nothing available. A decade earlier there were dozens on offer. Mark Ching and Ian Currie's offbeat *The Dorset Weather Book* with its pictures of row boats navigating the flood at Swanage Railway Station and frozen sea surrounding the pier in 1963 was a clear winner. As was Desmond Hawkins' *Dorset Bedside Book* with its poems by John Betjeman, descriptions of John Wesley having a hard time preaching at Shaftesbury, French attempts to land at Brownsea Island, and the hurdle-makers of Sixpenny Handley.

Jon Woolcott's *Real Dorset*, however, is no collection of curiosities. It's a psychogeography of a county, a personal adventure, a detailed track across one of Britain's most beautiful, varied, and accessible landscapes. Woolcott is the perfect companion. He's inside this country, this county. You'll get a full experience visiting where he does but there's no obligation. *Real* books are real enough on their own.

Peter Finch

Note

1 Borders might matter but boundaries can be vague – some say that Chesil ends at Abbotsbury where the Fleet tapers, the beach joins the mainland again and the pebbles change size, but technically it continues to West Bay, once Bridport Harbour.

INTRODUCTION: HEY, JUDE

For two centuries my family has been on the move, migrating, shifting. The Woolcotts might originally have been Dutch or Welsh, or something else, but two hundred years ago they sprang from Lympstone in Devon, and then to Somerset, before exchanging a rural life for London where my great-great-grandfather opened a cheesemongers in Drury Lane in the mid-nineteenth century. Since then, by degrees, we've been working our way back west. I grew up in Wiltshire, went to London for college and a life, then worked in Wiltshire while living in London, lived and worked in Wiltshire, lived in Surrey and worked in London, lived in Dorset and worked in London. I have lived half a life on elastic, springing east and west, and it was dizzying. Now the last of the Woolcotts – ours is a genetic dead end – are settled happily in a county mid-way between our alleged well-spring and the capital.

From the moment I moved here, Dorset held me firmly in its grip. It's a county of fields and farms, towns and a nearly-city, a fossil-studded coastline, heathland, woods and rivers, castles, drowned villages and burnt manor houses, quarries and sunken lanes, ghosts and myth, rebellion and ritual. It's the county of Thomas Hardy, John Fowles, William Barnes and Sylvia Townsend Warner, T.E. Lawrence, PJ Harvey and Billy Bragg. Its place names roll pleasingly around the mouth – Ryme Intrinseca, Langton Herring, Melcombe Bingham and Bingham's Melcombe. Just under 800,000 people live here.[1] Each and every one of us carries their own distinct vision of the county.

It's a popular place for holiday-makers, second-homers, and much, arguably too much, is made of its coastline – the road signs that welcome you to the county also welcome you to the Jurassic Coast, in some cases more than an hour's drive away. But it's always been the landscape – from the flat dairy-lands of the Blackmore Vale to the Purbeck Hills, the folded intimacy of the Marshwood Vale, the brackish stillness of the Fleet, the Blue Pool hidden in Wareham Forest, the towns and villages, which have drawn me, and hinted at a deeper, wilder story, behind the London-by-the-sea chic.

So it seemed to me that Dorset was ripe for a sort of psychogeography – a literary tradition that in essence is a sensitivity to the meeting point of place and history, finding meaning in the

everyday and making connections across time. Thomas Hardy revived the idea of Wessex, with Dorset at its heart, and re-imagined it – he wrote that his Wessex was a "partly real, partly dream country". Hardy's close relationship to the county still exerts a pull over Dorset, he lived in many houses across the county, settling finally in the house he designed for himself at Max Gate, not far from his birthplace. He's buried at Westminster Abbey, but his heart was always in Dorset, so after some post-mortem wrangling, that organ was interred alongside his first wife, Emma, at Stinsford, just east of Dorchester.

I have a terrible confession. I have something of a problem with Hardy, although it's only partly his fault. The vagaries of a 1980s school curriculum meant that I studied *Jude the Obscure* in a tedious looking Penguin Classic edition for my O-level English Literature. I hated the book, didn't buy the fatalism, and disliked the idea of Landscape as Character. It was long, confusing, moralising and deeply depressing. But I still took the subject to A-Level. Settling into the first day of the sixth form my English teacher was embarrassed to announce that one of our set texts for the next two years would be… *Jude the Obscure*. I drifted reluctantly back into the odd world of Jude, Sue and Arabella, stonemasonry and the dream of Oxford, of an unsuccessful defenestration, child suicide and pigs' penises thrown in a courtship ritual. I still hated it.

I found my own dreaming spires in the form of a now-defunct college of London University, and escaped Wessex. My first college girlfriend, an intense woman who made her own trousers out of curtains, turned out to have an unhealthy Hardy obsession, and soon I was back there, reading *Return of the Native*, immersing myself in *Tess* and earnestly discussing *The Convergence of the Twain*, Hardy's poem about the sinking of the *Titanic*. It was only after my native's return to the west that I began to understand him. The land really does shape the people in Dorset, partly owing to Hardy's own myth-making, but also in the folklore, customs, history, politics, all piling up around us. It affects us in our own ways, especially in our imaginations.

I've shuffled around Hardy for this book. I may have changed my mind about him, or at least his books, but I can add nothing to the scholarship, so here he appears as a phantom, a shadow on the page. I've found many others who have led me through the county – some on the page, some in person. Most obviously I was influenced by Frederick Treves, a surgeon to Edward VII, and author of *The Elephant Man*. His book *Highways and Byways in Dorset* was, in a sense, a sort of proto-pyschogeography, a partial and opinionated hymn to his home county. I have found much to disagree with in Treves' beautifully-written book, and a little to make fun of, but it's still a fascinating and unreliable shimmery reflection of the early twentieth century, as seen by an Edwardian gentleman.

City psychogeographers are wanderers, flâneurs, following their nose or a whim, down an alley, into a bar, poking around canal paths and gas cylinders – their rural equivalents require more purpose. I needed a car, my bike and walking boots to cover the ground, with the exception of the eastern conurbation of Bournemouth, Christchurch and Poole, where comfortable trainers were the order of the days. But Dorset is big, so I opted for depth, not breadth. The *Real* Books are not guides nor intended to be exhaustive. You'll find most villages omitted, some towns barely mentioned. This isn't to denigrate them – quite the reverse. I became frustrated with some of my predecessors' scant dismissive sentences on tucked-away towns or seemingly nondescript villages – they deserve better than a breezy drive-by description. In *Real Dorset* I wanted to go deeper, find the essence of a particular place, speak to people, linger at gravestones, sit silently in woodland, feel the buzz of Bournemouth or the wind on Black Down, find the stories that linger on the margins, just out of view.

When I told people I was writing this book, I was inundated with requests to cover a particular place, story, person, political event. It was a measure of how much the county means to people, how connected they are to the partly real or partly imagined. But *Real Dorset* is not a definitive portrait. It's specifically, singularly, my Dorset. It will have errors, you will certainly disagree with some of my impressions or conclusions, wish I'd spent less time on my hobbyhorses and more time on yours. It won't tell you where to find a footpath, the best place to buy a crab sandwich on the coast (although pubs occasionally feature), but I hope it might inspire you to seek out some of these places, or better still to find your Real Dorset, inevitably different from mine; and maybe there's a sequel already written in your heart.

Note

1 ONS Data 2021, including Bournemouth, Poole and Christchurch.

NORTH

BORDERLANDS: THE SHIRE RACK

One Wednesday in late July I found myself in a small and muddy car park in the RSPB reserve at Garston Wood. The few people here, men with long-lensed cameras and binoculars dangling from their necks, clanked through high grey metal gates to gain entry to the wood, twenty-first century kissing gates without the love. This remote and rural Checkpoint Charlie was designed, along with impenetrable stretches of stock fencing, to keep deer out of the reserve. But I wasn't here for the birds.

Dorset is hedged into a very rough diamond shape by the sea, by Devon, Somerset, Wiltshire and Hampshire. Its land borders are as intricate as its coves and harbours, and its inland history is every bit as compelling. Waiting for me in the car park was the energetic figure of Katherine Barker, a historical geographer who has researched this border for decades, recruiting historians, botanists and cartographers to trace a previously unseen history through the banks and dykes. We pulled on walking boots and scanned the dingy sky for signs of rain. Katherine is an enthusiast, a fount of knowledge, chatty and sharp-witted. She's introduced a new word to describe her field of study – hercology (from the Greek, *hercos*: boundary). She can't help seeing the signs of ancient frontiers in subtle landscape features: she told me that whenever she's out with her family and spots a tell-tale ditch or embankment her daughters will laugh: "Oh, mum's crossing a border again."

Katherine had agreed to show me the Shire Rack, the footpath that follows part of the northern boundary with Wiltshire. The Dorset Boundary Group has walked and surveyed almost all the 143-mile-long border, from Uplyme in the west to Bournemouth in the east, mostly with landowners' permission. They've found veteran trees, ditches and banks, unusual coppices, traces of ancient earthworks, scratching at layers of history, combining what they find on the ground with the written record. Katherine first stumbled over the old border in the writings of Bishop Aldhelm from the seventh century, recognising in the text a section of the border near Lyme Regis, sparking her years of research, walking, spreading the word.

I'll enthusiastically walk anywhere in Dorset but to do so in Katherine's company was revelatory. Walking with her was to walk also in the Middle Ages. Stepping off the quiet road and pushing through scrub we found ourselves on a narrow footpath leading gently uphill through cool woodland with views across Cranborne Chase, marked by beech and high chalkland. This Area of Outstanding Natural Beauty is remarkably empty of people, and aside from today's brisk wind and the occasional clatter of wood pigeon, quiet. We walked under the wood's dark canopy, but imagining the landscape centuries ago revealed open land, cleared of trees and busy, full of traders and merchants, crossing places for the materials of the medieval world, a contested zone.

We found pollarded hazel; Katherine speculated that this might be a descendant of ancient defensive structures; in Julius Caesar's *Gallic Wars* the advancing Roman army was surprised by sharpened hurdles on ridges of embankments. Ten years ago she brought the botanist and writer Oliver Rackham here and astonished him by taking him to a tree that she now showed me: an ash pollarded into three separate tall and dramatic trunks, like an out-of-scale espaliered fruit tree, quite unlike the familiar dome shape.[1] Its bark demanded to be stroked, and during a walk which was full of chat, ranging freely from medieval pandemics to the politics of land ownership, from the Civil War to academic conferences on the age of chalk hill-figures it was the only time we fell properly silent. Katherine leaned in towards the tree.

"Why don't you tell us your secrets?"

The ash, sacred to the god Woden, is decidedly unchristian, never used in church building in the British Isles. Despite our appeals to its spirit, it remained mute.

Katherine despaired of the lack of active woodland management in the twenty-first century – until recently a vital multi-purpose resource: flexible, tough and sustainable. In her wanderings across the Dorset boundary she had met just one hurdle maker still working.

A little further into the darkening wood she stopped and pointed her stick.

"There it is."

Across the ground, littered with branches which I'm sure Katherine would have loved to gather up for burning or building, was an earthwork, a coiled snake in the gloom. Pulling out my slightly damp Ordnance Survey map I could see that Mistleberry Camp was labelled in gothic script as a fort, but Katherine was keen to allow other possibilities.

"Everyone says these places are defensive, but they would have had many uses. This one was probably protective, like a pen to keep animals overnight."

The Church held lands across the border – at places like Shermel Gate, a little further on. These, said Katherine, were "the Travelodges of their day. Somewhere to stay the night, water your stock, say a prayer for the onward journey." I've stayed in many Travelodges and never overheard anyone praying, but sometimes I've been pretty sure that animals were loose. An appealing sense of mystery hung over Mistleberry Camp, occupying about two square acres under the trees' shadow. Katherine, I thought, would have preferred its original version, with the royal recorders passing this way, taking their notes. Domesday, she pointed out, revealed how well organised England was by 1086.

Our progress was slow. Once we'd started spotting little lumps and bumps, signs of the route of the ancient path, it was hard to stop. We kept talking and the centuries dissolved. The Norman Conquest detained us for a while – we discussed the decapitation of the Anglo-Saxon nobility and how Norman French words, to this day, have higher status than their Old English equivalents – parliament over meeting, lieutenant over sheriff. Still, the aristos and the more recently wealthy remain dominant in these borderlands; had I continued walking I would have threaded a way through lands owned by Viscount Rothermere and Guy Ritchie.

The trees overhead, and our chatter, hid from us the gathering clouds. When we finally regained the road, Katherine gleefully noted that the road on one side of the county border was recently resurfaced, but not on the other, the rites of the medieval border made modern through the medium of hi-vis vests and JCBs. A motorist stopped to offer us a lift, doubtless alarmed by two people spilling from a hedge to gaze at recent road repairs under threatening skies, but we declined. As we reached the car park the downpour began. Already soaked, we jumped into our cars and waved farewell through windscreens. Later Katherine sent me an email – the rain had held off so completely while we walked, she wrote, that Woden was clearly protecting us along this length of the Shire Rack.

WIMBORNE ST GILES

The countryside around Wimborne St Giles is tinged with Hampshire – the lanes are sandy, the New Forest is close. On the day before Queen Elizabeth's funeral, the flag on St Giles' church was at half-mast beneath the pale blue September skies. I propped my bike against the porch. I like to trace the history of a place through its church, the hints in the memorials, the graves old and new, the leaflets, the announcements of future events. But sometimes you need to look further afield.

One hundred miles away, in Piccadilly Circus, surrounded by digital advertising boards and some of the tackiest shops in the capital, tourists sit on the steps around the delicate statue of Eros, and rarely glance at the winged figure above them. The statue, his loins covered and bow unstrung, is a symbol of the city, adorning the masthead of London's daily paper, the *Evening Standard*.

Eros is not Eros. Unveiled in 1893 he was intended to be the 'Angel of Christian Charity', rather than a mildly scandalous God of Love. Officially known as the Shaftesbury Memorial Fountain, he was built in remembrance of the seventh Earl of Shaftesbury, Anthony Ashley Cooper, who died in 1885 after a long life of reforming public service – his campaigning work led to the abolishment of child labour following a series of mine disasters. From his original location in the centre of the Circus, the statue's bow was designed to point directly towards Wimborne St Giles, the family's home. But the angel has been moved several times, for war (when he was kept in Egham for protection), for the construction of the Underground Station (a short spell in Embankment

Gardens) and later for restoration, after which he moved a few yards south, so whether he still aims precisely at this corner of Dorset I can't say.

The lives of successive Earls of Shaftesbury haven't all been characterised by Christian Virtue. Tragedy, bad luck and a streak of poor decision making have all played their part.

In 1886 the eighth earl, under the stress of debt and mental illness committed suicide, shooting himself with a revolver while in a cab in Regent Street, not far from the planned statue to his father. He had only become Lord Shaftesbury six months earlier, and his wife, Harriet, had St Giles remodelled in the fashionable High Gothic style in remembrance.

Inside the church I found tombs for the family members, and a wide, heavy wooden screen reaching across the nave, obscuring some of the view. In 1908 soldering work sparked a fire which, in the words of a black engraved stone beneath the tower, 'completely destroyed' Harriet's work, and the church was rebuilt by the ninth earl (1869-1961), who was surprisingly long-lived given that he led one of the last cavalry charges in the First World War, under machine-gun fire.[2] His son was not so lucky, dying in 1947, but not before he had married and divorced the socialite and model Sylvia Hawkes who went on to marry both Clark Gable and Douglas Fairbanks Senior.

But it was the tenth earl, also named Anthony, whose life ended most dramatically and horribly. In later life he met a woman described in some newspapers as a 'high class prostitute' who eventually became his third wife. He was last seen alive in Cannes in November 2004 – his body was found in a ravine six months later, and in 2007 his wife and her brother were convicted of his murder, after it was proved that that she had visited the ravine just before the earl's death, despite her denials.

His son did not enjoy his inheritance for long, dying of a heart attack aged 28, just one month after the discovery of his father's body. Unexpectedly Nicholas Ashley Cooper, the second son, inherited the estate, becoming the twelfth earl. Previously a D.J. in New York going by the name Nick AC he excited some newspapers by his return to St Giles House, ("a tattooed young raver" – that's at least two things *The Daily Telegraph* isn't generally in favour of). But he's proven to be its saviour. The house had fallen slowly into disrepair and had not been occupied since the 1960s. His father's attempts at mitigation which had included demolishing a wing and taking down a tower, had remained unfinished – the house was not weatherproof and a tree was growing in one room. But slowly Nick AC and his wife have restored the house and its gardens, turning it into a business for conferences and weddings. In the course of the restoration of the garden a buried statue was discovered – a copy of Eros, where it now points back towards Piccadilly. The huge pile is invisible from the road, so to experience it you'll have to be invited, and I wasn't, so I cycled away.

HORTON TOWER

Eccentricity dominates this landscape and I was keen to get close to its most prominent feature – the Horton Tower. Follies are often pretty: grottoes or eye-catchers, towers or gateways, set in parkland around grand houses, or on distant hills. The tower at Horton is in the latter category, but it's not pretty. I leant the bike against a gate and walked across open ground to the tower. It was vast, red brick, triangular at its base but I could see the top two storeys were hexagonal. Its purpose, if it had one, is mysterious. It had been built, probably around 1725 at the behest of Humphrey Sturt of Crichel House, a few miles away. In a map of Dorset dated 1765 the tower is shown with a dome and cupola and labelled 'Observatory' but whether it ever had a dome or the illustration showed an unrealised plan is not known. It would have been a fine location. Twenty-first century night skies are bright with sodium and headlights' glare, the heavens littered with satellites and space junk, but this is one of England's darkest spots: Cranborne Chase AONB is designated a Dark Sky Reserve.

The Sturts' estate at Crichel, neighbouring the Ashley Coopers, had a similarly chequered history. Humphrey Sturt's son, also named Humphrey, enlarged the house, and around the same time as Joseph Damer drowned the original village of Milton Abbas,[3] relocated villagers in order to create a large lake near his expanded home, leaving only the parish church.

The final Sturt was Napier, Lord Alington, a jazz age eccentric whose lovers included Tallulah Bankhead, and who shot off his finger when he learnt of his brother's death. In the 1930s he brought impoverished men from London's East End to Moor Crichel to provide them with employment and fresher air. He died

in Egypt of pneumonia in 1940 after a flying mission, having failed
to bring with him sufficiently warm clothing. Leaving no heir his
title became extinct.

Horton Tower slowly decayed on its hill. Thomas Hardy lived
briefly in nearby Wimborne Minster and would have known it. It
might have been the inspiration for *Two on a Tower*, (in which one
of the characters is an astronomer, a literal star-crossed lover). But
that might have been Charborough Tower, more menacing even
than Horton, or The Hardy Monument (named after a different
Hardy altogether).[4] There was enough of Hardy the novelist in the
air for Horton Tower to be used as a backdrop for Terence Stamp
as he rode a galloping horse in John Schlesinger's 1967 film *Far
from the Madding Crowd*.[5] It attracted artists too: John Piper
photographed and painted the tower as it crumbled, rendering it
distant and amber, lost in darkness.

I touched the red brick of the tower's base: its glorious
monstrosity is safe now, used as a phone mast for a mobile network,
and therefore stabilised.[6] Having had quite enough of aristocrats for
one day I mounted my bike and wobbled away from the tower, less
sure of myself than Terence Stamp's galloping semi-hero.

BOOKISH IN LONG CRICHEL

The graveyard at Long Crichel, a village scattered along a lane, tells one story of the settlement. There were a few new graves clustered around the gate, the grass mown neatly. But the older headstones were mostly hidden by the long dry grass. The population of the village has declined steadily, there are too few local descendants to tend the older stones. The church was shy, facing away from the lane, and from the outside typically English Perpendicular – a square tower and grey stone. Stepping inside, it was if I had entered a completely different building, a beautifully painted and simple interior, light-coloured pews, the ceiling blue. The church had been unloved and slowly mouldering until it was rescued by the conservation organisation Friends of Friendless Churches, who spent years restoring it – I was lucky to find it so soon after the work was complete. Recent research has revealed that a trio of nineteenth century architects had first created this calmly intoxicating effect, including P.C. Hardwick, whose father designed the much-missed Euston Arch, which John Betjeman, in his role as protector of the nineteenth century's heritage, had tried and failed to save.[7]

My reason for visiting lay beyond the churchyard, where a path had been cut into the leggy grass leading to the rectory. This large house was once a retreat for artists and writers. In the mid-twentieth century it was owned by a succession of bookish men who invited some of the best-known writers, poets, artists and musicians of the day to stay. The food and company were good, the list of visitors impressive: Nancy Mitford, Benjamin Britten and Peter Pears, Somerset Maugham, E.M. Forster, Cecil Beaton (who rented Ashcombe, just over the border in Wiltshire),[8] Vita Sackville-West and Patrick Leigh Fermor. Even Greta Garbo put in an appearance, presumably alone. The owners, Eddy Sackville-West, Desmond Shawe-Taylor, Eardley Knollys, Patrick Trevor-Roper, Raymond Mortimer and Derek Hill were all gay but never in relationships with one another. In typically rebarbative style Evelyn Waugh called the rectory "the buggery house at Crichel" but Frances Partridge celebrated the atmosphere, writing "hurrah for homosexuality and also for the happy friendships between buggers and women." Mostly the occupants were known as The Crichel Boys or The Batchelors and the house was a refuge from an age marked by prejudice. Indeed members of the wider Crichel circle were instrumental in making a change to the law: Lord Montagu and Michael Pitt-Rivers were arrested in the 1950s in the midst of anti-gay hysteria and both served prison sentences, in turn leading to the Wolfenden Report, which recommended the decriminalisation of homosexuality.[9]

The comings and goings of the artistic set at Crichel predictably led to love triangles, hexagons, polygons, better explained with a flipchart than a paragraph. An example was Ralph Partridge, who later married Frances, but whose first marriage was to the artist Dora Carrington, even though she was in love with Lytton Strachey, who was gay and had a relationship with the painter Duncan Grant, whose lovers included Vanessa Bell and the economist John Maynard Keynes. Well, we've all been there.

A late visitor was the ex-prime-minister Edward Heath, who in the 1990s drove over from his home in Salisbury Cathedral Close and annoyed Derek Hill with his rudeness and by taking many tapes of classical music, but the whirlwind of visitors and minor scandals was by then over. The boys slowly died off[10] and their way of life was no longer sustainable. They had depended on domestic help for cooking and housekeeping; a more connected world had no need of literary salons dominated by snobbery and bitchiness. I could get no closer to the rectory than its low garden gate, and could hear no laughter tinkling from within.[11]

KNOWLTON: THE CHURCH
IN THE HENGE

Just off the B-road that runs from Wimborne to Cranborne was
Knowlton church, isolated: Saxon with a bit of late Norman, and
ruined, open to the elements. The lonely church would be
remarkable enough, but what's made it famous is that it sits
squarely in the middle of a neolithic henge.

This corner of Dorset is scattered with ancient monuments.
Almost totally invisible except in aerial photography in parched
summers or low winter light is the nearby Dorset Cursus, (from
Latin meaning 'course'), an earthwork that runs across the
landscape as a ten-kilometre-long double ditch, its meaning
unclear, although the southerly and older section aligns with the
midwinter solstice sunset. At Martin Down the Cursus meets the
imposing Bokerley Dyke, an Iron Age defensive ditch, later
reinforced by the Romans, who also built roads across this land,
running from the hillfort of Badbury Rings.

But Knowlton is the star of this landscape, much photographed
and written about. On previous visits I made straight for the
roofless church, but this time I walked the perimeter beyond the
embankment, anti-clockwise. I've never been alone at Knowlton.
There were people throwing balls for dogs and two drones buzzed
intrusively above me. The drones annoyed me more than the dogs,
although was I really any different, recording my experiences for
others? One man plucked his flying machine neatly from the air,
two other young men let theirs circle overhead and talked of finding
a good day to film at Old Harry Rocks on the Purbeck coast.

Knowlton is a mystery. Its earthworks were probably ceremonial
rather than defensive, but the shattered church is the puzzle, the
sacred over the sacred.[12] The countryside broadcaster Jack
Hargreaves (1911-1994), who lived in Dorset[13] devoted one of his
Old Country programmes to Knowlton. The film begins with him
leading a horse around the long pond at Ashmore, pipe stuffed in
his mouth, before he begins his exploration of the henge, built he
says, to keep the spirits in, not people out. At the northern edge of
the earthwork I came across two yew trees and pushed my way into
the hollow between them. This space was hung with many brightly
coloured ribbons, like Tibetan Prayer Flags, there were also
keepsakes: teddy bears and notes for the departed. Yew trees are

associated with the divine, found often in churchyards but also at earthworks, the sacred trees of the pre-Christian era.[14] Jack Hargreaves thought that these trees were the descendants of older yews, a deliberate connection to the wider landscape, the roads and burial mounds around the site.

The Christians used earlier religious sites for their churches elsewhere too, to stamp out pagan beliefs, the Roman Catholic church's final conquest, it's been assumed. But it's not that simple. Apart from anything else, historical paganism is so hard to pin down, so phantasmagorical. We know chiefly of its existence through Christian texts forbidding certain practices like digging up animal bones to ward off cattle disease, or the telling of prophecies. Medieval Christian chroniclers worried about the power of cross-roads, which at Knowlton would have been especially problematic, while Cnut, who died at Shaftesbury in 1035, outlawed worship of heathen gods, the sun, the moon, fire, flood, witchcraft and stones. But while we have the henges and standing stones, we don't know the practices. Paganism seems to have been a people's religion of landscape, customs and rituals embedded in particular places, and that shapelessness allowed it to survive, to duck under formal faith and keep magic alive. The church at Knowlton may not have been a Christian power-play but a continuation of the sacred under a new guise, a regenerative spot.[15] The votives in the yews continued that spirit in our supposedly godless age. A few yards further on I passed a couple arm in arm, facing away from me across the fields and I wondered if they were here to mark a private sorrow.

The church was abandoned sometime in the eighteenth century, but its existence also preserved the henge: its use meant that the earthworks weren't lost to the plough like much of the Dorset Cursus was. The relationship between the religions protected the site, and something of its mystery too. And no amount of drone footage or modern-day cycling flâneurs will eradicate that.

MYTHS OF GILLINGHAM

"The town has lost much of its ancient beauty." – Arthur Mee, *The King's England, Dorset*

"Gillingham is singularly devoid of architecture worth noticing." – John Newman and Nikolaus Pevsner, *The Buildings of England, Dorset*

"Not now so picturesque as it was…." – Michael Pitt-Rivers, *A Shell Guide, Dorset*

"Not pretty…" – Jo Draper, *Dorset, The Complete Guide*

In his tidy, welcoming office, lined with shelves of box files, John Porter, Gillingham Museum's Assistant Curator, sighed.

"We're definitely not on the tourist trail. Everyone goes to Shaftesbury and Sherborne and we're just this industrial place in the middle."

Dorset isn't all Instagrammable sunsets over Durdle Door, sunken ancient holloways, or The Shire Rack. Gillingham, Dorset's most northerly town, with its guttural hard G, unlike its Kentish namesake and nicknamed Gill by locals too busy for unnecessary syllables, has sometimes had a hard time of it. The most damning was Sir Frederick Treves in *Highways and Byways in Dorset* in which he described Gillingham as "a sprawling, uninteresting town with a drab church too large for it, and many new red-brick houses which are elemental in their ugliness." Fred never sat on the fence. But on this wet Thursday in early August, I had to admit the town *was* looking drab.[16]

John Porter was generous with his time and knowledge. I love museums in small towns, the enthusiasm, the typed signs, the lack of pretension, the crowding of exhibits in a limited space. The

Gillingham Museum is a wonder – one room in a modern building shared with the library, full of information, maps, photographs, an early fire appliance. John, a softly spoken Lancastrian who moved here in 2004, gave me a short history of Gillingham. I wanted to explore the town's industrial heritage. John gave directions, loaded me with local history books, journals and a Town Trail leaflet.

Outside the rain had set in, I zipped my jacket, hoisted my newly loaded rucksack. Looking for brick and chimney, water wheels and winches, almost immediately I was disappointed. From a supermarket car park I stepped onto a narrow footpath and immediately into an older, rural age. Just yards from the busy bypass were two perfectly preserved thatched cottages, their gardens full of wildflowers and a few hens, leading down to the River Stour, at this point only a gentle, narrow stream whispering through the town's centre. Over the river was a footbridge, until the 1990s the only way to access the houses. The western end of the town centre, hard by the bypass named Le Neubourg in honour of Gillingham's French twin town, was a quiet square with a Tandoori restaurant, a café, a pub and a road leading to The Backs, a little muddle of lanes tucked behind the high street, where I found the old town lock-up. Crossing the bypass I set off west, past the original town cemetery, now a public garden where the gravestones leant against the wall under a road sign advising motorists of the presence of Elderly People. The wildflower garden was a smudge in the old cemetery, mostly given over to long grass, aside from a few immovably large and sentimental Victorian statues of angels. More insect-friendly were the adjacent Cemetery Road allotments, brimming with August produce: courgettes, lettuce, runner beans and sweetcorn, sweet peas and peas, rhubarb and potatoes, swollen onions with fallen stalks. A notice on a shed warned me that there had been recent produce theft, a scarecrow pointed a shotgun made from a plastic tube.

Not far away was a long lane, which led me to the last building in Gillingham: Slaughtergate Farmhouse. There are rumours of darkness on the edge of town. In his *King's England* book on Dorset and surely with a delicious shudder, Arthur Mee wrote that Edmund Ironside "overtook" a defeated Danish army here and a bloody end ensued for the invaders.[17] But John Porter, who has always enjoyed debunking local myth, had set me straight:

Slaughtergate is simply a corruption of the Old English word for a muddy place. There was no feeling of ancient battle here; nearby I could find evidence only of an assault on the liver: forty empty vodka bottles lined up neatly along the base of a wall. This could have been a boast, or a cry for help.

My industrial perambulation had so far yielded only aching feet and wet socks. Walking back to the town along a busy road demonstrated that Gillingham now is mostly light-industrial, Dorset's White Van capital. But as I trudged damply along, I came across a large, confusing building, a Greatest Hits of architecture – yellowed stone, a bulky square tower, arched windows, a steeply pitched roof, iron railings and what looked like an attempt at a dovecote, a building of uneasy dreams. The Wyke Brewery had been the largest of the town's breweries, closed and partly demolished in the mid-1980s. The building had lost its original function, but its self-confidence was undimmed. In part of the old complex was a motorcycle showroom and obligatory café, an echo of local manufacturing history – W.H. Light.

Bill Light was a successful bicycle racer in the 1880s, just as the machine broke out of its aristocratic origins and became an engine for working class mobility. Retiring from competition he began making bicycles in Gillingham. His most popular model, The Magnet, was adopted widely by the Dorset Constabulary. Later, in his pursuit of two-wheeled perfection he also made motorbikes and sidecars, and sold petrol from the premises. W.H. Light and Co is gone now, replaced by a branch of Lidl in the town centre.

I had coffee in the café on the square. Steaming gently from the rain and wiping down my notebook, I fell into conversation with the owner, who had previously let the space out as a bar. "I had to kick them out," she said, "the usual problems." The café was also a gallery, which was thriving.

"It's great," I said, "to have this in somewhere like Gillingham."

"Somewhere like Gillingham," she repeated, wrinkling her nose slightly, a mild rebuke to my unthinking snobbishness.

Outside I walked to the green near the bridge past empty, derelict shops. Once there was a little row of workers' cottages and a pub here, knocked down and never replaced. In 2013 English Heritage declared Gillingham town centre a Heritage At Risk area. The residents have pride in their town, though, as demonstrated by the friendly café owner. I found a cheery, knitted post box topper with figures of athletes celebrating the delayed 2020 Tokyo Olympics.

In the Blackmore Vale, where elm persist, and cattle drink from streams' muddy shores, I've sometimes felt I have slipped into a painting by John Constable. The artist visited Gillingham on several occasions, painting watermills, rendering them as ancient buildings sliding into elegant disrepair, rather than engines of industry. He

painted the town bridge, daubing a few pedestrians, poplar, ash, an energetic sky, and trademark quaffing cow. The bridge had a proud new plaque celebrating this, made by the Local History Society, but the painter's viewpoint was gone, replaced by a small shopping precinct. For a few years, between the artist and the shops, this site was a theatre for dreamers – the Regal Cinema, a neat modern Art Deco affair, knocked down in 1972.

I followed the course of the river behind public toilets, through a car park, finding an impressive memorial to the dead of two world wars between parking spaces. Clambering over a low wall at the river's edge I peered through the trees towards the Town Mill. Built in the mid-eighteenth century, the mill processed raw silk from China, India and the Mediterranean. Workhouses in London supplied the women and girls for labour. Later years saw the buildings used as a corn mill. All that was left of this complicated history of empire and workers' exploitation were sluice gates and two large pipes arching into the water. The Town Mill fell into disrepair and in 1982, arson destroyed much of it. In its place was a large red-brick block of flats. It would have been, in John Porter's words, a flagship heritage attraction. When Treves, Pevsner and Mee wrote their books the mill was still standing, but they all chose to overlook it, noting only the traditionally pretty or the rural.

In 1856 the *London Illustrated News* ran an article celebrating the cutting of the first turf for the railway at Gillingham by a Miss Seymour, which she "accomplished in good style" before the chairman of the railway gave a speech, regretting that the south had been "beaten by the north" in the race to industrialise, but that all this was about to change. Gillingham's fortunes were transformed – much of the new industry gathered around the station. Finding it in a sprawl of retail units and For Sale signs, I was struck by the pungent smell, the unwelcome Proustian hit of 1980s school dinners, wafting from the food processing factory. Smells hang around here. The muddle of buildings across the road was once a bacon curing factory, killing 1300 pigs a week, and just a few yards away a glue factory, making the most of the porcine corpses. There's a Slaughtergate rumour hanging on like the smell: Oake, Woods and Co, the bacon curers, had been credited in local histories for their prescience when opening their premises *before* the railway arrived, but in fact they came after, snouts following the money, this myth also dispelled by John Porter.

The Up platform is too long for trains, the extra length was made for waiting milk churns; farmers, milking Constable's cows, benefitting from new markets. The station is much quieter than in its heyday, when served by two lines from Salisbury rather than the one that remains today. It had sidings for the brickworks, which still cut bricks by hand from the dense Dorset clay until the 1930s. Little remained of the brickworks' buildings, only preserved in the name of the light industrial park, also home to a nightclub called Legends, with a last-chance-saloon reputation. In place of the brickworks' chimney was a mobile phone mast. But sometimes, when leaving my car overnight in the station car park, I've returned to find a thin coating of brick dust on the windscreen, decades after the brickworks' closure.

Just before the train pulls into the station on the Down platform, near where Gillingham FC plays, the attentive passenger will spot an earthwork. I walked down a residential street to a royal palace. The rain had stopped, the air had lost its heaviness, but I was alone. I spread out my rain jacket and sat down. I was in King's Court Palace, commissioned by King John as a hunting lodge in 1199 in Gillingham's Royal Forest, but demolished on Edward III's orders in 1369. Treves described it as "The Sandringham of its day" – an exaggeration, given the number of royal retreats in medieval England. Nothing was left except the earthwork's square shape. At Clarendon Palace twenty-five miles away, which I explored as a teenager when it was still covered in woodland, portions of walls and cellars remained. But this was a near obliteration.

This might be Gillingham's problem. The museum is stuffed

with wonders, mementoes and photographs because it's the final bastion of memory. Gillingham came to believe its own press. When Arthur Mee made 'ancient' and 'beauty' synonymous, he dispensed with the rich complexity of the last few hundred years in a single phrase. The recently redundant was swept away: the brickworks, the Town Mill, the gasholders of the Gillingham Gas and Coke Company, the Regal, W.H. Light, even Constable's viewpoints were banished. We are left instead with unreliable stories like Slaughtergate.

The legacy of destruction is even built into my home. When my wife and I bought our house, in a hamlet five miles away from Gillingham, a new extension was in the process of being built. The builder, roll-up corkscrewing around the corner of his mouth, told me that the brick for the job had come from "an old pub in Gill", the impressive Royal Hotel, knocked down in 2004.[18] So when the time comes, please join the campaign to save Legends, the nightclub on the industrial estate.

SHERBORNE'S SLUMBER

In the early 1960s the poet John Betjeman, not yet the Laureate, made a series of short films about west country towns, dwelling on their architecture and people. Some of these films were found after thirty years lost in the archives and were re-released in the 1990s, introduced by the actor Nigel Hawthorne, dressed in a white suit and Panama hat.

Sherborne is the subject of one of these films. Betjeman's original voice-track remained lost so Hawthorne read the poet's words in a fruity baritone over tinkling light music. The experience of watching these films is slightly unsettling, a 1960s take on mostly ancient towns through the prism of the 1990s. Betjeman began his tour in the Abbey, originally a cathedral and now simply a very large parish church, before trawling the town's many schools, stopping to examine notable architecture. Betjeman had a miserable time at his own school, Marlborough, and some of his unhappiness rubs off in Hawthorne's voice-over, but the poet was in love with Sherborne, and I found it easy to see why. He called it a Junior University Town, and its several schools, public and state, dominate the golden-stoned town still. Sherborne School itself nestles up against the old abbey, making it impossible to walk around the outside of the whole church, as at Winchester, as at Salisbury.

Instead I walked into the Abbey porchway, where two mallards were drinking from a water bowl left for dogs at the entrance. The nave, and especially its ceiling, took my breath away. I stood, gap-mouthed, for a minute or so, before a friendly guide accosted me, handed me a leaflet and calmed me down.

"The fan-vaulting," I mumbled pathetically, like a junior Betjeman who'd read too much Pevsner.

The fan-vaulting is Sherborne Abbey's Big Thing. The fans swooped delicately above, umbrellas turned inside out in a perfectly placed symphony of ham stone.[19] It was complex, dizzying, and beautiful. Slightly stunned, I walked the Abbey's arcades. It was surprisingly busy – I wondered if the strange circumstances and terrible losses of a pandemic had effected this change, that people felt again the need to find sanctity or sanctuary. In one of several side-chapels I found a gravestone to a near namesake – John Walcott (ours is a west country name, even if our roots are elsewhere). In a transept was a broken stone commemorating a Great Hailstorm in May 1709, which caused a flood which erupted through the north door of the church and passed straight through the building, leaving at the south door, ripping up many of the paving slabs in its course.

The ruling family of Sherborne, the Digbys, possibly Dorset's largest private landowners (the figures are imprecise), loom large in the town. On the green was a tall obelisk, a sentimentally pious monument to George Digby who, in the nineteenth century, had made it his priority to restore the Abbey. One of the figures featured on the obelisk was of Sir Walter Raleigh, whom the Digbys replaced as owners of the castle after Raleigh's imprisonment and execution, a way perhaps of enveloping the national hero into their story. The current owner of Sherborne Castle, Maria Wingfield Digby, has even written a biography of the privateer, who neither brought potatoes nor tobacco to England, although he popularised them both. Close by were St John's Almshouses. In Betjeman's film the residents are pictured eating, gathered around a large wooden table. Betjeman thought they lived with the memories of the Dorset of Thomas Hardy, who had died only thirty-five years earlier, and he used this as a chance to quote one of his own poems, 'Dorset', which lists some of his favourite village and town names, before its sting in the tail – foreseeing the death of his contemporaries.[20] Frederick Treves, writing comfortably in Hardy's lifetime, thought too that the almshouses sheltered those who spoke Dorset's "rare, enchanting dialect" through "toothless mouths".

After the dissolution, after The Flood, Sherborne, on its surface, returned to a sort of ancient slumber. Many of the streets appeared little changed from Betjeman's film, a little more traffic on the A30 running through the town, but none on the High Street, now pedestrianised. The Conduit, a shapely stone affair resembling a small poultry cross where monks once washed, was fenced off for restoration, sackcloth draped over it, giving it the appearance of a scone on the turn. A man sat on a platform, using a small trowel to slowly scrape away the dirt of the centuries from the stone. The aim, he told me, was to prepare The Conduit for another few hundred years, not to make it look new. It was painstaking but rewarding work, he said. Above us, from a little window to the left of a gateway leading to the Abbey green, a life-size doll, possibly once a tailor's dummy, looked down upon us.

At the top of the high street was an imposing three storey Palladian building gazing imperiously across the town: this was Sherborne House, and has a long and occasionally illustrious history, originally medieval and then owned by the Digbys who endowed it as a school. Betjeman was fascinated by the building and its ornate staircase which climbed beneath a mural by Sir James Thornhill, the artist who decorated the dome of St Paul's Cathedral. The schoolchildren were not allowed to touch the mural under any circumstance, according to one ex-pupil who met the future Poet Laureate in the headmaster's study. This schoolgirl was Katherine Barker, who had walked with me on The Shire Rack.[21] The school closed and became Sherborne's Arts Centre but became so dilapidated that it featured in the TV programme *Restoration*, in which buildings at risk were offered a chance to win funds to save them. It didn't win, but I found the building shrouded in fencing – a huge project to restore Sherborne House was underway.

Betjeman was always going to be a sucker for Sherborne, inevitably summoned by the Abbey Bells, but it's drawn other architectural afficionados too. In *Father to the Man*, a 2007 film, Jonathan Meades recounted his childhood and how travels with his father across southern England shaped him and his tastes.[22] He began the film outside the New Sherborne Castle, the last place they ever visited together. Meades is not Betjeman, his tastes, like his suits, are sharper, his attitude lugubrious, pointed, more critical. He banishes romance from the stones – buildings don't literally hold memories he tells us, but our memories of them help make us who we are. Many, Meades included, think the New Castle a strange piece of work, a post-Elizabethan lodge, facing the Old Castle which, having been besieged twice by the New Model Army was finally destroyed in 1645. The lodge was turned by the Digbys into the New Castle during "a brief period in English design", as Meades tells us, "when the fantastical became the norm", and which he finds both "sweet" and "sinister". The New Castle sprouts griffins and beasts; the nearby ruin of the Old Castle was reduced to the function of an eyecatcher for the new occupiers.

Sherborne's tourist brochures don't describe the New Castle in the same terms as Meades, preferring to stress its Capability Brown landscape, which keeps new development in check. Instead the town emphasises its friendliness and human scale. On the 'Discover Sherborne' website the residents wrote about why they love it – each of them holding their fingers together to make the heart shape so popular on social media. The first of these was Maria Wingfield Digby, standing slightly awkwardly in her home, next to a suit of armour, talking of the appealing scale of 'Sherbs' from the comfort of an estate judged to be around 13,000 acres.

The townspeople on the website were right – Sherborne was supremely pretty, the stone warm to the touch and to the eye, compact and friendly. But it also carried a tang of aspic – the A30 was long ago superseded by the faster, more direct A303, and Sherborne became marooned. Yeovil, a short distance away in Somerset, grew instead, and the town that was once a cathedral city draws tourists and architectural critics, but no longer the masses.

HINTON ST MARY

A few miles south of Gillingham, but a world away, was the village of Hinton St Mary, which I cycled to under a hot and leaden sky. It was a blink-and-you-miss it sort of place, nearly subsumed by Sturminster Newton, on a little ridge overlooking the River Stour. I turned off the B-road to discover somewhere that appeared to be

twinned with St Mary Mead, just before the decorous murder. It
was a picture-postcard village made of the sort of stone that writers
like me can't help but describe as honeyed, a network of lanes so
quiet that a green woodpecker was quite undisturbed as I pedalled
past. It felt an affluent place where little happens – the parish
website reported that teaspoons were running low in the village hall.
The hot spot was the White Horse pub, doing a brisk lunchtime
trade. Beyond St Peter's, just up the lane, the burial ground
carefully mown to leave sprays of wildflowers between the graves,
the manor house loomed with its own gate to the churchyard. The
laughter from the garden beyond gave away a wedding party. I
found the church an empty, elegant jumble: the nave is nineteenth
century, the tower fifteenth century, the font even earlier, but older
still is the reason I came to Hinton St Mary. When Frederick Treves
dismissed the village as "uninteresting" he could not have known,
but in 1963, while digging foundations for a new barn a blacksmith
uncovered the remains of a Roman villa and a spectacular mosaic
floor. Amongst the tessellated mythical creatures was a face
identified as one of the earliest representations of Christ. The
British Museum was alerted, the floor transported to London. I
found a board explaining its significance in the tranquil garden next
to the pub. But what remains of the villa was otherwise invisible, the
site covered by a field of munching horses, a small outhouse and a
gallery devoted to equine paintings.[23]

The mosaic had been found on land previously owned by the
local landowner, George Henry Lane-Fox Pitt Rivers, who had
abandoned the family seat at Rushmore and made his home in
Hinton St Mary. The writer Patrick Wright had told me of a rumour
– in the war years George had arrows cut into his crops on the land
around the village, pointing to Bristol to give guidance to Luftwaffe
bombers. There was a parallel rumour associated with Springhead
just a few miles from here, the home of Rolf Gardiner, who
allegedly cut a swastika into woodlands on his land, but almost
certainly didn't. Was north Dorset really a hotbed of Nazi
sympathisers? George certainly was – caught up in the eugenics
movement, he published anti-Semitic works, attended rallies in
Germany at the invitation of Goering, gave speeches blaming the
Spanish Republicans for the bombing of Guernica (demonstrating
that fake news is nothing new), entertained Oswald Mosley and was
interred for two years during the second world war. His dedication
to the cause of genetic purity didn't extend to his own personal life.

Married twice, he left his second wife for a younger woman improbably named Becky Sharpe, and later had a long relationship with Stella Lonsdale, who had been accused of spying for both the British and the Germans. After George's death in 1966, Stella was responsible for selling some of the collection of Augustus Pitt Rivers, George's grandfather, known as the father of modern archaeology. Since then the Pitt Rivers Museum in Oxford has attempted to recover these artefacts.

The heavy clay soil of the largely flat Blackmore Vale means that dairy farming dominates the patchwork of small fields, the hedge boundaries punctuated by oak trees, under which cattle shelter for shade in summer. So, amongst all these cows, where were the crops which hid George's arrows? At the end of a lane leading eastwards from Hinton I bumped my bike onto a wide track which led me gently downhill for half a mile. I have rarely found a spot so quiet in southern England, the track alive with insects, sparrows chattering from the hedges. I saw a snail so big, its shell so glossy, it looked like an escapee from the set of *The Magic Roundabout*. As the track wound down I found myself in a large open bowl in the landscape and fields sown with maize. It wouldn't have been hard, in this silent place, away from the village and miles from a road, to implement a 1940s fascist-friendly version of a crop-circle unnoticed. One local, years afterwards, had dismissed the idea and scoffed at George's ability: "he couldn't have planted a crop to save his life." I could find no evidence for the crop-meddling, or some of the other more extreme rumours circling George, such as him founding a school solely for the education of the many children he had fathered.

This murky history is largely missing from the local record – George is roundly ignored on the village website, and if he's remembered in Dorset at all it's because much of his land was broken up on his death allowing local people and communities to buy land previously leased. I didn't take this silence to be a sign that anyone here ever took him seriously or wanted to cover up his sins but rather that he wasn't worth bothering with.

At the back of the church, close to a path that ran between the nave and the wall of the manor house's garden I found a plain square grave. Peering closer I could see the name: Rosalind Pitt-Rivers. Rosalind was George's second wife. The union did not last long – by 1937 they had separated. She graduated in 1930 with a first-class honours degree and became a prominent and pioneering biochemist who did much research into the thyroid hormone. At the end of the second world war she was briefly posted to Belsen, just after the death camp's liberation. The horrors she witnessed, the appalling consequences of a warped world-view, reportedly remained with her for the rest of her life. This quiet and unassuming woman was the real hero of the family, now tucked away safely in this pretty village. It's Rosalind who was celebrated in Hinton St Mary's parish newsletter, *The Mosaic*, which I thought was just as it should be.

THE BONAPARTE OF STALBRIDGE

Stalbridge, on paper, didn't look promising. Writers have swept through the little town and breezily dismissed it. One, writing in the 1990s, described it as an "uninviting narrow hole".[24] Sir Frederick Treves, his book bouncing around heavily in my rucksack, was also less than fulsome. He liked the land around here, calling it "comely". But when it came to Stalbridge, while he quoted John Leland who had described the town as "praty" (pretty), Treves thought it was more like Hull, which presumably wasn't a compliment, unless Treves was fond of eastern ports. I parked near the triangular green and aside from the chattering of starlings from a tree, found it quiet, unlike my dim memories of Hull. I walked into town. This was no narrow hole, but instead one long street, a crowded throng of vernacular architecture, cheek by jowl, brick by stone. Like many of the Blackmore Vale's towns it was built on a ridge, and the buildings were mostly grey, reflecting the sky blankly. There was a slight tang of ancient decay – a wistful stillness. Many of the shops had closed a long time ago, the buildings were now homes with outsized windows originally designed to show off wares. The main street was also an A-road, the pavements were narrow, lingering wasn't tempting. But a cycle shop was bright, the butcher's pies looked enticing and the car park of the independent supermarket, where there was also a place to tie up your horse, was full.

Further on, jutting out precariously into the road and protected from traffic by large wooden blocks was a lichen-speckled needle-like market cross, badly eroded by weather – so spindly that a gale in 1949 blew its top off. Almost all the engravings were rubbed out by the centuries' weather, not even its original date is known. Behind the cross, set into a wall, was a plaque placed by "Christians in Stalbridge" to mark "the two thousandth anniversary of the birth of Jesus Christ." The plaque was keen on the idea of One God, but Dorset Christians haven't always been hospitable to their near co-religionists. When John Wesley came to Stalbridge and stood at the Market Cross to spread the word of Methodism in August 1766 he was met with a hailstorm of stones and rotten eggs. While Methodism spread in Dorset amongst a new, generally progressive middle class, the staunchly Anglican squirearchy hated the new religion, as did the very poorest.[25]

The church of St Mary occupied a high point, raised slightly above the rest of Stalbridge. Inside it was empty and calm, cast iron candlesticks and a large organ, its pipes painted vibrant blue and yellow, a bright spot in a much-restored space. In one dark corner, I found something which had drawn Frederick Treves, fascinated him, repelled him. In the greyness of the day and with no lights on in the church I tiptoed closer, edging my way past the pews.

Hidden shyly in the corner was a tomb, the figure of the deceased lying on the large slab in the typical fashion of the later Middle Ages. But the shock value came from the body itself – naked, the corpse represented as decaying flesh. Treves went so far as to call it "gruesome".

I'm easily spooked, I dislike horror films; only a few years ago a friend jumped out at me as we were exploring a ruin, and I'm sure my screams echo there still, but this 'cadaver tomb' was something of a let-down: a few ribs showing meekly through the thin chest, a decorous cloth over the thighs. I thought about Treves standing in this spot, a Victorian trying to understand a stone carver from four hundred years before him, and me, trying to understand them both.

Cadaver tombs are relatively rare. Why did the sculptor represent the deceased so nakedly, so honestly? Churches are no strangers to the gruesome – grotesques and beakheads adorn their exteriors or entrances, sometimes held to be symbolic of the space between the temporal and the divine, on the outside of the building. But this was deep within the church, hidden but present. I was perplexed, but not shocked.[26]

The Victorians knew their way around death: their mourning clothes, sentimental deathbed paintings and elaborate gravestones. But Treves was horrified by this realistic depiction of a corpse, and I wondered if this was because its honesty was transgressive, breaking through the comforting rituals of his age. I hoped Treves was less squeamish in his day job as a surgeon. The most perturbing part of the church for me were the few shelves of an informal lending library on the way out, which offered many books by Dan Brown.[27]

In the porch, alongside the parish notices was a large, wooden framed sign high on the wall and inscribed with careful nineteenth-century script. It was headed 'Benefactions to the Poor of this Parish', and set out how William Boucher of Thornhill

House, on his death in 1836, had left a legacy for three "poor persons" provided they were Anglicans and "of honest life and conversation". The charity, whatever its religious and moral stipulations, the Victorians being obsessed with the idea of the Deserving Poor, would have been welcome. In the early nineteenth century the Blackmore Vale was one of the most deprived areas in England and Dorset was notorious for low agricultural wages.

At the end of the large churchyard which had spread slowly up the gentle slope, were newcomers' ashes, marked with fresh gravestones. The field beyond was occupied by a few shiny stand-offish horses, and a donkey wearing a coat decorated with cartoon dogs, who trotted over for a pat and to establish if I was carrying carrots.[28]

Fifty metres away was an earthwork marking the site of Stalbridge House. Little is known about the house, but it was once the residence of the seventeenth-century scientist Robert Boyle, whose work on air pressure gave us the eponymous law. He was unduly modest about his large Jacobean House, describing it in a letter as "my own ruined cottage in the country". Boyle was an important figure, a founding member of the Royal Society and the author of many books, but for a man whose work would presumably require calm concentration, he seems to have been rather clumsy – suffering many accidents while living in Dorset including nearly drowning while crossing a river on horseback and narrowly avoiding being crushed by a collapsing ceiling.[29]

But his calamitous habits didn't cause the destruction of the

Manor – that was quite deliberate, pulled down in 1823[30] by Lord Anglesey to fund building works at nearby Milborne Port. The demolition of this "fine old family mansion" as one anonymous letter to *The Times* described it, was one of many grievances that the townspeople levelled at the aristo's land manager William Castleman. But why should the population of Stalbridge care about the fate of a mansion which they could never set foot in? The answer lay in the town's history, and because Dorset's rural poor felt a sense of place, not as an abstract concept, but a real, living, meaningful connection to the land. For all its poverty, the Vale lived in people's hearts, finding expression in folklore, customs, ancient rights and obligations. At Mappowder, a few miles south, the people believed that the common land was haunted by hedge-pigs – the ghosts of Gypsies who had been driven off the land. In these delicately balanced communities it mattered that the poor were paid properly, that they had access to land to graze their animals and grow food, and that in winter the forests provided firewood to warm homes. Each parcel of land, every copse, every stream, held meaning. The land held the stories.

William Castleman set about making himself thoroughly unpopular by disrupting this fragile order – enclosing the land around Stalbridge Park, depriving local people of this source of firewood. He sold off silverware which had been used in town celebrations, so when the house came down it was proof that this outsider had no regard for the community; one anonymous letter to his absentee landlord boss, Lord Anglesey, invoked the nineteenth century's favourite bogeyman: Castleman was "worse that Bo____te".[31]

Despite the enclosure the locals continued to harvest wood: pruning trees, removing elms which had come down in gales, minor acts of sedition. Castleman was outraged, employing informers and later armed watchmen to patrol the plantations. But the town was adamant in its defence of the ancient rights. It was almost impossible, Castleman reported, to recruit special constables to police the land. And then, in 1830, Swing came to Dorset. The rural riots began in Kent, but soon spread through England, reaching Dorset in November. The new threshing machines were the target, letters signed 'Captain Swing' were sent to farmers and machinery wrecked. A typical incident took place at Pulham where a group of around fifty protesters destroyed a draining machine. On the whole, Swing rioters, despite their threats and the attacks on property, weren't violent mobs – protesters were careful to refer to their customary rights and often wore their best clothes, a mark of the solemnity of the occasion.

A group of protesters from Henstridge, just a few miles north, tried to persuade the residents of Stalbridge to destroy farm machinery, but instead Stalbridge people turned out in their finery, decorated their hats with laurel leaves – a symbol of radicalism and independence, occupied the park of the demolished manor house and lit bonfires.

Castleman made short-lived amends, employed more local labourers and constructed ten new cottages for the 'best' of the workforce, although the new houses were initially shunned. Resistance continued through the decade – in 1837 almost the whole town came out on New Year's Day to gather firewood in the Park, following a major storm which had blown down trees, and were only thrown out after a small riot which wounded some of Castleman's agents. The land agent had significantly underestimated how the idea of place mattered to the residents, and how intertwined it was with the complex relationship between rich and poor in nineteenth century rural England. At Great Wishford in Wiltshire, the ancient right to collect firewood in Grovely Woods is asserted still every Oak Apple Day, when a group parades through the village shouting "Grovely, Grovely and All Grovely!"

I walked back through the churchyard. The new cottages eventually became accepted as part of the fabric of the town – I found gravestones of some of the residents – and eventually the customs, just like the carvings on the market cross or the history of the cadaver tomb, faded.[32] I slipped down a long grey alley between two low dry-stone walls and as it turned a right-angled corner I came across that most domestic shrub, the laurel, growing wild, a shining wood running along the park side, in some places toppling the stones. The memories may have faded, but the laurel remained, a symbol of past rebellion, and a battle lost.

I came to a break in the long and crumbling park wall. The footpath here led me directly to the middle of the park, close to where the house had once stood. There was no-one around on this high grazing ground, and no donkeys to accompany me. I stopped under a tree, picked up a stick and shoved it into my rucksack – kindling for my fire that evening.

Back in the town I found the street where Douglas Adams had lived – seeing a cottage being demolished nearby had inspired the opening chapters of *The Hitch-hiker's Guide to the Galaxy*. Boyle's "own little ruined cottage" left its mark more resolutely with two huge gate pillars on the main road, topped with lion's heads. One had clearly recently become dislodged and was turned slightly towards its companion, as if muttering that it could remember when it wasn't all fields around here.

Stalbridge has no railway station now, although a rail timetable in a noticeboard on the main street told me where I could next get a train to London from. The brief entry for Stalbridge in the 1966 *Shell Guide to Dorset* read "its station stands in a field" and it did once.[33] All I could find, between warehouses and factories on the edge of town, were two sunken rails running across the road, embedded in the tarmac, a minor rumble under tyres. It was worth finding out more.

SHILLINGSTONE AND THE TRAILWAY

"No more will I go to Blandford Forum…" *Slow Train*, Flanders and Swann

In the distance, from the busy platforms of Shillingstone Station the hillforts of Hambledon and Hod rose dramatically. Wheeling my bike around the piled-up luggage on porters' trolleys I found a wheezing train, about to pull away. This was the Pines Express, the daily service that snakes through England from Manchester, taking holidaymakers to the coast at Bournemouth, bringing noise and cheerful bustle to this quiet Dorset village. Through a smeary train window I saw a couple in their early seventies who had found a relatively quiet corner in the packed train. They smiled uncertainly and I waved back. The man stood and slid open the narrow top window so we could speak. Tall and broad in a woollen suit, a pipe sticking from his breast pocket, he introduced himself as Frank, his wife, who remained perched on her seat, was Lily. She was slight, wearing a wide-brimmed hat and dark green dress. They had been staying in Bath for a few days, visiting Lily's family, and now were looking forward to a week in Bournemouth, enticed by the bright poster which advertised the resort as the "centre of health and pleasure". As we were speaking came the shouts, the whistle, the steam, the smoke, the chug, the vanishing.

★

Shillingstone Station closed in 1966, along with the rest of the line, the Somerset and Dorset Joint Railway, the victim, along with much of Britain's network of branch lines, of a civil servant's report.

The Somerset and Dorset Railway had a local nickname: the Slow and Dirty, but it brought people and possibilities, opened up new markets for farmers, offered a means of escape from a hard rural life, the chance to marry someone not from the same village. It connected the Bristol Channel and Bath to Bournemouth, and for 71 miles slipped through the Somerset coalfields, the Blackmore Vale and on towards the coast, crossing and recrossing the Stour.[34] By the mid-1980s, Shillingstone Station was in a sorry state. The last train was the demolition train. The signal box was taken, the rails removed, leaving only the platforms and station building. For many years it was left to crumble. Elsewhere it's hard to tell that a railway once ran through the county. Whole stations and halts were removed, bridges blown up, rails ripped away. Sometimes tell-tale signs were left – sunken rails crossing roads, mysterious wide avenues over fields, collapsed or collapsing huts for workers along the route, a decaying platform glimpsed through undergrowth. In one domestic driveway there's a set of level crossing gates.

When I first moved to Dorset I bought a custom-made Ordnance Survey map with my house at its centre. Spreading it over the duvet one weekend morning as I sat in bed with coffee, I spotted the faint line of the old railway. Later that day, following the trail as best I could by bike, I fetched up on the banks of the Stour river, running brown and fast, a few miles from Shillingstone, where the footings of the old railway bridge stood either side, and I could go no further.

Beeching had his way, the Pines Express is gone, but I found Shillingstone Station busy. The old buildings had a new lick of paint, there was a café inside and another in a restored railway carriage on the platform, a shop in the waiting room sold books and railway memorabilia. New tracks were laid, extending enticingly a few hundred yards in each direction towards Blandford and Sturminster Newton. There were even diesel and steam locomotives, in various stages of repair. At the far end of the platform a man was sitting on a bench, his little terrier in a pink collar tied to fencing while he painstakingly stencilled the letters ESSO onto an oil tanker hitched to a newly painted shunting engine. Shillingstone was reborn, after a fashion. But most of all, some of the route of the Slow and Dirty had a new use.

Waiting for me at a picnic bench on the platform was Joe Hickish. For fourteen miles either side of Shillingstone the route of the railway is now a path – the North Dorset Trailway; Joe is the chair of the trust that oversees it. It's his group which constructed a sparkling new bridge running across the river where once I came to a muddy stop. Joe had cycled to meet me from Blandford, our bikes leant together against a lamppost. He bought me a cup of tea and explained their mission – to link up the full length of the old railway, from coast to coast, make it accessible for walkers, cyclists, horse-riders and mobility scooter users. An energetic wiry man, active in local politics, wearing an Always European wristband, he conceded he was unlikely to see the project completed in his lifetime. The trust negotiates with landowners, persuading them, bit by bit, to reopen the old track bed. The next target was the section from Sturminster across fields to Stalbridge where I had found the old rails embedded in tarmac. I imagined cycling that forbidden flat land. On a satellite map the route of the railway is still traceable, tantalisingly within reach, but there's many a slip.

A few weeks earlier I had found myself in this farmland, delivering a parcel of books to someone who had ordered them from the publisher I work for. The address was a bungalow across a broken cattle grid. The owner was a woman who had farmed here for a lifetime and looked much younger than her 86 years. I said she lived in a beautiful place but she replied, "I know that now, but we just worked every day all day and never noticed." She said it had all once been Pitt Rivers land. I suggested to Joe that when the land was in the hands of one family the negotiation would have been simpler. Perhaps, he acknowledged, but these old aristocrats were a hard bunch, unlikely to surrender without a difficult compromise.

There's competition for the young Trailway. There are more books on the Somerset and Dorset Railway than any other closed branch line, online documentaries follow in detail the old route, some mournfully contrasting footage of the railway in use with its

later derelict condition. The Wikipedia page for the Somerset and
Dorset is as long as that for William Shakespeare. I understand this:
as a teenager I spent a few too many wet weekends on windy
platforms, cold fingers clutching a pencil and locomotive book
looking for the rare and not so rare.

At the top of the narrow staircase in the Blandford Forum
museum I'd come across a large model railway, a replica of the
station at Blandford, now a car park. The model was excellent and
lacked the infelicities which had plagued my own attempts in my
parents' hot loft, where I spent long hours piecing together Hornby
OO tracks while placing monstrously out of scale farm animals on
papier-mâché hills. The Blandford version was perfection, carefully
detailed, tiny hillocks of ballast by the trackside, authentic road
vehicles, a perfected, glossy vision of the 1950s. The museum
manager told me that one evening she took a phone call from one
of the men (and they *were* all men) who had made the model.

"What time do you open?" he asked.

She replied "10 am."

"Could you be there tomorrow at 9.30 instead?"

"Er, why would that be?"

"I want to see off the 9.45 to Wimborne."

Pinned up near the old waiting room at Shillingstone Station, a
notice explained that the eventual aim for the railway was to run a
full service to Sturminster Newton, along the same route as the
footpath, bringing steam back to this landscape for the first time in
decades. But given that Joe's group had spent years negotiating for
a modest path, I wondered if this grander scheme was anything
more than a pipe dream, a last burst of nostalgia running on fumes,
a simulacrum of an idealised lost past.

As I left I met a couple eating sandwiches under the station's
canopy. Two identical e-bikes were propped by the side of their
picnic table. They were on holiday from the Wirral, younger and
more active than Frank and Lily. They had spent the last two weeks
in the south-west. I asked them about e-bikes. Glancing at my
skinny legs the woman told me how they extend the range of a day's
ride, and how it's sensible to take the battery's help on hills. They
had loved their holiday, marvelled at how these old railway lines can
connect places.

I cycled home in the hillforts' shadow and thought about the
Trailway: carbon-free transport for those on holiday, for walkers,
commuters or kids going to school, without risk from traffic. The

tracks laid by previous generations have gone, leaving memories and quiet paths. But it was also a glimpse of a more hopeful future.

HAMBLEDON AND THE THIRD PARTY

On the day I moved to Dorset, in the rush of removals vans and searching for the kettle, I allowed myself to stop and take in the new view. The neighbours had left a bag of runner beans harvested from their garden dangling from the handle of our front door as a welcome gift, the lane was deathly quiet. In the distance over the flat land was a large grey-green shadow on the landscape, Hambledon Hill, Dorset's most impressive hillfort,[35] a huge, ribbed upturned bowl of green and ditch.

I had arranged to meet Haydn and Sheila in a muddy layby in Child Okeford, at Hambledon's foot, to explore some of Dorset's less remembered history: the alternatively rebellious seventeenth century Dorset Clubmen, which the couple have devoted years to researching. The sunny midweek February day had tempted few walkers, we were mostly alone. Taking a short footpath through a field we approached the hill from the north.

I once wrote a newspaper article about a bike ride through the Blackmore Vale; the picture editor illustrated it with a photograph of Hambledon's huge banks and ditches. Shortly afterwards I had an email from an 'ancient engineer' who claimed that the terracing on the hillfort could only have been constructed by an invading

Chinese army, the Ancient Britons not possessing the technology required.[36] While I considered this unlikely, the massive, vertiginous fortifications are nevertheless otherworldly. It's a hillfort that's attracted much attention, from historians, archaeologists, antiquarians. On 29th May 1996 the musician and deep-time enthusiast Julian Cope, best known as the singer in the band The Teardrop Explodes, who has subsequently carved an idiosyncratic and self-willed career as artist, historian and writer, visited Hambledon Hill. We know the date because he carefully recorded field notes in his magisterial book *The Modern Antiquarian.*[37] Cope described Hambledon as "sheer magical heaven" although he thought the large defensive ditches "ugly". I'm more relaxed about Hambledon's immensity – it's what first pulled me to it. John Piper painted the brooding hill in 1945,[38] and Gordon Haskell, who was briefly in the prog-rock band King Crimson, released an album called *Hambledon Hill* in 1990 – the title song is an atmospheric, charming slice of folk-pop.[39]

The ditches are relative newcomers in Hambledon's long life. Hambledon, and its close neighbour Hod Hill, are both chalk outcrops of the eastern fringes of Cranborne Chase. Hillforts generally occupy the borders of the high chalklands, points of division between landscapes.[40] Hambledon was in use five thousand years ago, probably as a seasonal gathering point and a burial place, only later defensively. Over the millennia occupation ebbed and flowed. Excavations found evidence of grazing wild aurochsen, the now extinct cattle. It was *only* around 700 BCE that the banks and ditches were piled up.

Haydn and Sheila came across the history of The Clubmen almost by accident. A few years previously they had helped research a book on the Levellers, one of the radical sects of the English Civil War – our only proper revolution[41]. Their research focused on Dorset, and especially on The Clubmen. Our popular imagining of the Civil War might now be restricted to the Cavaliers ("Wrong but Romantic") and the Roundheads ("Right but Repulsive"),[42] but its politics created many complex interweaving factions: the Levellers, Diggers and Ranters, all revolutionary in one way or another. But while only a small proportion of the population actively took sides, and even fewer fought, the war killed around 100,000 people, and had a widespread impact, owing to the armies from both sides traipsing through the countryside, taking what they wanted or needed. The Clubmen who were active mostly in the south and west, were heartily sick of the incursions, the theft of livestock, the pillage. Embodying the idea of 'active neutralism', The Clubmen were a new force in the land, a Third Party, arming themselves for defence. Both Royalists and Parliamentarians recognised the threat.

Throwing themselves into The Clubmen project, Haydn and Sheila created videos, commissioned artists to draw maps, created a website to gather and disseminate information about the movement. Hambledon Hill was the site of the Dorset Clubmen's last stand, their final confrontation with the Parliamentary forces. Haydn and Sheila guided me up Hambledon's slopes – this approach, they believed, was where the dragoons of the New Model Army, under the command of a promising Lieutenant General for the Parliamentary forces, Oliver Cromwell, ascended the hill. I asked Haydn why he thought it was here that they made their advance against The Clubmen.

"I've been round and round the hill, looking," he said, "the contemporary accounts describe the dragoons climbing the hill, three abreast, and this is really the only place they could have done so. And then I met a man here, a retired army officer, riding his horse, and he said that his daughter used to collect musket balls from this exact place when she was a kid." Frederick Treves was inclined to agree, writing that there was a spot between the villages of Shroton and Child Okeford where the attack seemed most probable.

Where The Clubmen's history has been recorded, it's not always been kind, Treves being an example. Over the course of a few pages he employed every rural stereotype he could muster:

> … despairing yokels … uncouth … lumbering quotum of red-faced countrymen … poor red-faced clumsy patriots … muddle headed… Well-meaning but ridiculous.

Sheila and Haydn's research revealed something quite different. The Clubmen, representing all elements of society, carefully worked out strategies and alliances, petitioning both sides to navigate the complicated political landscape of the 1640s, hoping to shorten the war.

We reached the top of the hill, its wide undulating plateau empty aside from a few sheep, the views stretching westward to faint, distant hills. From the northern edge of the hill we could see the whole fateful landscape of August 1645 – the hills of Shaftesbury and Duncliffe, the land towards Sherborne, where a solar farm now sparkled.

On 2nd August 1645 a number of Clubmen were captured at Shaftesbury by the Parliamentary forces. Angered by this, a large group of Clubmen, wearing white ribbons, met at Duncliffe – a prominent wooded hill, notable now for its springtime bluebells. The negotiation here between the locals and Cromwell seemed to result in truce, except that just a few miles away, a few thousand Clubmen were gathering on Hambledon.

Haydn didn't believe that the Clubmen were out for a fight. They had their firebrands, notably Thomas Bravell, the rector of Compton Abbas, just south of Shaftesbury.[43] Parliamentary sources described him as 'Malignent', but taking on the highly trained, disciplined and battled-hardened New Model Army would have been foolish. The Clubmen weren't named after makeshift weapons (a misunderstanding that might have led Treves and others to consider them unsophisticated) but because they formed an association, a club. Sheila and Haydn believed that they were cornered and took to the hill as refuge.

History is written by the victors and we have only Cromwell's account. There was some attempt at discussion, ended by the Clubmen firing shots at the Army, the musket balls found centuries later by a little girl playing on the hill. What ensued was a few hours of terrifying combat, as the New Model Army destroyed the opposition – killing "not a dozen" in Cromwell's words, many of them fleeing helter-skelter down the embankments to escape. Haydn and Sheila took me to the relatively flat area at the top of the hill where they thought the final battle took place, patrolled by sheep, a kestrel swaying unsteadily in a nearby tree. Around us were the topmost pilings of the earthworks but even in the stillness, the thought of the noise, confusion, terror, was vivid and chilling.

The Clubmen's legacy is contested. The Tolpuddle Festival, founded to celebrate the unionism of the Dorset labourers, was largely uninterested, but allowed a Clubmen banner in their annual march. From across the political divide Haydn and Sheila had been contacted by some "UKIP-y types", looking to co-opt the Clubmen to their cause, which they resisted – the Clubmen were no little-Englander separatists, but prepared to work with all sides, wanting stability rather than disruption. We talked about how hard it was to draw parallels with our times, seventeenth century politics tightly bound with what we'd now see as obscure religious arguments about the possibility of earthly perfection.

We came down the hill faster than we had climbed it. A friend of mine says that Dorset villages have the names of faded Hollywood Stars, living out their final years drinking heavily at the poolside: Hazelbury Bryan, Glanvilles Wootton, Buckland Newton, Lytchett Matravers, Wynford Eagle. Iwerne Courtney would be the most raddled of the lot, all tall tales and scandal, but everyone I know calls the village Shroton, the village with two names. We crunched the gravel to the door of St Mary's church. After the battle The New Model Army brought the ringleaders of the Clubmen to St Mary's and locked them in overnight. In the morning Cromwell took to the pulpit and lectured them on their misdeeds. The cowed rebels promised not to repeat the escapade and were released. Outside Haydn showed me where he thought the dozen or so Clubmen who had been killed were likely to be buried, in unmarked graves.

Hambledon wasn't quite the last of the Clubmen – the terrible harvest of 1648 saw widespread hunger and anger; the Clubmen rose again across the south and west, before final defeat at Burford the following year. But the thread of individuals' subsequent lives wove different paths. Thomas Bravell lost his living at Compton Abbas but was reinstated in 1647. Another leading light, Thomas Frampton, left England in 1655 for Aleppo in Syria, returning to become Bishop of Gloucester, but on the ascension of William and Mary found himself once more on the wrong side of history, ending his life as a parish priest.

There was nothing on the ground of this – the National Trust's sign at the foot of Hambledon made much of the nature and nothing of the rebellion, the graves of those killed were invisible. But Haydn and Sheila's efforts to revive this history could yet teach us something about the spirit of localism, collaboration and mutual aid embodied by The Clubmen, rooted in a sense of place and an emphatic rejection of war.

SHAFTESBURY'S VAGUE IMAGINING

My mother made a late and unhappy marriage to a man with whom she shared interests but not temperament. Habits kept them together, chiefly camping trips in France, made several times a year. But age was catching them, and they no longer had the stomach for tent pegs and arguments about groundsheets. As a solution mum had set her heart on a particular type of small campervan.

On one of their visits to see us my wife Helen and I took them to Shaftesbury, our nearest town. As we were leaving our car, another vehicle caught mum's eye and she grabbed the arm of her husband.

"Look Trevor. It's a Romahome!"

She strode off across the car park, Trevor in reluctant tow. Accosting the owners she asked to be shown every feature of the van, and they obliged. Over the course of twenty long minutes, Helen and I lingered a short distance away while bedding and chemical toilets were explained. The car park was full of tourists; every two or three minutes we were approached, always with the same question.

"Where's Gold Hill?"

Shaftesbury's modern fame is due to the director of the dystopian masterpiece *Blade Runner*. Years before he turned Harrison Ford loose in a futuristic Los Angeles in his adaptation of Philip K. Dick's *Do Androids Dream of Electric Sheep*, Ridley Scott made a TV advert which has gone on to be named one of the nation's favourites. In the opening scene a young boy pushes a heavy black bike up a vertiginously steep cobbled street, the basket full of loaves of bread. The baker boy leans his bike against one of the neat, thatched cottages, delivers his load and freewheels down the hill, before being rewarded with a slice of Hovis and butter at his boss' house. The closing caption tells us that "Hovis is as Good For You Today as It's Ever Been". This soft-focus slice of rural nostalgia was filmed on Gold Hill but has in the public imagination somehow translated Shaftesbury to Yorkshire, possibly owing to the soundtrack: Dvořák's mournful Largo movement of his symphony *From the New World*, played on brass instruments, an echo of a colliery band. But the accent of the voice-over is unmistakeably, exaggeratedly West Country.

Frederick Treves began his Dorset book in Shaftesbury, briefly referring to Gold Hill, with an accompanying sketch which renders the hill steeper still. For Treves, it was just one of many of the town's pleasures, as it was for Michael Pitt-Rivers in the *Shell Guide*. But since 1973, when the advert was aired, Shaftesbury has made the most of it – the image of Gold Hill appears everywhere, from the town council website to tote bags, cards and prints, and it's the star of thousands of Instagram posts. Hovis supplied an enormous plastic loaf, proudly on display at the top of the hill and the excellent museum, also on Gold Hill, has a replica of the bike used in the advert. In 2017, in a move that can only be described as 'meta', Evans Cycles commissioned an advertisement in which the members of a local cycling group each try and fail to climb Gold Hill before finally a middle-aged man dressed in a flat cap and tweed suit, a basket of bread on the handlebars, makes the climb easily on an e-bike. This man was the original boy from the Hovis ad.[44]

Almost all the images of Gold Hill are taken from the same spot: the hill curves, the cottages face the cobbles, below is the green floor of the Blackmore Vale. Some of the houses would have been both living space and workplace for the women who worked in Shaftesbury's button-making industry, wiped out by mechanisation in the early nineteenth century, plunging the town into one of its periodic declines.

Standing at the top of the hill I could see that the cottages had no opposite neighbours. Instead there was a huge, buttressed, grey stone wall, rearing high above. This was almost all that remains above ground of the massive abbey complex which gave Shaftesbury its pre-eminence, making it, for a few hundred years, Dorset's most populous and important town. Some of its fame was due to a murdered teenager.

Shaftesbury is Dorset's only hill-town, giving it a perfect defensive position. At its westernmost point are the earthworks of the former castle, but despite the road signs welcoming the visitor to the Saxon town, nothing remains of the old 'burgh'; instead historians have relied on the accounts of contemporary or near-contemporary chroniclers, and some informed guesswork to recreate it. The twelfth century historian Geoffrey of Monmouth claimed the town was founded by King Lear's grandfather around 950 BCE, but Shaftesbury is King Alfred's town. He founded a nunnery for his daughter Aethelgifu in the town, but its big moment came over a century later. In 978 The young King Edward, aged just seventeen, was murdered at Corfe Castle, possibly by Aelfthryth, the original wicked stepmother. The king was apparently prone to violent rages, nevertheless rumours of miracles associated with Edward's body began to surface, and having been hastily interred at Wareham he was reburied at Shaftesbury with great ceremony the following year. Not long afterwards, possibly in response to calls for 'native saints' he was canonised. Shaftesbury became a pilgrimage hotspot, one of the great shrines of England, helped along by William of Malmesbury writing that one of Edward the Martyr's lungs was still pulsating in a glass jar, a good 250 years after his death.

The town had twelve churches, chantries, mints and the vast abbey itself, the richest Benedictine nunnery in England. This would have pleased my mother and her husband, both devout Roman Catholics when they weren't bickering or buying campervans.

The ruins of the later Norman abbey church lay in gardens behind Park Walk at the top of Gold Hill, just small piles of stones representing pillar footings, although recent archaeology has since established that the abbey buildings, built and rebuilt, ran wider underground. These gardens, overlooked by a slightly forbidding statue of King Alfred, were modest, but in its heyday the abbey would have been visible for miles around. I'd come across a digital model online which, despite a LEGO-like tendency, hinted at its scale. Glimpsed from the still largely forested valley it would have been a dramatic testament to Alfred and his daughters.

Alfred dominates Wessex, the supposed site of where his troops mustered before defeating the Danes at the battle of Edington is marked by the triangular folly tower built on the Stourhead estate by Henry Hoare in the eighteenth century, and is a constant presence in the northern vale, a Rapunzel-ish tower, poking through trees on the hillside. It may not be in the correct spot, even the site of the battle is still contested; the tower was a way of making history, of creating a lineage of English greatness. The truth is less convenient. Alfred defeated the Danes, or at least kept them out of his part of England, but they were soon back – Cnut raided Wessex in the early eleventh century and made it his own, using it as a base to attack London, and eventually becoming England's king, dying at Shaftesbury in 1035.

Shaftesbury's dominance did not last. It was hit badly by the plague that arrived in Dorset in 1348[45] and pilgrimage fell out of fashion. The abbey keys were handed over to Henry VIII's commissioner on 23rd March 1539, and soon after its dissolution it was demolished. Marooned on its hillside, Shaftesbury declined. Medieval Shaftesbury is almost all gone – the town today is an eighteenth and nineteenth century idea of itself. In Hardy's last, and arguably most depressing novel, *Jude the Obscure*, Sue jumps from a surprisingly low first floor window in a suicide attempt in Shaston, the author's version of Shaftesbury. The site of the fictional event, appropriately close to the ambulance station, was marked by a blue plaque. Hardy describes the town as the "queerest and quaintest of spots" and that any visitor would be driven to "pensive melancholy" at the thought of its vanished glory. But these were the years before Hovis. On a recent dark winter's day I poked around the graveyard of the former church of the Holy Trinity, a Victorian replacement of an earlier church and found gravestones lying flat or propped against the wall of the abbey gardens, and felt Hardy's chill. Other writers have reflected on the town's literal cold, Richard Ollard going so far as to complain that it's "windswept".

By the nineteenth century, its button-makers consigned to the sewing box of history, Shaftesbury was little more than a large village; the position which had once made it so important was now a disadvantage. It's hard to build railways on hilltop towns. The nearest station was at Semley but that closed in the 1960s and is now identifiable only by a few buildings by the side of the track. But Shaftesbury Station exists in fiction. In one novel, longlisted for the Booker Prize, a character takes a train to Shaftesbury. It would be wrong to carp – the author told me she had chosen Dorset precisely because she knew nothing about it and was able to superimpose her book on the landscape – after all this is a partly real, partly dream land, and her novel is very good.[46]

For a century the town was owned by the Grosvenor family, bought to ensure their candidates were successful in local elections. This met with some resistance in the town, the Grosvenor Arms becoming a focus of rebellion as the landlord denied the supporters of reform access to the inn. Eventually Shaftesbury's reforming Methodists worked with the Grosvenors to bring a water supply to the town, to rebuild homes and establish a hospital. The Grosvenors replaced the Town Hall, building it right at the top of Gold Hill. I was once told that this was to block a ley line which might otherwise bring bad luck. The theory of ley lines, invisible straight connections across the landscape between hills or churches or other notable features, was first proposed by Alfred Watkins in his book *The Old*

Straight Track, but evidence for the siting of the town hall for this purpose is lacking beyond vague reports of a Shaston Eagle grouping of ley lines which fold out from the town, having made a direct line from Glastonbury.[47]

The lost glory of Shaftesbury was a "vague imagining" (Hardy again) but in the 1930s a lead-lined casket was discovered, containing human remains, assumed to be those of Edward the Martyr, the lungs now so decayed that they could no longer inflate and deflate. Since then, curiously, a group of Russian Orthodox brothers at Brookwood in Surrey have come to revere the remains of this hot-tempered teenager as holy relics. The abbey, so long lost to time, has re-emerged in Shaftesbury's history. And with it, new rumours, new stories.

Many towns have tunnel-fables. Books have been written on London's underland, its alleged sunken streets and very real Roman temples. I've heard talk of chambers beneath Bridport being used for firearms practice by the police. So too does Shaftesbury. One story is that at the abbey's dissolution a priest hid many of its treasures in a network of tunnels, but died before he could tell anyone their location. I've walked the streets noting the depth of the cellars beneath grills in this high town, and wondered. Most evidence for the streets beneath our feet is scant, based on hearsay from friends of internet friends, but in an interview for Shaftesbury's local radio station, Alfred FM, a local councillor gave a plausible account of being taken to a forty-foot-long tunnel on

Tout Hill. Even the Neighbourhood Plan, devised by the council, makes provision for the possibility of their existence.

Given that the existence of tunnels is alluded to in the historical record, and that access to a vast hillside abbey might well have required tunnels as access points from the vale below, to deny the possibility seems premature. In Shaftesbury's long history relics and abbeys, buttons and tunnels are apt to be lost, forgotten and rediscovered, turned up afresh, made to mean something different, shovelled up and slipped down. But it will always have Hovis.

LARMER TREE GARDENS: END OF THE ROAD

It was around 11.30 at night when I stopped to examine the small, octagonal folly in the Larmer Tree Gardens. I was a little too full of gin and 'half and half' cider – half a pint of cloudy dry cider with half a pint of medium, bought from a double decker bus. With a group of friends I've come to the End of the Road Festival almost every year since it began in 2007. I've seen some remarkable artists, old favourites and new discoveries: David Byrne, Patti Smith, Low, Johnny Greenwood, Yo La Tengo, Gwenno, She'll Stop at the Bridge, Arlo Parks, Are You Swedish?, John Grant, St Vincent, Coelacanth? Coelacanth!, Little Simz, Hurray for the Riff Raff and Richard Dawson.

The folly is *just* across the border in Wiltshire, a matter of a few yards – the county line slices the site neatly in two, running up the middle of the road that festival goers enter by. Frederick Treves wasn't bothered by this – including in his Dorset book a description of the gardens as they were in the early twentieth century. The festival is dotted with art, carefully woven into the woodland walks; inside the folly was a series of test-tubes lit delicately, visible through the windows on each side of the structure, its classical decoration topped off with an inscription in Latin: Augustus Pitt Rivers Erected 1880.

I needed to sit down. I'd already walked a long, stony, straight path past rows of tents, the hum of the onsite generators and drum beats slowly fading, to another folly. This one was 65 feet tall, ochre and pale brick, four pillars reaching to a high platform and topped with five domes, as if imported from a Mughal past. I walked

around it, prevented from getting close by temporary fencing and a deep trench. New follies are rare in England now,[48] but this one was built in 2009 by William Gronow-Davis, who told *The Daily Telegraph* that it "finished off" his estate and therefore justified the expense. In the daylight it's unmistakeable, gaudy, but at night, during the festival, it made a kind of sense, and it's *just* in Dorset.

A couple, probably in their 60s were sitting at a picnic table drinking wine and were congratulated on their elegance by two passing younger people who were then offered a biscuit. It's that sort of festival – nobody was 35 years old, they were 65 or 18, 55 or 23. The crowd was slightly self-consciously bohemian, gentle middle-aged musos, bouncier kids. It was fashion for all times and none, happily mismatched.

William Gronow-Davis was the partner of Michael Pitt-Rivers or to give him his full name: Michael Augustus Lane-Fox Pitt-Rivers, son of the failed fascist George,[49] great grandson of General Augustus Pitt-Rivers, who made the gardens and carried out archaeological digs across his estate. Modern archaeologists may blanche at the general's interventions, sometimes reconstructing sites to better suit his sense of the past, but still he's known as the 'father of modern archaeology' and his name lives on in the famous Oxford museum. Not far from here, close to a golf course, he excavated a Roman farm and large tombstone-like slabs were installed, pointing to wells and giving a short history.[50]

Michael Pitt-Rivers wrote the *Shell Guide to Dorset* and was responsible for rescuing the gardens and their various follies and buildings from ruin after they fell into disuse following the general's death in 1900. The gardens were made not solely for the general's pleasure but also for the entertainment and education of the working classes, for whom he laid on entertainment and picnics, using the stages and buildings he built here. They came in their hundreds, on bikes and by charabanc from Salisbury railway station. This sense of magic and mystery clung on through the years of neglect: the film director Ken Russell remembered coming to the then decrepit gardens as a child in the family Austin Seven, eating cucumber sandwiches amongst the decaying buildings, returning as an adult to use Larmer Tree as a set.

I sat on the trampled grass under lights from food stalls to take some notes, drank red wine from a can and thought that this was the noisiest outdoor space I had been in for months. I was practically invisible – the peacocks that roamed by day and squawked by night were the most extravagantly attired, but only just. An older man, dressed entirely in tweed and carrying a silver topped walking cane walked past me: he wasn't the general, but he could have been.

When Pitt Rivers dug into the ground on his estate he may have found, along with the pottery fragments and brooches, a time portal which is not yet closed. If a late Victorian group had arrived at the festival, breathless from their ride from Salisbury, hot in woollen and crinoline, what would they have thought? Their dress would not have marked them out amongst the beards and dungarees, the formality and the glitter. On its last night the festival has a controlled fin-de-siècle atmosphere.

Maybe our time-travellers would have thought this was the End of Days, although they would have been comforted by the familiar sight of a helter-skelter in this southern English Brigadoon. Would we really be so unfamiliar to one another? The atmosphere of the late-night woodland discos isn't that different to the brass-gilded pubs which the temperance movement so disliked. The twenty-first century revellers would have seemed unnaturally healthy, mostly, but otherwise identical. In the Larmer Tree's half and half borderland we might have already met both our history and the times to come. In a hundred years, after wars, pandemics, a realignment with nature, someone returning to this magical place would still encounter the present, the past, and in the sky a sliver of the future moon.

Notes

1 Oliver Rackham's *The Ash Tree* was his final book, completed and published just before his untimely death. See *The Ash Tree*, Little Toller Books, 2015, paperback edition, 2017.

2 This action, carried out in Egypt was considered a success, even though the Queen's Own Dorset Yeomanry lost 30% of their men.

3 See the Central section of this book.

4 See the Folly Flaneuse, an excellent website about follies, for more on Horton. If this is your sort of thing, it's well worth signing up to the newsletter, a lovely slice of history and mystery delivered every Saturday morning: thefollyflaneuse.com/horton-tower-or-sturts -folly-horton-dorset/. For more on the Hardy Monument, named for Nelson's Hardy, see the South Section of this book.

5 This adaptation starred Julie Christie as Bathsheba, alongside Peter Finch, Alan Bates and Stamp. In the same year as the film came out, The Kinks released 'Waterloo Sunset', in which "Terry meets Julie" every Friday night at the eponymous station, a reference to Christie and Stamp.

6 For a good, brief history of the tower see *Discover Dorset, Follies* by Jonathan Holt, The Dovecote Press, 2000, pp 34-35. I was lucky enough to run into the author when we were both exploring the landscape around William Beckford's Fonthill, in Wiltshire.

7 The very solid Euston Arch once stood at the entrance to Euston station but was demolished in 1962 when the station was remodelled. The stones were dumped in the

River Lea, and only rediscovered during another great infrastructure project – the construction of the Olympic Park for London 2012.

8   Later home to Madonna and Guy Ritchie – Ritchie still lives on the estate and has opened a brewery: Gritchie.

9   Michael Pitt-Rivers was also the author of the *Shell Guide to Dorset*, and later married Sonia, Orwell's widow, although the marriage was not a success. See also the section on the Larmer Tree Gardens in this book.

10 Eddy Sackville-West, so much a hypochondriac that he was the model for Davey in Nancy Mitford's *The Pursuit of Love*, died on the toilet in 1965, just like Evelyn Waugh in 1966.

11 For an entertaining account of the life around the house see *The Crichel Boys* by Simon Fenwick, Little Brown, 2021.

12 The site was extensive, constructed first in the late neolithic period but used again in the Bronze Age as a funerary complex with at least 170 barrows.

13 Hargreaves' ashes are scattered on Bulbarrow Hill, close to where he lived. For my walk over Bulbarrow see the Central section of this book.

14 For more on the cultural and religious associations of the yew see the magnificent *Flora Britannica* by Richard Mabey, Sinclair Stevenson, 1996, Chatto and Windus, 1997 pp 28-35.

15 In *Churches in the Landscape* by Richard Morris (J.M. Dent and Sons, 1989) he discusses at length the adoption of "pagan" sites by Christians pp 57-74.

16 My first impressions may have been influenced by a small contretemps in the supermarket car park just before my meeting: a woman had nearly run me over, going the wrong way towards the exit, and when I remonstrated with her told me to bugger off and said that if she had been younger she would have physically assaulted me.

17 The *King's England* series is characterised by a tendency towards nostalgia, and was contemporaneous with the Shell Guides, which I prefer. Both series were influenced by the Highways and Byways books, of which Sir Frederick Treves' Dorset is the best written, in my opinion.

18 For a photo of the large pub, for which only a few bricks would have been needed for the modest extension, see *Around Gillingham* by David Lloyd, p 19.

19 Simon Jenkins says he "would pit Sherborne's roof against any contemporary work of the Italian Renaissance". See *England's Thousand Best Churches* by Simon Jenkins, Allen Lane, 1999, Penguin edition, 2000, p 161.

20 The poem appeared in *Continual Dew*, published in 1937, and is collected in *John Betjeman's Collected Poems*, John Murray, 1979, pp 40-41, although Hardy, the last of those names, had already died.

21 For Katherine's History of Sherborne House see www.sherbornehousedorset.org.uk /history-full.php, and for her account of our walk see The Shire Rack section of this book.

22 This film was part of Meades' *Abroad Again* series. His memoir *An Encyclopedia of Myself* expands upon this and is brilliant. Co-incidentally, Meades' mother, whom he writes about movingly, was my teacher at primary school, years before he was famous.

23 Some recent research has indicated that there was probably never a Roman 'villa' here at all, but the mosaic remains an important discovery.

24 *Dorset* by Richard Ollard, Pimlico, 1995, p 91. It's hard to know why he included a place he says so little about, except that he points readers in the direction of Jo Draper's *Dorset* – but even she writes that the town's main attraction is that it's "old fashioned" and "rather plain".

25 See also Bridport section of this book.

26 One theory is that cadaver tombs were a *momento mori*, to remind the living that death was around the corner, that purgatory was real, that they should pray for the departed's soul and that they should live a good life.

27 In the once bafflingly popular novel *The Da Vinci Code*, now mostly confined to charity

shops and holiday cottages, one character, an evil Roman Catholic priest, repeatedly whips himself.

28 The donkey was called Doris.

29 I'm grateful to Catherine Speakman aka Tess of the Vale for her pointing me in the direction of Boyle's Klutzy habits; for more on this see www.dorsets.co.uk/stalbridge

30 Or thereabouts. Archaeological work on the site in 2019-2021 isn't precise but the team working on the site speculated that by 1825 the last vestiges of the manor house, above ground at least, were gone.

31 Bonaparte clearly being the worst word imaginable.

32 The excellent Stalbridge History Society website keeps the memories alive – and lists the residents of the cottages in the nineteenth century, and notes that the date carved onto the houses – 1863, is erroneous.

33 For an excellent, short history of the Shell Guides and their guiding principles see *The Thirties, An Intimate History* by Juliet Gardiner, Harper Press, 2010, pp 247-249.

34 The Pines Express never stopped at Shillingstone but I hope that Frank and Lily, my grandparents, who came for holidays in Bournemouth, would have at least appreciated the views of the hillforts from the speeding train.

35 A personal opinion.

36 It's hard to know where to start with this. My correspondent worked closely with the now discredited historian Gavin Menzies (1937-2020), whose book *1421: The Year China Discovered the World* was a bestseller when published in 2003, but a 2012 article in *The New York Times* reported that it had been ranked as one of the worst history books ever. A review in *History Co-operative* carefully weighed its merits and concluded that while it was useful to counter Euro-centrism, it was rubbish. historycooperative.org/not-rewrite-world-history-gavin-menzies-chinese-discovery-america/.

37 *The Modern Antiquarian* by Julian Cope, Thorsons, 1998. His visit to Hambledon Hill is on page 132. I urge you to get a copy of this extraordinary and only relatively eccentric book if you can. It's learned, brilliant and captivating.

38 The painting is now at St Cross College, Oxford.

39 I have found several other pieces of music also called *Hambledon Hill* – Andy Wilkinson's is plodding rock while Tim Souster and the Smith Quartet's is terrifyingly discordant but thrilling modern classical music. Hawkeye and Hoe's song is about The Clubmen and quotes directly from their manifesto.

40 I have left Hod Hill out from this book, one can only find room for so many hillforts, but its history, first as a bustling Neolithic settlement and later as a Roman fort is fascinating.

41 At time of writing.

42 These were the descriptions of the opposing sides in the Civil War in *1066 and All That* by W.C. Sellar and R.J. Yeatman, the classic that lampooned the way history was traditionally taught.

43 Bravell's church is gone, replaced in the nineteenth century, but its tower and graveyard remains, as does a distinct atmosphere, it's worth looking out this secluded hamlet.

44 I've cycled up Gold Hill two or three times, on a 'normal' bike. It's a bloody horrible climb.

45 See chapter on Weymouth in this book.

46 For the interested it's *Almost English* by Charlotte Mendelson, Mantel, 2013.

47 *The Old Straight* Track was first published in 1925. Watkins observed that many ancient landscape features were organised in straight lines. His theory was based on the idea that these would act as navigational or processional routes for ancient peoples, but in later times the New Age movement, as it was first called, took the theory further, proposing that ley lines were routes of Earth Energy. A recent investigator has pointed out that one could draw regular shapes across the land, only using the sites of closed Woolworth's stores as key junctions. This sounds like a perfect new psychogeography: bigthink.com/

strange-maps/527-the-st-michael-line-a-straight-story/.

48 The last folly tower of any significance was Lord Berners' at Faringdon in 1935. *See Lord Berners: The Last Eccentric* by Mark Amory, Chatto & Windus 1998, Pimlico, 1999 pp 149-150.

49 See the Hinton St Mary section of this book.

50 Woodcutts Roman Farm, accessible via a footpath. Those in possession of a smartphone can download the Time Travellers of Cranborne Chase app to see an Augmented Reality version of the farm in the first century CE. More info: cranbornechase.org.uk/time-t raveller-locations-in-the-landscape/

SOUTH

WEYMOUTH: THE SWEET TOWN

One hot, humid Friday in mid-July I cycled to Weymouth. Between houses, graveyards and the reedy waters of the River Wey I slipped in, never once sharing my route with a car. In 2012 the town hosted the Olympic sailing events; this network of busy and ingenious bike paths was part of the accompanying infrastructure work.

A wide, curving beach and the confident eighteenth and nineteenth century buildings exuded settled superiority, but Weymouth has seen better days. George III visited in 1789, having heard of the water's curative properties, and took enthusiastically to the new-fangled bathing machine on this and his many subsequent visits. I found a large, badly proportioned statue near the Promenade devoted to him. Across the hazy bay towards Osmington I could make out the huge chalk figure of George on his horse, walking *away* from the town, a strange slight. The town's heyday was in the early twentieth century. In *Highways and Byways in Dorset*, Sir Frederick Treves wrote that the town was "incommoded by its exceptional popularity, which is well deserved and is vouched for by a crowd of many thousands of visitors every summer." Pushing my bike, I walked into the network of narrow streets behind the Esplanade. Here buildings crowded close, the stand-offish seafront forgotten. I found betting shops, places to get phones unlocked, or tattoos inked, intermingled with Costa, Starbucks, Café Nero. This is a shut-away place, difficult to leave. Some districts of Weymouth are desperately poor: adjoining neighbourhoods have life expectancies as much as ten years apart.[1] I was struck by the number of mobility scooters – their riders weren't all old, but ill, pale and stuck here. The Olympic legacy only goes so far. Weymouth is marooned, hindered by an unhelpful reputation.

For all that, I'm fond of the town. The seafront was glorious. The beach was teeming, the deckchair company was doing a roaring trade, dogs and families danced gingerly in the surf. I sat on the edge of the Esplanade, legs dangling above the sand, unwrapped my cheese sandwich and didn't mind that it was slightly warm and squashed, gulping it down with tepid water. The British were doing what they love: getting on the outside of European lager in the heat, laughing and turning beetroot. A funfair wafted eerie music across the promenade. Everything was primary colours, bunting flapped on guesthouses' railings.

Under the surface Weymouth's history speaks of the radical and the rambunctious – in 1826 the local populace, deprived of the vote and deeply distrustful of an alliance between conservatives and liberals, hijacked the hustings, preventing the few entitled voters to enter, until dragoons barricaded the town hall against the protestors.

I was apprehensive. When my mother died she left many clothes. If I had taken them to a charity shop close to home, I'd certainly see people, maybe people I *knew*, in her skirts or coats or blouses. So I drove to Weymouth and left a huge pile of garments at the Sue Ryder shop. This was my first visit since. I glanced a little nervously at what people were wearing. But I was here for something else.

The sea was once Weymouth's fortune, important long before George III made it fashionable – Daniel Defoe described it as "a sweet, clean agreeable town, well-built with many substantial merchants in it". Cross-channel ferries no longer run but the waterway was full of boats and a few rusted, purposeful trawlers. The harbour bridge's arch cracked open to admit a high-masted blue yacht, gliding imperiously through town, followed cheekily by a small *Swallows and Amazons* style boat with ragged red sails, packed with people and a barking, happy dog. The bridge spans the water between Old Weymouth and what was once Melcombe Regis. Melcombe was subsumed into Weymouth in the seventeenth century, but previously the two competing ports faced each other across the narrow waterway. Shipping had made the towns rich, but the sea brought more than trade.

In May 1348, a ship docked at Melcombe. On board was a sailor with an unknown illness.

The Black Death was a rampaging monster. It spread fast and killed as much as sixty per cent of Europe's population, falling hardest on the rural poor, reshaping society forever. Daily life broke down. It was assumed to be God's punishment for humanity's sins, it had no cure and no prevention. Fleas killed their host population of black rats, turning next to humans, bites drained to lymph nodes causing buboes to swell at the groin, armpit, thigh or neck. Death was swift, painful, all but inevitable. The Plague was a watershed; everything was before or after. Sometimes there were too few living to bury the dead.[2]

I visited the small museum, tucked away in Old Weymouth. Here I found a photograph of a plaque set into the quayside across the water, commemorating the plague ship's arrival. At the desk I asked the two friendly volunteers where it was. The women were unfazed by my request but neither knew. "I've definitely seen it," said one, "I'll find out because I'll be asked again." They must get a lot of this sort of thing.

Outside I set about looking for the plaque. It was still hot and busy along the street overlooking the water, crowded with wandering shirt-sleeved groups, pubs spilling onto pavements, tents setting up for a seafood festival. I wondered if I was attracting attention, searching behind overflowing wheelie bins, upsetting gulls. Nothing here. I cycled away from the hubbub, carefully avoiding the hazardous old tram tracks. I poked amongst the weeds sprouting through cracked tarmac in the harbourside car park. Where was it? I wondered if the plaque had been removed by the Tourist Board, trying to dissociate the town from one of history's great disasters. But finding these few words would have proved little and feeling the rising urgency of a long ride home through the evening I remounted, little suspecting that in a few months this town, and much of the world, would be silenced by a new pandemic.

KEEP PORTLAND WEIRD

Before I lived in Dorset I worked with a gentle, well-read and intelligent man, perfectly suited to his job marketing novels at a chain of bookshops. I liked him a lot although I was a less than perfect manager for him – I was too impatient, too obsessed by minutiae. One day, close to Christmas and staring through the office windows towards a bleak view of the M4 flyover at Brentford, I asked him about his festive plans.

"I'm going to stay with my sister in Dorset," he replied.

I responded enthusiastically. It sounded like an excellent escape from the clutches of his boss. But Rodney shuddered.

"It's Portland," he said. "Such an odd place. There's a big prison and no trees."

This didn't sound like Dorset at all.

Frederick Treves likened the outline of Portland to Monaco, conjuring a Mediterranean outcrop overlooking a tideless, sparkling sea. As I drove across the causeway from Weymouth on a rare sunny day in early January, the grey bulk of the island growing slowly larger, I tried to see what Treves had seen, but with little success. The closer he got the less he liked it, describing the small island as a "dismal heap of stone". His journey across the exposed land would have been slower than mine, but faster than it would have been sixty years earlier, when the only connection to the mainland was across the long pebble arm of Chesil Beach. Portland, like Purbeck, is not strictly an island. Queen Victoria had been violently seasick while making the crossing by boat and some have said that the works to connect it by road, finally opened by Prince Albert in 1849, were a result of her experience. If so, the cost of settling the monarch's stomach was high – the project took twenty-five years, resulted in the deaths of many workers and the accidental burning of a wooden lighthouse.

Passing the marina I finally reached the town of Fortuneswell. Its long runs of terraced housing, here crowded onto the steep slope, are typical of Portland. Treves had been unimpressed by Fortuneswell ("like the island, ugly"). Geology forced strangeness onto the island. Fortuneswell's church is not built along the traditional east-west axis, because it would otherwise slide down the hill, and the main street is shored up on one side by walls dating from the eighteenth and nineteenth centuries to prevent landslips.

I drove up a steep hill and emerged onto an exposed, somewhat desolate plateau, and as Rodney (and the sixteenth century traveller John Leland) had noted, almost treeless. Everywhere was whitened rubble and blocks of stone.

Even if you've never been to Portland, it's likely that you'll have been inside it. Portland stone built our cities, especially London, a city shaped by Dorset. Its potential was recognised by William I – Portland is the first entry in the Dorset section of the Domesday Book, when the island boasted 14 cattle, 27 pigs and 900 sheep, but importantly the King reserved Portland for himself, rather than parcelling it out to his Norman nobility. Some of the Tower of London, his great building project, was extracted from Portland quarries. The Great Fire of London was a disaster for the capital, but its aftermath was boomtime for Portland. St Paul's Cathedral was dug from the quarries here; walk from Waterloo station through the windy ICI complex and you're walking through Portland, stepping inside the Tate Gallery is to lose yourself in Portland, Broadcasting House beams radio from stone cut from its quarries, Senate House, London's impressive University building is Portland too. Commonwealth War Graves commemorate the dead with slabs of Portland and New York's U.N. building is faced with Portland stone. Even the coming of concrete couldn't dent Portland – briefly the island manufactured Portcrete, used to build Centrepoint on Tottenham Court Road in London.

The industry scarred the island, made its landscapes. Quarries in use or disused, all the associated paraphernalia and danger. At the top of the hill the road bent sharply to the left, but had I made the journey 25 years earlier I would have followed New Road along the coastline, before the crumbling earth forced its diversion inland.

I left the car at Wakeham, crossed the road, passing a slab which commemorated the spot where stone for Whitehall's Cenotaph was quarried, a memorial to a memorial. The plaque also grumbled about the destruction of a thirteenth century chantry by Cromwell's troops – Portland was, almost alone in Dorset, loyal to the crown in the Civil War, and held out, securing a relatively generous settlement with the eventual victors.[3]

I found a little lane, slipped past a house named Well-Beloved, in tribute to Hardy's Portland novel, and walked beneath the arch of Rufus Castle, a ruined twelfth century lump, patrolled by gulls. Beyond and below was the shining sea, and I wondered if Treves' Monaco comparison held water after all. In a semi-circle looking out to the sea were benches with little brass name plaques – many of Portland's departed Loved This Place and today or yesterday someone had left a bouquet of cellophane-wrapped lilies on a bench with a message for Dave from his sister. A few yards away two women wrapped in winter coats were chatting, complaining about the gifts they had each been given for Christmas. "My chutney drawer is full" one said. I took steep steps towards the cove below, meeting a couple in their 60s or 70s coming the other way. I commented on the fine weather, which in summer tempts little lizards to bask on the steps.

"About bloody time," said the man, with the weary air of someone about to write to his MP.

"I'll need the kiss of life at the top," said the woman, a few yards behind.

I passed a shaded area with two more benches, fresh bouquets left on their seats, the trees dangling many ribbons of remembrance. A few steps further led me to a clearing of broken walls and shattered leaning gravestones with the curling fonts of the eighteenth century fading into their surface. This had been St Andrew's Church, abandoned in 1750 when it became clear that landslips would soon wreck it. One grave bore a skull and crossbones, the burial spot for a pirate, it is alleged. Chutney chatter was a simple, welcome way of breathing life back into this place. I walked down to the shingle beach, the clack of wet football-sized pebbles beneath my boots. The beach-huts, clinging to the slopes and warily keeping their distance from the sea, were simple garden sheds, which struck me as being Very Portland. Friends once spent two nights in one of these and told me that storms sometimes sweep away the huts. In defence the owners had made breakwaters from the rocks, piling them in front of their huts, creating barren front gardens.

I scrambled up the slope from the beach, finding myself on Penn's Weare, a pockmarked landscape of rubble and low thorn threaded with tiny winding paths between the cliffs and the sea. I came across a carefully constructed mizmaze of stone, was pleased to follow its one true path to the small cairn of rocks at the middle. Half a mile later I ate a sandwich overlooking the sea near the whim where stone was once lowered into boats. I admired a seal's head bobbing a few yards out before realising it was only a dingy buoy. Taking new, still narrower paths back to Rufus Castle I found myself in thorny dead end after dead end, occasionally meeting other walkers, also lost in this strange labyrinth. Briefly I was joined by a dog who had decided, quite wrongly, that I was a better bet than his bearded twenty-something owners squinting at the maps on their phones in the sunlight.

Finally inland, or as inland as one can be on Portland, I came across a working quarry where large rocks were spray-painted with their weights, and beyond found two round stone bases, the only remnants of all Dorset's windmills, their sails long gone, creeping housing development slowly stealing their scrubland but leaving the wind, faintly redolent of Greek islands under the azure sky.

At Southwell, where the Portland accent was said to be so rich that Anglo-Saxons would have understood residents today I drove through an estate of 1970s bungalows to the business park, stopping close to the high chain-link fence. This large collection of grey buildings was once the highly secretive Defence Research

Establishment. In the early 1960s, the cold war raging, it became the centre of a spy scandal when two employees, Ethel Gee and Harry Houghton, were arrested for passing state secrets to the Russians; both were imprisoned.[4] 'Reds Under Beds' tabloid hysteria ensued, and in this case Harry and Ethel were very much in the bed together, being lovers. The Portland Spy Ring even prompted a feature film, *Shadow of Treason*, released in 1964. Finally, after a slightly pompous speech in parliament by the MP for South Dorset, Evelyn King,[5] pleading for clemency, in 1970 the pair were released. Houghton later wrote an autobiography *Operation Portland*, before slipping into obscurity; they lived out their lives in Poole – Ethel died in 1984, Harry in 1985.[6] The defence establishment left Portland in 1995 when the naval base which dominated life on the island closed, but Portlanders have a sense of history, and a sense of humour. I saw one road in the business park was named Espionage Way. It's these oddities which have given Portland its singular reputation and the proud bumper stickers: 'Keep Portland Weird'.

Everywhere is five minutes' drive from everywhere on Portland; I was soon in the square at Easton, a small triangular park, a neat lawn, wide paths, a tree fern, benches, an Edwardian clock tower. Although sheltered from the wind, on this cold day it was almost empty, but it wasn't always peaceful. In 1803 a Navy press gang were fought off by a group of Portlanders on the site of the park, knowing that a fifteenth century Royal Charter meant the Admiralty had no jurisdiction on the island. During the struggle three men were killed, and a woman later died from her wounds. There was nothing to mark the 'Easton Massacre' although if I had wanted to discuss it I could have sat on a bench with a cheerful blue sign attached which announced it was a 'Happy to Chat Bench'. Instead I drove to St George's Church at Reforne, more safely inland than the ruined St Andrew's, which it replaced. Two horses grazed in the field opposite – descendants I guessed of the quarry-working animals who had dragged stone from the pits along railway tracks.

Some years ago I took a trip along the Dorset coast in a fast motorboat, which I boarded at the marina. The skipper, a Portlander, told me that his neighbour, a retired quarryman in his eighties, had never once left the small island, not even to venture as far as Weymouth, inhabited by Kimberlins, the name given by the islanders to outsiders. Portlanders are insular, by definition, but there was evidence at St George's of events further afield. In the packed graveyard one tall memorial commemorated Charles John White "supposed to have perished off the New Zealand coast" in 1882, and Edwin Egbert White who was "accidentally killed", also in New Zealand. Staying on Portland might well have been preferable. But this little spit of land nuzzling the sea has always been connected – the Romans were here, the Vikings made raids at Ope Cove, and the Saxons settled widely. In the twentieth century the island became a huge marshalling yard for troops amassing for the D-Day landings. During the preparations African-American soldiers operated smoke-generating machines to hide the harbour from enemy reconnaissance planes, earning themselves the nickname The Smoke Screen Gang. As elsewhere in Dorset, when local people met with the racism of white American officers, they were often appalled – the landlady of the Cove Inn on Chesil Beach told white officers who objected to her friendship with a black G.I.: "black or white, you're all the same to me".

As I mooched through the graveyard I spotted a small sign

directing me to 'St George's bomb site'. In July 1942 a Luftwaffe bomb fell close to the church, blowing out windows, scattering gravestones and bodies, leaving a crater. By all accounts the smashed graves were dramatic testimony to the raid. A few years ago the volunteers who look after the church, now in the care of the Churches Conservation Trust, created a small circular memorial set into the ground where the bomb fell. A typewritten sheet of paper, encased in plastic and set in a bamboo frame beneath a flag of St George both explained the memorial and somewhat ruined its effect. I thought it would have been better to leave the shattered graves, to let history to leave its raw mark, but that's just a Kimberlin's view.[7]

I have no religion but I love churches, their air of calm purpose, the history and stillness, as if all time is compressed into the space. St George's took my breath away. The simple whitewashed walls overlooked grey wooden pews. The two pulpits either side of the narrow aisle were like exhausted boxers at the end of a bout, leaning towards one another. In July 1776, the same month that the United States declared its independence, St George's was consecrated by the Bishop of Bristol who was carried across the waters from the mainland at shoulder-height.

St George's escaped the Victorian enthusiasm for restoration. Owing to uncomfortable pews and absentee parishioners attendances had always been low, so it was spared. It's no longer in use but remains consecrated. I was distracted by the sound of a bell tolling from the small tower at St George's western end. A volunteer was demonstrating it to two visitors, pulling the long rope, the mournful low clang muffled inside the Georgian church.

"It was rung six times for the death of a man, three times for a woman," he told them.

As I was listening I saw a plaque commemorating the Easton Square Massacre, listing the names of the dead. It had been unveiled in 1978 by a rear admiral, the Navy having taken only 175 years to acknowledge their error. Above it hung the Blue Ensign, a naval flag.

Outside in the sunshine a volunteer was talking to another couple about the upkeep of the graveyard.

"I must say 'No Mow May' was a nightmare last year. By June it was like we had never been here," she said.

The neat grass was firmly under control now. They might have learnt from the pretty sprays of wildflowers at Hinton St Mary,[8] or failing that, by using the services of r★★★★★s.

Known on Portland as 'long ears' or 'underground mutton' the islanders consider it bad luck to say the name of warren-dwelling, grass-nibbling animals. This stems from the belief that burrowing r★★★★★s cause rock falls, endangering the quarry workers. This is no long-forgotten superstition – in 2010 the comedian Mark Steel came to the island for an episode of his long-running radio show *Mark Steel's In Town,* which both celebrates towns or districts and gently teases their inhabitants. He spoke about the superstition and some of the audience jeered him. The publicity posters for the animated film *The Curse of the Were-R★★★★t* were adapted for use on the island, omitting the offending word and instead reading "Something Bunny is Going On".[9]

It was time to leave the churchyard and see a quarry, even if I risked meeting some r★★★★★s. I walked into Tout Quarry. My friend Neil[10] trained as a geologist and spent his working life attached, symbolically at least, to the underland. He once came to Portland for a weekend; having had several pints in the nearby George Inn, he decided to take some night air. Drawn to the old quarry he stumbled around before slowly realising he was surrounded by monsters: animals heads, an octopus perched on a rock, a hull from a Viking ship.

Tout Quarry has been a nature reserve and sculpture park for nearly forty years, but the 'interpretation boards' are kept to a minimum – this is a living landscape, and all the better for it. I followed the footpath into an open stony arena and everywhere was art – surreal and phantasmagorical, realist and abstract. Faces popped from the rock. I found a fireplace etched into stone, a leaping fish, a huge chair, an owl. In one corner, visible from a grassy platform I found a figure of a man, Icarus like, falling through air, held in stone. This was 'Still Falling', carved by Antony Gormley. Portland's value to the world was in exporting itself, and sometimes, as at the Frolic, a vanished group of standing stones, it destroyed its own history, but at Tout creative energy was restored to wonderful effect. This was a place to linger, but the winter light was failing, and I had one more place to explore.

I parked close to the Portland Heights Hotel, built on a disused quarry, above buried tunnels and stables and looking shut up for the winter. My feet were getting cold as the sun dipped behind me, but I needed to see The Verne. It was impossible to miss, a massive earthwork dominating the whole north of the island. I walked down a lane to a wide, deep moat separating me from The Verne. Across the divide was a concrete footbridge, leading to an arched door set into the earthwork, above it the initials of a monarch and the date of its construction 'VR 1881' chiselled into stone. My way across the footbridge was blocked by a locked steel gate. The Verne was originally constructed to house up to 3,000 army personnel on its 56-acre site, built by Royal Engineers and convict labour. It had a hospital, canteens, a gymnasium, even a cricket pitch. Prisoners were later brought here to work the quarries, later still it served as a Young Offenders Institution.

Several years ago, on a cold winter's evening, driving home across the spine of hills which divides Dorset's north from its south, I saw a car stopped ahead of me, hazard lights blinking. I pulled over to find a woman by the side of the road. A car immediately in front of hers had hit a deer, leaving it dying by the roadside, but she would not leave it. We found a blanket from the boot of her car, covered the animal to keep it slightly warmer, and waited. The woman was initially wary of me, but as we talked she told me about her life – she worked at The Verne, then a centre for housing 'illegal' immigrants, offering them training – she taught some of the inmates how to cut hair. These were uneasy, divided years around the time of the EU referendum – had it been light we would have seen the 'Vote Leave' signs nailed to trees on the farmland across the road – and she sometimes encountered locals who loudly disapproved of her work. While we were talking another car pulled up and a man rushed towards us, a small torch aloft, looking anxiously in the dark towards the bloodied blanket.

"I'm a doctor," he gasped, and then, "Oh, it's a deer." We waited until the police arrived with an animal dispatch team.

The Verne no longer holds those who make perilous journeys from war-torn countries or failed states. Multiple brightly coloured warning signs screwed to the wall by the footbridge warned me not to fly a drone over the wall, that there were regular dog patrols, that any attempt to smuggle contraband would be met with prosecution. The Verne is now a prison, one inmate at the time of my visit being ex-pop star Gary Glitter.[11] An article in *The Sun* called The Verne "Paedo Alcatraz", housing "580 sex beasts", going on to claim that the living arrangements were "cushy", although from where I was standing, the complex was forbidding and dark. I walked down steep steps to the grassland below and looked back, a series of chimneys protruded from the earthwork. Feeling distinctly unwelcome and small against the scale of the prison, I returned to my car. As I clicked it unlocked I was greeted by a small and friendly dog, its quivering, snuffling nose investigating my legs. At the other end of its lead was a slightly harassed-looking young woman, a baby strapped to her in a papoose, and in a remarkable act of multi-tasking, also flying a drone. For a moment we watched the little aircraft together as it hovered above our heads, beneath a cloud of rooks.

"Is it difficult to fly?" I asked.

"This one's fairly easy – it's not one of those really sophisticated ones." she replied. "It was a gift, and I'm terrified – I know it cost £450, so every time I take it out I'm sure it's the last I'll see of it."

I mentioned the 'No Drone' warnings on the prison wall, just a few hundred feet away.

"When I turn it on I get a warning I'm close to a Red Zone – if I fly into it the drone will drop to the ground." The light failing further, I wished her a good afternoon and set off home, taking a steep and narrow road downhill, the shape of the prison slowly diminishing in my mirror.

The last of the sunlight sparkled on the pebbles of Chesil as I left Portland behind. It's many things, this strange outcrop, where we have dug our cities, exported criminals, defended ourselves and where spies have hidden. It's the perfect counterweight to Dorset's rural prettiness. It's not Monaco, nor a Greek island, our metaphors are not enough. Portland defies comparison, is peculiarly particular, only and gloriously itself.

THE VALLEY OF THE STONES

Dorset's high chalklands run in a broad swathe, North-East to South-West. Where the land falls fast away towards the coast is the densest concentration of archaeological sites in the county. I had arranged to meet Martin Maudsley at the Hardy Monument, which dominates much of the south and west. The monument is named for Thomas Hardy, but not that one. Thomas Masterton Hardy was

captain on HMS *Victory* – he was Kiss-Me Hardy (not Kismet
Hardy, whatever the Victorians would have preferred to think). His
monument is a slab of Victorian Brutalism, supposed to resemble a
telescope but more like an enormous pepper-grinder.

The weather was warm, the grass leggy and limp, the nettles
spiteful. The view towards the coast was hazy, a har-like mist
tumbling in over the bracken-feathered hills; the brackish Fleet river
behind the long shingle of Chesil shone flatly back at us. Martin
knows Black Down intimately, each year he takes a midsummer
nocturnal walk from his home in Bridport to Maiden Castle,
crossing the Down.

Martin and I are both blow-ins: he's a Lancastrian who made his
way south, via Norwich and Bristol, before settling here with his
family. He had, he told me, found his real home in Dorset –
something the place confers on you, if you're lucky. Martin has
made his living from the land too – as a storyteller, a conjuror of
legends, new and old. As he explained as we made our way through
a conifer woodland, for him this practice is a way of "re-storying the
landscape", the imagination as connective tissue, linking us to
nature, history, the earth itself. He has brought people of all ages to
Black Down, especially school groups, asking them to engage
directly with what they find, and creating myths to unlock
imaginations.

It's a rich landscape for his work. We came across a slab of
lichen-speckled stone inscribed HELL STONE ONLY. Up the
long-grassed path we found it, the first of our afternoon's
congregation of stones: a dolmen, several huge stones capped with
another, creating a chamber beneath. The Hellstone once was a
Neolithic Long Barrow. When the monument for Kiss-me Hardy
was only fifteen or so years old the Hellstone was recreated, the
capstone replaced in an approximation of the neolithic, the
Victorians re-storying the past.[12] We crawled inside the space,
although I was mindful that the 150 years since its renovation was
a blink of history's eye and it might choose now to slip and crush
us. I took a photo of the pepper-grinder on the hill and squeezed
back out. It's not hard to see why it's a focus for folklore, and even
though Dorset has largely avoided directly naming the devil in its
place names, the Hellstone has been considered the devil's quoits.

Twenty minutes' walk away through the mist Hampton stone
circle would have been easy to miss had we not been looking for it,
a few low stones by the path arranged in a circle, marked by a solid

iron sign inscribed in block capitals which in its uppercase
certainty, announced that stone circles were 'CONSIDERED TO
HAVE HAD A RITUAL SIGNIFICANCE'. The circle had also
been subject to more recent meddling – a hundred years after the
Victorians heaved the capstone over the Hellstone, the boulders at
Hampton were replaced in what was thought to be their original
positions. Martin and I discussed the purpose of stone circles: they
were probably multi-purpose and adaptable places: for ceremony,
calendar setting, community decision-making, for making trading
agreements, marking boundaries, for feasting. Martin and I finished
our sandwiches sitting on the stones.

The Grey Mare and her Colts was slightly harder to find – a low
mound, once probably high, at one end a collection of horse-tooth
stones, gathered together on the hill. It's likely the Victorians opened
the tomb, but left only vague notes about their findings, suggesting
pottery and human bones. Martin spotted a spark of yellow flower
between two of the massive stones.

"That's goldenrod – it shouldn't grow here."

I gently lifted the stem and found that its base had been wrapped
in damp tissue – this was a memorial or votive of some sort. I
replaced it and we moved on, from dolmen to circle, barrow to
circle.

There's been speculation that this path, co-opted into the South
Dorset Ridgeway, was once a processional route, part of an ancient
ceremonial landscape, although each conglomeration of stone and
earth was built at different times. At the remote Kingston Russell

stone circle, lying at the confluence of footpaths the sun broke
through, bathing us in light and eventually sweat. Kingston Russell's
stones now lie flat but were impressive still: two days after visiting I
met a couple who celebrated the summer solstice here, preferring it
to better known monuments. There was a legend that if one walked
anti-clockwise around the circle three times and counted the stones
the devil would appear. On a stone opposite us was a single
wheatear, which as we walked around the stones, hopped to a
neighbouring stone, the bird and us making a single circuit of the
circle. I didn't count the stones, just in case.

We tacked our way carefully down steep slopes to a farm track, a
single stabled horse, a pile of farm rubbish, open empty fields.
Quite suddenly a presence was at our heels, an unexpected panting.
No spirit or phantom, but an unaccompanied dog. Minutes passed
before its owner appeared from a house hidden by a copse. As
friendly as her dog she told us she and her husband had planted the
woodland thirty years ago – the whips that made the wood had
arrived in just two plastic bags.

The ritual landscape had its source near here – a dry, deeply
carved valley formed by glaciation and an ice age's retreat, leaving
boulders and stones pockmarking the land – The Valley of the
Stones. This was a quarry for the Neolithic and Bronze Age, where
nature had flung the specimens onto the earth, ripe for barrows and
circles. From the valley's bottom the stones on the hillside above
looked like lightning-struck sheep.[13] Martin had mythologised the
landscape in a story as 'A Game of Stones', in which two giants
hurled rocks at one another, a fight to the death. One stone, which
Martin pointed out to me, was all that remained of the defeated
giant's nose, poking through the earth.

We had walked through an emptied land, the circles and barrows
abandoned, but at Winterbourne Abbas is the Nine Stones, a stone
circle which can be glimpsed from a speeding car on the A35. Local
folklore has attributed these to the devil, his wife and their seven
children. On one visit Martin met a man from the Netherlands, as
direct and straightforward as the national stereotype. This was the
Dutchman's second visit – years earlier, while standing directly in
the centre of the circle he had experienced a time-slip. He saw the
landscape as it had been millennia before, the Durotriges
tribes-people around him.[14]

It's possible that there was once yet another henge, about a half a
mile further west of the Nine Stones, referred to by the seventeenth

century writer, John Aubrey. If so, it was dragged away, probably for building material. The only clue to its once possible existence is the Broad Stone, which lies at ground level, on the A35's verge, in approximately the right spot.[15]

Not all the monuments were in decay, or traditionally mysterious. Our final stop was close to the Hardy Monument, at a stone circle only four years old, a henge surrounded by wooden benches, a single grey menhir at its centre. Martin was asked to conduct a ceremony at the new circle's opening, at Summer Solstice Sunrise in 2018. It had been an anxious morning – Martin waited with a druid and the engineer who had designed the placing of the stones. Finally, the sun's rays pierced the space between supporting columns, casting its light on the stone at its centre. The three people: the engineer, druid and storyteller were elated, much as their Neolithic forebears must have been. In concert with the barrows and henges from Hellstone to Kingston Russell the new circle made a bowl-like shape on the map, south of the Valley of the Stones, a modern equivalent for the megaliths, a worthy replacement for Aubrey's lost henge by the side of the A35.

CLOUDS HILL

The tiny and isolated white and almost windowless house sat in a woodland bowl, within earshot of an A road. This was Clouds Hill, a property so small that visitors buying their ticket from the National Trust booth in the car park would have to wait if more than a small number were inside at any one time. The heritage bodies who look after stately homes and castles like to create a phantom illusion – that the long-dead owner has simply slipped out for a moment, leaving a radio playing, a half-drained glass of whisky on a desk, a coat thrown over a chair, the sound of a crackling fire from the grate. It's rare for it to work. But at Clouds Hill history was tangible.

Clouds Hill was the last home of T.E. Lawrence, Lawrence of Arabia, the celebrated soldier, writer and archaeologist whose exploits in the First World War earned him many accolades and whose legend was further enhanced by David Lean's 1962 film which starred a blue-eyed Peter O'Toole, looking remarkably like his subject. Clouds Hill had nothing of the widescreen: it was a two-up, two down affair – Lawrence's book-filled bedroom below, and a sitting room in the eaves. He made himself a hero with *Seven Pillars of Wisdom*, his self-mythologising account of his desert battles in the First World War, in which he fought alongside Arab forces against the Ottoman army. His move to Dorset was, in some senses, an attempt to regain some form of anonymity, using aliases to join the Tank Corps and the Airforce, latterly as Aircraftman Shaw.

Lawrence or Shaw or Ross, depending on when you met him, was a complex character. Born out of wedlock, as they used to say, in Tremadog, Wales in 1888, Lawrence was itself an assumed name, which might have bequeathed a shifting sense of his own identity, and a relaxed association with the literal truth. The impact of his military career is still hotly debated on internet forums devoted to military history, but there's no doubt he had extraordinary charisma. In *The Lion and the Unicorn,* George Orwell's spirited essay espousing left-wing patriotism and celebrating English culture he called T.E. Lawrence "the last right wing intellectual".[16] The question remains: how right wing?

In his upstairs sitting room Lawrence entertained military colleagues, with whom he did not always get on, but also writers, including, in his final years, Thomas Hardy. One close friend was Henry Williamson, author of *Tarka the Otter,* and a fascist sympathiser. Rumours spread about Lawrence's involvement with the Blackshirts and linger still, the most pernicious being that Williamson hoped that Lawrence would become the English Führer should the German invasion come. If this was the case, Lawrence was a security risk.

On 13 May 1935, Lawrence crashed his motorbike close to his home near Bovington Camp, on a road that no longer takes the same course. Six days later he died of his injuries. His funeral at Moreton was attended by many people, including Winston Churchill. Questions have remained over his death, some theories alleging that he was assassinated by the Secret Service. Even while he was lying in hospital, his brother was forced to deny that Lawrence had recently visited Berlin.

A recent feature film proposed the assassination theory, but the evidence is purely circumstantial.[17] As I stood in the small upper room at Clouds, I thought more about Lawrence's relationship with the military and with Dorset, and more about how Dorset itself is intertwined with the military.

Lawrence had come to live here because the Tank Corps at Bovington was close-by. This part of Dorset, stretching across the sandy, easily burnt Wareham Forest, to Winfrith Newburgh and to Tyneham, has a deeply ingrained relationship with the military, stretching from well before Lawrence's time.[18] As I drove the roads around here, I saw brightly painted Gypsy caravans and grazing horses on the wide verges but the most notable features were the fences, the barbed wire, the locked gates and the road signs warning of tanks. The crunch of gunfire is common, some roads open only at weekends.

TYNEHAM

The most famous example of Dorset's military landscape is Tyneham, a tiny village a mile from the coast between Lulworth and Kimmeridge. Lulworth has its cove and its castle, roofless now since a fire ripped it apart in 1929, Kimmeridge has a beach and a folly tower on the cliffs above, relocated by the Landmark Trust a few years ago to prevent it falling into the sea. But Tyneham is a gap, a shell, a smashed place.

No-one can quite agree on where Purbeck starts, a titular isle that's not an island. The only time a ferry is required is if you come from Poole. It might be that the border to the mythical isle is a small stream at Lulworth, some claim it's further west,[19] but Tyneham's loneliness feels like the borderland between Purbeck and the rest of Dorset. Frederick Treves kept a house at West Lulworth, and in *Highways and Byways* told of how he, the famous surgeon, had been summoned to tend to the injuries of a girl who, in September 1892, had fallen nearly 400 feet down the cliffs at Lulworth Cove, but survived, her clothing catching on the rocks and slowing her descent.[20] But Treves didn't mention Tyneham, something which would be inconceivable today.

In 1943 the tiny village was evacuated, the residents relocated and the land taken by the military for manoeuvres, for training. They have never been allowed to return. Tyneham, and its grand house have slowly become a ruin. Access to the village is tightly controlled.

Visiting was a fascinating experience. Tyneham's heart was a line of terraced cottages, roofless, the fire grates exposed, the ceilings missing, small front gardens a tangle of weeds. The buildings were made safe, the old phone box restored, the schoolhouse now a small museum. Shells and their casings were on display. It was also busy – I visited in late summer: part of the appeal was the curving pebbly beach at Worbarrow just down the lane, but aching nostalgia was also in the air.

Lilian Bond grew up in Tyneham's Elizabethan manor house, now a hidden wreck in the woods. She left the village in 1914, when she was twenty-seven, and wrote an elegiac memoir of her time in the village. It's sincere and concerned with the lives of ordinary people, but it's shot through with wistfulness, speaking of her gratitude for the "good years of freedom in the clean, cool Purbeck air". That the community was never allowed to return was outrageous, and the evacuation, carried out in extreme secrecy, left deeply traumatic marks. In 1948 the Labour Government, facing the uncertainties of the Cold War, decided to retain Tyneham for the army. Some of the inhabitants were resettled to a small council estate at Sandford near Wareham, the road re-named Tyneham Close. Tellingly the residents often said that they were happy with their new lives and the conveniences denied them in an isolated village. But since then many articles and books have promoted the idea that Tyneham represents a lost land, an arcadian dream. My edition of *The Shell Guide to Dorset*, published nearly twenty years after the government had made the evacuation permanent was direct on the matter: it was "intolerable to Dorset people". Tyneham's ruination has allowed a projection of an idealised deep England myth onto a place that the army had preserved in aspic. The legend of T.E. Lawrence, alone in his retreat at Clouds Hill, the once and future saviour of England, had powerful similarities with this sense of Tyneham's fate, part of the long and tangled relationship of Dorset with the military, and our sense of who we are.

CHALDON HERRING AND BURNING CLIFF

There's nothing truly wild in southern England any more: Dorset is a managed landscape, profoundly human. But it's still possible to find remoteness between the Isle of Purbeck and Weymouth's sprawl, a sequestered place tucked into hills and close to the coast, private but exotic: Chaldon Herring, sometimes also known as East Chaldon.

I left the village on foot, heading along the lane towards West Chaldon; behind the old vicarage, rooks noisily established their order of things. This empty land suggested the sea. Plastic sheeting laid over the fields to warm the soil for crops was like the swell in a storm, an approximation of the real thing two miles away, the foraging rooks imitating gulls. West Chaldon, under the long-nosed hill of High Chaldon, is now a few houses and a farm, but once formed part of a larger settlement, Holworth, deserted in the fifteenth century. I thought the ebb and flow of human life was written dramatically into this empty landscape. Just north of Chaldon is the grouping of barrows known as the Five Marys – although there are in fact six of them. When excavated in the 1860s by the exiled Bourbon princess, the Duchess of Berry, the graves of two adults, one male and one female, were discovered, both in sitting positions, stag antlers resting on their shoulders. The barrows had fascinated Frederick Treves, writing that the spot must have been chosen to be as near to heaven as possible, and as little in touch with the earth – I don't know the extent to which ancient tribes thought of the sky as a repository for souls or their gods, it's more likely that the high lands were simply where people lived and buried their dead.

From West Chaldon I climbed through grassy fields, the way marked by occasional lonely fingerposts, crooked and diminutive angels of the south. Closer to the coast was a building so neatly thatched that I assumed it must be a house, but closer inspection revealed it to be a barn, still in use, the yard recently stamped by cattle. I joined the South West Coast Path, marvelled at views towards Weymouth and Portland and found St Catherine's by the Sea, a tiny wooden church in a patch of woodland high above Ringstead Bay, serving a small, scattered parish and offering a few minutes rest and contemplation for walkers.

I had not chosen my day perfectly. As I reached the more exposed ground on the coast-path, the rain began, pleasantly cooling at first, and then a squally barrage of water, soaking me completely. The land on the undercliff is known as Burning Cliff – for several years in the 1820s the shale below ground burned and smouldered, a sign of the coastline's active and valuable geology, but the rain today would surely have extinguished it. I paused at the isolated White Nothe cottages close to the cliffs – built as coastguards' houses, the exposed line of houses was, in the 1920s and 30s, occupied by the writer Llewelyn Powys and his wife, the American novelist and feminist Alyse Gregory. Powys would sometimes be seen wandering the downs, dressed in a cloak, possibly on the way to visit his lover, another novelist, Gamel Woolsey[21]. Chaldon Herring and the land around it attracted a group of writers and artists centred around the Powys family –

Llewelyn's brothers, John Cowper and Theodore both lived in the village, Theodore fictionalising it as Folly Down in his novel *Mr Weston's Good Wine*. Two of the Powys sisters, Philippa and Gertrude, a novelist and artist respectively came to live there too. To add further spice to this already heady mix, the novelist Sylvia Townsend Warner and her partner, the poet Valentine Ackland came to live in Chaldon Herring. The two women were drawn to communism by the horrors of the Spanish Civil War and attracted the attention of MI5. Ackland and Townsend Warner were energetic presences in the village, organising dancing on the Five Marys as a republican alternative to George V's Jubilee celebrations in 1935. MI5 were confused by the women, first believing that Ackland was a man, and were further baffled by Townsend Warner's double-barrelled surname, thinking her to be two people. Townsend Warner is buried in the churchyard at Chaldon Herring.

I was getting very wet. In front of the cottages was a squat brick pillbox, hunkered against the elements. Purbeck and near-Purbeck bear the marks of a military-industrial legacy – Tyneham, Bovington, the nuclear reactors on the Heath at Winfrith Newburgh, in the process of decommissioning. But the pillbox had found new uses: I met two people sheltering from the near-horizontal rain, with grins that said they had the makings of a good weather-based anecdote.

I stopped to eat my cheese roll in a grassy bowl along the clifftop in the comparative shelter of a tall stone obelisk – one of two built in the eighteenth century which together formed a navigational aid for shipping. As the rain eased, spectacular views to rival Sussex's Birling Gap were revealed, a curving coastline and bright white cliffs.

A small slab shaped disconcertingly like a headstone invited me to take the Smugglers' Path to the undercliff, also warning that it was a 'Steep Hazardous Route'. On this occasion I avoided the criminal path and kept going to Bat's Head where the view east revealed one of Dorset's best-known sights: the massive rock arch of Durdle Door at the far end of the beach.

DURDLE DOOR

The final episode of *Doctor Who* to feature its first female lead, Jodie Whittaker, ended in a burst of CGI and forced emotion on a dramatic coastline, as the Doctor regenerated into an earlier version, David Tennant. For a few seconds it was possible to see that the Doctor and the TARDIS were perched on top of Durdle Door. In Dorset this prompted not only interest, but outrage. In 2020, as the first Covid lockdown ended and the weather warmed, thousands of people went to the beaches, causing anxiety that they might further spread the deadly virus by mixing too freely. At Durdle Door the release from home-bound lives led to reports of drunkenness and minor scuffles on the beach, and also of 'tomb-stoning' – the practice of throwing oneself from the arch into the waters, in some cases encouraged by the crowd below. Two people, misjudging their leaps or finding the sea less deep than they had thought, were taken to hospital by air ambulance. So when Durdle Door appeared on television screens, the actors superimposed in the place where tomb-stoners had leapt, it provoked a storm in a TARDIS.[22] James Weld, the owner of the beach and its surrounding landscape including Lulworth Castle, was furious, fearing it would draw people to risk life and limb and stretch the emergency services still further. He accused the BBC of "duplicitous and dishonest" behaviour in failing to reveal why they had requested permission to fly a drone over the beach. I can't help thinking that this was something of an over-reaction: the construction of an enormous car park, a holiday park complete with its own pub, and an annual music festival[23] held on the Weld estate, might have more of an impact on visitor numbers than a few seconds of television aired just as it became too cold to contemplate a swim.

I walked through the well-kept holiday park, where a children's play area featured a wooden model of Lulworth Castle, roofless like the original which is now partially restored. Historically the Welds were keen to keep commoners at arms' length, going so far as to relocate the village of East Lulworth in the eighteenth century, which was felt to be a little *too* close to the ancestral home, and I noted that the holiday park was safely out of view.[24]

My walk took me back through an open empty landscape alive with lark-song, to Chaldon Herring. The Five, or six, Marys appeared on the horizon above, and guided me back to the village, once scandalised by poets, but now comfortable with its history – the Friends of Llewelyn Powys meet in the pub annually and are met always warmly.

SURREAL SWANAGE

Very occasionally, I have been described as a 'Nature Writer'. I'm not, I'm far too hazy a naturalist, too likely to mis-identify plants and animals, even if I'm fascinated by them. But the most obvious tell is that, unlike every nature writer who's ever mused over a murmuration or worried about a butterfly, I don't really like cold water swimming, or wild swimming as we now have to call it. I'm just not that hardy.

But I do like the seaside. I like deckchairs and sand, I like gulls, I like chips as much as gulls like chips. Swanage is a perfect seaside town. One hot early July evening, just as the town beach was clearing, Helen and I arrived. We spread out beach towels, Helen swam and I thought about swimming. Across the bay was the Isle of Wight, the chalky Needles weren't visible without binoculars, but in Purbeck they have an answer – the stacks of Old Harry Rocks, one of which I could see in the distance beyond the sedate pier, a structure without Amusements or a Fairground. I left Helen and Old Harry to it, and walked through the little town.

Swanage has always been strange and wonderfully so. Frederick Treves, writing in the early years of the twentieth century could remember it as a "queer little town" of cottages, a place made prosperous by fishing and its quarries. But he feared for Swanage, for development, he worried that red brick would overwhelm it, that a gas holder would soon be installed.

He need not have worried. Swanage retains its character. A new series of beach huts had recently been completed, the eyes on the pedalos winked at me. Swanage never got too large: it had the spirit of a seaside town just before the Spanish costas took hold, before cheap air travel, reliable sun and the promise of the exotic. The beach and the quayside were full, seemingly with visitors from London and the south-east. One shirtless man spoke excitedly into his mobile: "It's brilliant here, I'm going to love it."

Swanage has a Folk Festival held in a seafront marquee and a twice-yearly Blues Festival, conducted mainly in small venues and pubs. But Swanage's individuality lies also in its buildings. In the 1860s George Burt, a successful building contractor who'd made his fortune in London, began bringing bits of the capital back to Swanage. His goal was to drag the little coastal town from what he had decided was its torpor, doing so with energy and imagination. His marks were everywhere: along the harbour beyond where the stumps of the old pier still stood, was a curious clocktower, a tall Gothic base and four delicate columns meeting below a cupola, but with no clock face. Built to commemorate the life of the Duke of Wellington it had once stood on the old London Bridge, and without Burt's intervention might now be standing in Lake Havasu City, Arizona.

At the edge of The Downs, which swept upwards towards the coast path was a round amphitheatre, made from grass banks and a large circular pavement, guarded by two columns, also brought here by Burt. Turning back, past where people were gathering on the quayside for fish suppers, I made my way past the neat 1960s polygonal library up the narrowing High Street to find the strange Purbeck House, a tall tower with embattlements and a stubby pepperpot structure overlooking the street. It was striking if hardly harmonious. Burt had allowed his magpie tendencies to have their full expression at Purbeck House: the marble chips in the walls came from the steps of the Albert Memorial in Kensington Gardens, then under construction, and other features came from Billingsgate Market and Millbank Prison.

On this part of the hill Swanage was losing its seaside character and becoming more like the queer old quarrying town of Treves' memory. I turned back. In my enthusiasm to find Burt's house I had somehow missed the Town Hall further down the hill. This once simple nineteenth century civic building had been adorned with a balcony supported by stone cherubs and fussy columns, the whole façade seemingly too tall for the original structure and too pompous for its purpose. Burt had taken this seventeenth century frontage from the Mercer's Hall in Cheapside, and brought it to Swanage by ship.

Burt bought the Durlston Estate, planning to create a whole new suburb of the town, which remains unbuilt, but he had his architect design Durlston Castle, overlooking the wide bay towards Wight. Below the castle, demonstrating his ambition, is a massive Purbeck stone globe, on which you can trace The Places You'll Go, or not go. Burt didn't always find a use for his curios, some of his salvage was simply left in the fields around the town, to be discovered by the artist Paul Nash in 1935, who photographed and published them in the *Architectural Review*, describing the town as a "Surrealist dream". Nash and fellow artist Eileen Agar met in Swanage, had a passionate affair, and in creating new work inspired by the Dorset town made Surrealism a very English art form, freed from its Parisian roots.

Standing above the town on The Downs, my back to the sea, and the sun casting longer evening shadows, Swanage looked like a pretty, idealised seaside resort, a scene from a twentieth century children's adventure story, which in fact it was. Enid Blyton came here frequently and used the Purbeck countryside as inspiration. You wouldn't recognise the area from her books; Blyton's descriptive phrases for the landscape are generic, not specific. As Peter Fiennes pointed out in his book *Footnotes*, Blyton described views as 'lovely', farmhouses as 'old', the sea as 'blue', and had no interest in summoning a Spirit of Place.[25] In doing so she conjured a myth of the bland English rural which persists to this day, somewhere for us to put nostalgic dreams, a vague place where nothing changes, and nothing should change.

But despite Blyton the weird still crops up in this part of Purbeck, sometimes on the map. There are three Norths: Grid North – the line on a map which points towards the North Pole, True North which follows the lines of longitude northwards, and Magnetic North, which wanders slightly. On Wednesday 2nd November 2022, for the first time in British mapping history, the three Norths converged at Langton Matravers, just outside Swanage, tantalisingly close to Burt's globe. BBC Radio Four reported that cartographers had converged on the village that morning and interviewed a Scout Leader, presumably because he owned a compass. The convergence was the starting point: the three Norths joining together for a journey through the country, reaching Poole by Christmas, and then across the land, agreeing for a few years on the one real North.

I met Helen on the quayside, we bought fish and chips and sat on benches surrounded by happy tourists and were unmolested by gulls, who kept a distance that their cousins in Lyme Regis would not. We found a column, topped with cannonballs, a Nelson-imitating gull perched on its pinnacle. This was erected by Burt's uncle, John Mowlem, to commemorate a 'Great Naval Battle' fought by King Alfred against the Danes in 877 CE, although as Helen pointed out, given that this was significantly earlier than gunpowder, the cannonballs were anachronistic.

This is all part of Swanage's unusual charm, the reason that Londoners are drawn here, at home amongst the scraps of their city. Swanage and the strange, mined landscapes of Purbeck, from Old Harry to Kimmeridge aren't vague imaginings, they're far more Eileen than Enid.

Notes

1   From an article in *Dorset Echo*, 20 July, 2018. The data comes from an ONS study, published by Dorset Council at mapping.dorsetcouncil.co.uk

2   An excellent overview of the Black Death can be found in Philip Ziegler's book of the same name, published in 1969. Since he wrote the book the estimates for the percentage killed by the disease have increased. For more on the rural impact of the Black Death see the West Milton section of this book (West).

3   Like Sherborne, although the inhabitants of Dorset were often annoyed by both sides.

4   There's a good, brief summary of the case on the MI5 website: www.mi5.gov.uk/portland-spy-ring

5   Evelyn King was first a Labour MP and then switched to the Tories. Alan Clark, hardly a reliable moral arbiter, later called King a "nasty old buffer".

6   MI5 are pretty pleased with themselves for breaking the spy ring but both the *Guardian* and the BBC believe that the ring could have been broken years earlier: www.bbc.co.uk /news/world-africa-49804965

7   Other Kimberlins have found inspiration at St George's, including John Piper, who sketched the graveyard and painted details from the tombs in 1954.

8   See the North section of this book.

9   This has a whiff of an excited PR team at Aardman Productions about it.

10 See the chapter on Bulbarrow and Elisabeth Frink in the Central section of this book.

11 He was released in February 2023, but was recalled to prison in March.

12 When Julian Cope, the Archdrude himself, visited the Hellstone on 28 May 1996, he was

more generous towards the restorers. See *The Modern Antiquarian*, Thorsons, 1998 p 214.

13 At Thorncombe, on the Dorset-Somerset border, sixty sheep were killed by a lightning strike in June 1914.

14 Visions of the past are not uncommon around ancient monuments. In Adam Thorpe's memoir *On Silbury Hill*, he too experiences a time-slip.

15 In *Prehistoric Dorset* John Gale writes that the Broad Stone is also missing, but various local news outlets have reported on the Broad Stone's sorry state, and moreover, in *The Modern Antiquarian* Julian Cope is pictured sitting on it, wearing sunglasses.

16 Orwell's view that socialism and patriotism are perfectly compatible is one that's also held by Billy Bragg, who wrote about it in his book *The Progressive Patriot*. Billy lives on the Dorset coast.

17 Nick Churchill's article on both the film, *Lawrence After Arabia,* and the theory, is nicely balanced: www.nickchurchill.org.uk/the-later-life-and-death-of-t-e-lawrence/

18 In the late nineteenth century the army acquired one hundred acres of land around Bovington.

19 In an article for the *Guardian* I suggested that Purbeck, or at least its character extended a mile or two further west, and received several letters of complaint.

20 There's another story of a child surviving an unlikely fall in Dorset – at the great house at Milton Abbas, where the child's skirts acted as a parachute.

21 Woolsey later married the travel writer Gerald Brenan.

22 I am indebted to Helen Baker for this pun.

23 Camp Bestival.

24 In turn, the Welds, who were Roman Catholics at a time when the old religion was a risky business, feared reprisals from extremist Protestants, and during the Gordon Riots of 1780 they worried that the unrest would spread to Dorset. There's a Catholic chapel in the grounds of Lulworth Castle, only given permission as long as the design did not resemble a church.

25 Peter Fiennes book is terrific, and covers writers from Celia Fiennes to Beryl Bainbridge.

EAST

BROWNSEA ISLAND

It was one of those school-years facts which cling on to into adulthood. Along with the formation ox-bow lakes, squares on the hypotenuse and the number of miles to the moon, for those in the south, was the size of Poole's natural harbour – the second largest in the world, beaten only by Sydney. It lent the town on its north shore a mythic status, at least in my mind, as did the presence of Brownsea – a small wooded island in the harbour, just a mile and a half long.

When Celia Fiennes, the pioneering traveller, came this way in around 1700 she referred to Poole only as "a little sea-port town". Fiennes, always curious and enthusiastic, was much more interested in the copperas workings on Brownsea Island, which she described in detail, and praised the lobster, crabs and shrimp in her writings: "I there eate some very good." Brownsea is a peaceful spot and a sanctuary for red squirrels, but over the centuries it's been a focus for curious misadventures and eccentric owners. Henry VIII built a defensive blockhouse on the island as part of his channel defence system, in the eighteenth century this was converted into an elaborate sham castle. During the mid-nineteenth century, when the island was still known as Branksea, it was bought by Colonel William Petrie Waugh and his wife Mary. Mary was a keen geologist and was sure she had discovered deposits of valuable china clay on the island. Having obtained a survey which confirmed their hopes, the Waughs immediately began work. The sham castle was remodelled[1], the church rebuilt, and hundreds of workers were brought in. They constructed a new pier on the west of the tiny island and even a small village, Maryland, named after Mary.

But it wasn't china clay; the Waughs had borrowed heavily to finance their operation but the deposits on Brownsea were suited only for bricks and drainpipes. One legend, which has hallmarks of the apocryphal, runs that in 1857 a group of merchants came to Brownsea from Poole to ask Colonel Waugh to become their parliamentary candidate, but he was away so Mary greeted them. Being rather deaf she misunderstood the reason for their visit and assured them that they would be paid, if only they were patient. This spooked the creditors, and shortly afterwards the Waughs fled to Spain. The pottery stumbled on without them, but by 1888 it had folded, though even today fragments of inferior clay pottery are found on Brownsea's shoreline.

In 1927 Brownsea was bought by Mary Bonham-Christie, a reclusive figure who engaged in an early form of rewilding, letting nature take its course and freeing the farm animals to roam over the island. She moved out of the castle into a more modest residence and threw the estate workers off the island. When war came the island was used as a reception and processing centre for thousands of refugees escaping the invading German forces in northern Europe. To protect nearby Poole from the attention of bombers a technician from Elstree Film Studios was brought to Brownsea to create the illusion of the sleeping port under attack, fires flickering from below. The deception was successful: the Luftwaffe destroyed the ruins of Maryland, reducing it to a few bricks. In 1961, with Bonham-Christie's health declining she moved from the tiny island, but died just hours after reaching the mainland. Her son applied for permission to build four hundred houses, was refused, and so gave Brownsea to the government to settle his mother's inheritance tax. In turn the government passed it to the National Trust, its custodians today, along with the Dorset Wildlife Trust. The island has never been in safer hands.

Brownsea is hugely popular with day-trippers. In my youth we came here repeatedly, a place that was perfect for small-scale childhood adventures, for poking about, and finding quiet spots. It's also a woozy place for me. Once, on an organised trip to the island I became ill, had to sit alone on the pews in the rebuilt church, exhausted and faint. Later, deposited by the bus a mile from home, I somehow stumbled back to our bungalow, stopping every few yards to lean into privet hedges to rest. I had developed pneumonia, an aftershock of a more serious illness which had me hospitalised a few weeks earlier and from which everyone had assumed I had recovered.

FRAGMENTS OF POOLE

Poole and Brownsea, one a busy port, the other a small and almost empty island are wholly different, but are tied together by history – Brownsea is in some senses microcosmic of its bigger, uglier cousin. Standing on Poole's quay in blustery sunshine, I found myself face to face with a statue, the 'Hero of Mafeking', Robert Baden-Powell, dressed in scout uniform and sitting on an upturned log. As a child I had a colourised postcard of him, short-sleeved and arms crossed, a paternal smile on his tanned face. I don't know why I found it such a compelling image – maybe because we didn't have family photos on display at home: no weddings nor christenings; to have the constancy of Baden-Powell, a man who died nearly thirty years before I was born, gazing out into my bedroom was somehow a comfort.

In 1907 Baden-Powell brought a group of twenty boys to a camp to the south side of Brownsea. The experience convinced him that a movement based on the practical outdoor life, a code of conduct based on self-reliance and patriotism, with a dollop of imagery borrowed from Kipling's *The Jungle Book*, would be a huge success. He was right, scouting grew quickly and internationally, separate divisions created for girls, for younger children and for those on the cusp of adulthood. My trip to Brownsea which ended with pneumonia had been with the cub scouts. When I recovered, I put Baden-Powell's postcard in a drawer. He would have been disappointed with my weakness.

Baden-Powell was a complex character – he founded an important youth movement but was also an imperialist whose troops committed atrocities in Africa, and he regularly used racist language. During the 2020 Black Lives Matter protests which followed the murder of George Floyd, the council decided to remove Baden-Powell's statue to prevent it being 'targeted' and rolled into the harbour, like Edward Colston in Bristol. Outraged by the suggestion that the council might 'give in' to protestors a group gathered around the statue to prevent removal and to protect it from hypothetical attack. Instead the statue was boarded up for a few months and then the hoarding removed. I noted that Baden-Powell was ignored by the passers-by today, and no-one stopped to clean the gull shit from his left shoulder.[2]

Fear of the mob is nothing new in Poole. During his exile

following the French Revolution, Charles X, the ultra-conservative Bourbon monarch, sought refuge in Lulworth Castle further along the coast, but was reportedly unnerved by the sight of a large crowd on Poole's quayside who may, or may not, have had revolution on their minds. They might also have been influenced by drink[3]: I was struck by the number of pubs in this most ancient part of Poole, and by how busy they were at lunchtime; the King Charles offered "home-cooked food" and claimed to be haunted.

By the time that Celia Fiennes gave her ride-by assessment of Poole, the town had long been in the ascendancy. Its harbour was always its fortune – a boat over 2,200 years old, carved from a single tree trunk was discovered there in the mid-1960s and was subsequently preserved by soaking in concentrated sugar solution, before being displayed in the town museum. Poole fought off competition from the Saxon town of Wareham, which lost out when the River Frome silted up. Edward I had also spotted the harbour's potential and in 1286 instructed the constable at Corfe Castle to establish a new city on the opposite southern shore, naming it Villa Nova. There were to be "sufficient streets" for merchants, a weekly market and a church. That too failed, and Villa Nova lives on only as Newton Bay, close to the oil wells which form part of the largest onshore oilfield in Western Europe, and a single isolated house.

Poole flourished through sea-trade, especially with Newfoundland (salted fish), and the Mediterranean (wine, olives, dried fruit). Frederick Treves, writing in his *Highways and Byways* book, was enchanted by Poole's "romantic and adventurous" history, its pirates and smugglers, and mentioned its involvement in the slave trade, something which the guardians of Baden-Powell's effigy might have considered. The pages in Treves' book devoted to the town have dark sketches from the Age of Sail.[4] But Treves also noted that its more recent buildings were "featureless", a result of unregulated building in the early nineteenth century, in Poole's boom-time. Walking the back streets that lead down to the quayside I could glimpse still narrower alleys, stone-built and leaning inwards, guarding their secrets. It was obvious that Poole had taken a series of batterings.

The Luftwaffe took an interest: in the Second World War Poole was bombed several times. The most deadly attack came at midday on 27th March 1941 when a single German bomber, aiming at railway bridges, hit instead the gasworks' canteen,

killing thirty-three workers. Post-war redevelopment was less
than kind to old Poole, in well-intentioned slum clearances many
older buildings were lost. In the *Shell Guide to Dorset*, re-issued in
1966, dedicated to "all those courageous enemies of development
to whom we owe what is left of England", I found a photograph
of Blue Boar Lane, but I couldn't locate the little street today,
although I did find a pub named the Blue Boar, presumably close
to its location. In his memoir the film-maker Derek Jarman
remembered school trips in his art master's Rolls Royce from his
school in nearby Canford. He wrote that the car was old but
could still manage 70 miles an hour along Dorset's lanes. They
were drawn especially to Poole's demolition sites to scavenge old
doors, which Jarman would decorate.[5] Much of Poole's centre
had been knocked down and rebuilt, but on my visit I found the
planners had not thought to better accommodate the railway line
– a level crossing ran over the busy pedestrianised street,
regularly holding up shoppers waiting for a train to pass. Bad
luck and carelessness played its part too: on 21 June 1988, an

explosion and subsequent fire at a chemical works on West Quay
Road resulted in one-hundred-foot-high flames and a
mass-evacuation. A staff-member at the excellent museum told
me that she had been in hospital when the accident happened,
having just given birth to her son, and everyone was ordered to
stay inside to avoid the toxic fumes. Poole has survived all this,
just.

I'd come to the museum to find out more about Poole's industry.
Brownsea had proved a dead end for the Waughs' pursuit of riches,
but the clay beds of Dorset were the making of one company and
one enigmatic woman. Since Neolithic times potters working on a
small scale were a feature of the landscape of south and east Dorset,
focusing on the town of Verwood, especially.[6] In 1915, Gertrude
Sharp, a young woman studying at the Royal College of Art,
married John Adams, a ceramicist and potter. Arriving in Poole they
joined forces with Cyril Carter to make a new range of decorative
wares. Truda, as she was better known, became the company's Art
Director. The company had been previously known for its tiling
work, especially popular with breweries wanting to make their pubs
stand out – on the quayside I had been struck by the shining olive
green of the Poole Arms, characteristic of the pottery's style, and by
the two swans facing one another above the door of the Swan Inn,
now boarded up.[7]

Under Truda's direction the company, Carter, Stadler and
Adams, developed an astonishing series of Art Deco vases and
plates: bold, colourful, botanical designs twisting around geometric
patterns, all painted by a talented group of women. Truda divorced
John Adams and married their business partner Cyril Carter, yet
somehow the three of them continued working together. But, aside
from this detail, almost nothing is known of Truda. Only one
photograph of her exists and the staff member I spoke to in the
museum hadn't heard of her. It's been speculated that she was
deliberately left out of history, a woman taking full creative control
of a business, gathering other women around her, and succeeding.
The company no longer makes pottery in Poole, but aside from the
pubs, there were signs of this rich heritage around the town, a mural
celebrating D-Day on a shopping centre entrance, and a striking
section of black tiles with a floral motif that once adorned a corn
merchants shop, relocated when the town centre was redeveloped
in the 1960s.

Poole was like that – its museum was a wonderful repository of

its past, but with the queasy exception of Baden-Powell this
working port didn't strike me as especially interested in the niceties
of its past, letting history's shards gather on the shoreline, a
hotch-potch practical town and like the seaplanes that once
lumbered over the harbour and the ospreys which have now
returned, gazing always out to sea.

SANDBANKS

I drove through Lilliput, a suburb of Poole, named in a roundabout
sort of way after the land in *Gulliver's Travels*, not because Jonathan
Swift took any direct inspiration from it, which Poole council once
claimed, but because Isaac Gulliver, Dorset's apparently gentle
smuggler king, had lived here. Before it was given its diminutive
name Lilliput was known as Salterns; in the later part of the
sixteenth century a group of alchemists calling themselves The
Society of New Arts settled here, hoping to make their fortune not
by turning iron into gold, but more modestly by turning iron into
copper. They may as well have hoped for gold, but although failure
was inevitable it took some years before the last alchemists left
town, no richer and probably no wiser.

Frederick Treves, usually something of a completist, didn't mention Sandbanks or its previous name, Parkstone on Sea, in *Highways and Byways in Dorset*. In the first decade of the twentieth century when Treves published his book the drooping teardrop peninsula which forms the northern part of Poole's natural harbour wall was simply a rapidly eroding group of sand dunes. It had one hotel, one house and for many years the coastguard station was a beached gunboat from the Crimean War. When I was growing up in the 1970s and 80s Sandbanks had a reputation for comfortable but still affordable middle-class affluence, restrained villas lining its streets. But then something strange happened to this modest sandbar, a quirk of economics which transformed it. Driving the one-way system that runs clockwise around the tiny peninsula took me less than five minutes. In small places, space comes at a premium. In 1998 it was calculated that if one worked out the value of each square foot of a two bedroomed flat Sandbanks was the fourth most expensive place to live on the planet.

Millionaires like nothing more than other millionaires. Within a few years Sandbanks was full of enormous new seafront houses. I had an inkling of what to expect – sandwich boards on Poole's quayside promised not only boat trips along the coast beyond the chalk stacks of Old Harry, but also a one-hour cruise of 'Millionaires Row'. My first sight of Sandbanks was a fish restaurant owned by an affable celebrity chef. The sandy suburb was harder to hate than I would have liked, but only because a show of privacy and security is highly prized amongst footballers, football coaches, football commentators and ex-managers of football teams.[8] Walls and high wooden gates blocked my views but I could glimpse the neo-Palladian, a hint of New England and quite a lot of Florida. I drove around three times, and then took the chain ferry to Studland, a five-minute ride that cost £5 to leave the island – it was worth it.

There have been rumours that the same property speculators who continue to find new ways of developing Sandbanks, despite spirited local resistance, have also eyed-up Studland beach – the long, wildlife-rich nature reserve that reaches up to nearly enclose Poole Harbour. I was pleased to be on the Isle of Purbeck, thankful that Sandbanks hasn't yet stretched across the harbour mouth and that Villa Nova remained a monarch's dream.

BOURNEMOUTH'S BANGERS

When Ed found me, I was photographing a mermaid on the seafront. Chained to a railing with padlocks, and made of metal she had a clown's face, long lashes, a sly smile and was carrying a shield emblazoned with the words "Let's Play". All along the length of railings were informal pieces of street art, a few yards away was a yellow and black steel bikini, glinting in the sunlight.

Ed and I drank weak coffee in the almost empty café of the eccentrically loveable Art Nouveau Russell Coates Museum and Gallery. We've known each other for nearly twenty-five years, since we worked together in a bookshop that's long gone. Ed had been at art college in Bournemouth, but had rarely returned – he and his wife Rose live now in north Devon where he works as a copywriter, writing novels and short stories in his free time, and she as a wildlife ranger. Rose's life has been adventurous – she had come to Bournemouth with Ed but elected to spend the day with old colleagues from her years working as a skydiver and parachute packer for the armed forces.

I had left Frederick Treves' book behind; in his day I would no longer be in Dorset, but in Hampshire. In 1972 the Local Government Act scythed Bournemouth and Christchurch from Hampshire and incorporated it into Dorset, creating the county's only urban conurbation. This still rankles with some. A few years ago my wife and I took a taxi home after a night out. Helen's better at talking to taxi drivers than I am, and soon they were chatting about football while I glazed blankly into the darkness. He was an AFC Bournemouth fan and Helen ventured that it was good that Dorset had a successful team. The taxi driver took a long breath. Bournemouth, he said firmly, was not in Dorset, it was in Hampshire and no amount of politicking could change that. How he felt about the subsequent creation of a new authority which brought together Bournemouth, Christchurch and that Dorset interloper, Poole, into one large council is unknowable but predictable.[9]

So Treves was at home, and I had with me instead D.H. Moutray Read, the pen name of Rose Moutray Read, the author of *Highways and Byways in Hampshire*. Pleasingly the Hampshire volume was every bit as eccentric as its Dorset equivalent – it had 400 pages, but as she explained in the preface Moutray Read chose to omit almost all the New Forest and the whole of the Isle of Wight, "for lack of space". She didn't dwell on Bournemouth, referring to it as a "fashionable health resort" but first-hand experience had made her wary of it in winter: "one of the most cheerless and sombre places it has ever been my lot to live in." But she did enjoy the chines – the gorges that carry bubbling waters to the sea, a notable feature of this friable landscape. And in the book's pages I found early stirrings of what we'd now call Nature Writing – Moutray Read was a horticulturalist and a sensitive writer who conjured landscapes with ease.

When her book appeared, Bournemouth was still a new town. Its first house went up in 1810, built on flat land in a valley close to the sea, but it was only in the 1840s that this village started expanding.

There's nothing really old in Bournemouth, and that, together with its somewhat haphazard approach to development, gave the town its character. Bringing one heavy book with me for a long day's walking wasn't enough – I had also packed the Hampshire edition of the *Buildings of England* series, by Nikolaus Pevsner and David Lloyd. If you ever feel short on opinions of the merits of individual buildings, one of Pevsner's books will sort you out. I could imagine Pevsner and Lloyd rolling up their sleeves when it came to this unassuming seaside resort. All the Good Architecture, they proclaimed, was confined to the churches, and then they set about some notable errors – the Pavilion which dominated the land behind the seafront quite innocuously I thought, was "lumpish". The small village of Talbot built for the poor, including cottages, a school and almshouses was "wild and ignorant", although they had more time for the Talbot Heath School for Girls which was "surprisingly acceptable considering its architect."[10] What Pevsner really enjoyed hating was the Victorian expansion of the town, especially the domestic architecture. The architect Christopher Crabb Creeke, who designed many of the houses and hotels was thought to be "not talented".[11]

Ed wanted to show me the 1990s, not the 1860s, and had planned the walk meticulously. His student life, he told me, was not characterised by academic diligence and his part-time jobs were always short-lived. In this town of hotels he'd be sacked from a silver-service job most weekends. But it was in Bournemouth that Ed first developed his high-wire approach to creative practice. He wanted to write plays but knew he had to outwit his inner slacker. His solution was to book a venue for the play, then, having created his own deadline, would write furiously, recruit a cast, persuade the theatre or arts centre to supply the lighting, sound and backstage crew in exchange for a cut of the ticket sales. He'd direct the play himself, sometimes also taking a role. Every performance I attended of his elliptical, social-realist plays was sold out. In later life this DIY punk spirit has filtered into Ed's approach to his novels and collections of short stories, overseeing every aspect of the books himself, creating his own imprint, editing and organising the printing and distribution.

Ed is chatty, observant, self-deprecating and grateful for the way that life has treated him. A long walk through his 90s revealed a lost Bournemouth. Strolling east through wide streets between tall buildings ringed with palm trees doing reasonable but modest

impressions of L.A.'s Chateau Marmont, we passed a
Weatherspoons named after Pevsner's bête noire, Creeke, and then
through a series of underpasses where graffiti implored us to Fuck
Boris. As the town faded into redbrick houses we came to a
four-storey cheese-wedge building covered in scaffolding, once
called The Hothouse, where Ed used to put on DJ nights, now
renamed Alt, its posters featuring an astronaut on a floating
skateboard.

Tucked neatly into a side-street across the road was the railway
station. Pevsner described it as an "odd design" but in the calm of
a Saturday morning, bright sunshine filtering through the glass
ceiling and narrow windows, casting strong shadows from the
ironwork above, this seemed to us the best of Victoriana. It was also
the most important building in Bournemouth's history – the reason
that the town grew so quickly from nothing in the nineteenth
century. I tried to imagine the bustle of the Pines Express in the
heyday of the Somerset and Dorset Joint Railway, the
holidaymakers disembarking at this, their final destination. And
amongst them an older couple, Frank and Lily, her petite and quiet,
careful and organised, him tall, a strong jawline, his pipe glowing, a
limp from a war wound. Both clutched leather suitcases tied with
straps, knowing their way because they came here every year, to the
same hotel with the dark wood panelling and revolving front doors,
which their tiny grandson found fascinating and strange, and better
than the windy beach.[12]

The Pines Express is long gone and its spirit didn't stay with us as we left the station. Soon we were in narrow, busy streets. Every shop was different from its 1990s incarnation, said Ed. Takeaways had replaced places where once you sat to eat. But gentrification remained at arm's length. Bournemouth and Poole are notably younger, more diverse and poorer than the rest of Dorset, the Covid pandemic had hit the conurbation harder than the rural areas, the same inequalities exacerbated, extended, more deeply embedded.

Ed's a record collector; we share a fondness for late 80s and early 90s Daisy Age hip-hop, though his knowledge exceeds mine – during our walk he gently corrected me on the release date of *Three Feet High and Rising*. All the record shops he haunted in his student days were gone – he showed me the site of one which had been run by break-dancers, now a bubble tea shop named Yunique. Taking inspiration from Pevsner's umbrage Ed was also keen to show me his own architectural horror, although he warned me that I might be sick on the pavement.

The building was a concrete 1960s multi-storey car park, a gentle upward curve allowed vehicles to gracefully ascend the slope, a hint of the space age and of an abandoned utopian dream; it wasn't so bad. Except that, as an afterthought, the architect had added two storeys of now damp-stained flats onto the top floor, as if a toddler had wedged LEGO bricks onto it, and not well. This student accommodation was called The Outlook, high above the carwash and the takeaways. Back on the main drag we passed For Your Eyes

Only – 'the ultimate table dancing club', permanently closed with whitewashed windows, one smashed. The streets were busy with people in rugby tops in preparation for a Six Nations match, the Irish bar had inflatable goalposts emblazoned with the Guinness logo outside its doors, above us red brick and vertiginous half-timbering, nostalgic for a past that Bournemouth never possessed, but pleasing anyway, whatever Pevsner thought. A blue plaque marked where the composer of *Jerusalem*, Hubert Parry, had been born, in 1848, not long after Bournemouth's beginning, but the building had been replaced in the meantime, as had much of the original town. Bournemouth is always in flux, new shops, new takeaways, closed table-dancing bars.

In a street dominated by the tall grey spire of St Peter's church Ed showed me a frozen yoghurt shop. Neither of us have a special interest in yoghurt at any temperature, but amongst his other interests Ed is a cinephile – he has thousands of films in his collection. Yobu Frozen Yoghurt was where the minor horror movie, *K-Shop*, was filmed. In the film antisocial customers of a kebab shop become another customer's next meal.[13] There may be an aura of menace in this part of Bournemouth – the Godmother of horror fiction, Mary Shelley is buried in St Peter's graveyard, alongside her husband Percy's heart, in a grisly twist that seems to be relatively common in Dorset. Hardy's heart is interred in Stinsford, while the rest of his body is in Westminster Abbey. Whitchurch Canonicorum is the burial spot of the founder of the colony of Bermuda, George Somers, but his heart remains in St George's in the north Atlantic.[14] Later I checked a map for the relative locations of these hearts without bodies, or a body without a heart, and found an Old Straightish Track, a slightly wobbly cardiac ley line, running from Bournemouth through Stinsford to Whitchurch. In Mary's case, her burial in St Peter's was a second attempt. Some have claimed that it was her last wish to be buried in Bournemouth (and who wouldn't want that?) but in fact her preference was to be with her parents in St Pancras, London. Her son considered the churchyard there to be too full already so had her dug up and re-buried in Bournemouth.[15] He was right to do so – the coming of the railway later disrupted the churchyard and many bodies were disturbed, causing a national scandal. A young architect working on the railway was asked to create a new scheme for the churchyard. His response was to have many of the tombstones rearranged around a tree – the architect's name was

Thomas Hardy, not yet a novelist; the embattled tree is now known as the Hardy Tree. Ed's schedule did not allow for graveside loitering, but Mary's spirit was kept alive by another Wetherspoons, The Mary Shelley, opposite.

Bournemouth has attracted artists and writers and not just in death. Aubrey Beardsley came to Boscombe for his health in 1896 to recover from tuberculosis, having rejected Dieppe, as he owed money to a hotelier there. The house he rented is gone, as is his later residence close to the second pier, but I came across a large mosaic nearby ('sponsored by Tarmac Construction Ltd') representing one of his less erotic illustrations.

We were soon in the long narrow strip of gardens gently sloping to the bandstand, where the narrow River Bourne was innocuously channelled. It was a busy, profoundly controlled space, of winding paths, monuments, a one-time aviary on the slopes. Ed had once seen the disgraced TV entertainer Michael Barrymore in the gardens, and nearby we found a small lump of stone commemorating the birth of Prince Andrew, the words on the plaque scratched out and spray-painted. A gull pulled its lunch from a plastic bag left on a bin.

What is Bournemouth known for? Its sandy beaches, pier, and for many, its night-time entertainment – the streets were full of bars and clubs. For decades the town's most famous venue was The Winter Gardens. Originally built in 1875 as a glass and ironwork exhibition space with strong echoes of London's Crystal Palace, it was replaced with a brick building in the early twentieth century. If you hung around Bournemouth in the 1960s and 70s you'd have been able to see an astonishing line-up of musicians at the Winter Gardens: Petula Clark, The Beach Boys, Pink Floyd, Cat Stevens, David Bowie, King Crimson, The Kinks, Yes, Van de Graaf Generator, Genesis, Elton John, Queen, Black Sabbath, The Clash, Richard Hell and the Voidoids, The Cure. At a concert headlined by Buzzcocks in November 1979, Ian Curtis, lead singer of the support act, Joy Division, collapsed backstage after their show; Pete Shelley of Buzzcocks asked the audience not to block the doors as an ambulance was on its way. Even the Beatles performed here, in 1963. Whether they spent much time in Bournemouth I don't know but four years later the band squeezed one-time resident Aubrey Beardsley into the cast of characters on the cover of *Sgt. Pepper's Lonely Hearts Club Band*. I never saw any of these bands in Bournemouth – the best I managed was Frankie Goes to

Hollywood in April 1985, when they were touring their album *Welcome to the Pleasuredome*.[16]

In search of The Winter Gardens we crossed the road next to the Royal Exeter Hotel, which has at its heart Bournemouth's first house. But The Winter Gardens were gone. In their place was another car park; a large pile of rubble nearby marked where more recent demolition had taken place, taking with it a restaurant called Funki Griller, and a bar called the Lost Paradise.

The Winter Gardens' fate was sealed by the arrival of a new monster. Close by was the Bournemouth International Centre, a sprawling, domineering red-brick building whose guiding aesthetic was a combination of an insurance company's head office and a Cold War era bunker. It opened in 1984; overnight The Winter Gardens became redundant, closing after Ken Dodd's summer season. Various attempts were made to save it, but in 2006 it was demolished.

On the grass opposite the site of The Winter Gardens and the Lost Paradise I noticed peculiar but unmistakeable lumps and bumps beneath our feet – we were standing on an old crazy golf course, abandoned. We walked its holes, greens and unplayable fairways, which took us nearly two minutes.

We stopped for lunch and beer in a café around the corner from a bar themed to a cheery version of the 1990s, brightly coloured murals of antique mobile phones on its windows. Ed remembered seeing Dogburster, a Death Metal band, around here, in his 1990s.

"What were they like?" I asked

"Like every other Death Metal band."

Ed ordered a hot dog, which the café's menu had mysteriously failed to call a Bournemouth Banger.

We walked off lunch along the busy seafront, Hengistbury Head in the deep distance. We stopped to admire goats who were tackling the scrub on the steep slopes above the brightly coloured beach huts. I was keen to see, and maybe take a ride on the East Cliff funicular railway. I remembered my grandparents, Frank and Lily, riding the blue railway-compartment-like cars down to the sands, that glorious, shared sinking feeling in the pit of their stomachs.

But the funicular was gone, its steep tracks overgrown with grasses and the carriages missing. In 2016 a landslip overwhelmed it, a century-old attraction left to the sands. The goats are the only animals sure-footed enough to cope these days.[17] Ed and I didn't get as far as the consumptive Aubrey Beardsley would have managed. We walked up one of the zig-zagged paths to the top of the sandy cliff and back to Bournemouth. We needn't have worried about crazy golf dying out – close to the pier was a huge course, complete with fake battlements, crowded with families.

Tired from the day's tramping, its peculiar and unexpected connections, but happy to have spent longer together than any time since the 1990s, Ed and I said our goodbyes and he went in search of his sky-diving wife. Making my way past the supine bulk of the International Centre I found a survivor of the spirit of an older Bournemouth. A simple sign on a garden wall read 'Court Royal Home for South Wales Convalescent Miners'. Originally run jointly by the National Union of Mineworkers and the Coal Board, it was now a hotel catering solely for ex-miners from Wales and their families. Bournemouth is a town for the Day Tripper, a town to be torn down and rebuilt on its shifting sands, a place for the fleeting experience, for forgetting. But this modest hotel represented something more tangible, something about community, for the longer-haul, a rare and important survival.

CHRISTCHURCH'S MODERN GROTESQUES

Neither my arrival, nor that of two peregrines, were entirely welcome at Christchurch Priory. I had stepped from bright late March sunlight into the shade of the high porch. But a service was about to start and a sign mounted on a lectern at the entrance to the church told me visitors were not permitted to enter. A visitor leaving the church told me to take no notice: "they let me wander around," he said.

At the back of the nave I was met by a small group of people surrounding a middle-aged man in a cassock, who grew slightly red-faced.

"I wondered if I might look around?"

The churchman's eyeballs puffed.

"No, you can't. There's a service about to start." He looked at his plain-clothes assistants. "Isn't the sign out?" They assured him it was. I began to retreat. He looked me up and down warily.

"Well, you'd be welcome to join us. Or you could come back later."

As I was leaving a woman from the group stopped me, and offered to show me the Priory tower, for just a small charge. I agreed enthusiastically, gratefully, and we returned to the nave, where the indeterminately-ranked cleric was even less pleased to see me than he had been a few seconds earlier.

"He would like to see the tower..," began the guide.

"Well he can't. We've got peregrines nesting there."

I practically jogged back through the porch, apologising, saying that I didn't want to disturb the falcons, because I didn't. I was again followed by the guide who offered to show me the outside of the church instead.

Christchurch Priory is long and low and very, very old. William

II, better known as William Rufus,[18] gave the original structure to
Ranulph Flambard, who knocked it down and began rebuilding. In
the twelfth century it became an Augustine priory and over the
centuries was granted to other royal associates, rebuilt and
extended, was dissolved under Henry VIII, its ancillary buildings
destroyed, but reconstituted as a church. The result of this
continued monarchical meddling was a building which had little
overall cohesion but was fascinating, nonetheless.

"I want to show you the modern grotesques," said my new
companion. "Most people miss them."

We looked up at the grotesques, more commonly known as
gargoyles (technically speaking gargoyles disperse rainwater,
mostly through their mouths, grotesques don't). Heads and faces,
monsters and animals, gurned down at us. My guide, a woman in
her sixties, clearly enjoyed showing people these details. Some of
the grotesques were carved only in the 1990s, and some were even
more recent. I was shown one of the current canon and of Donald
Bailey, designer of the Bailey Bridge, a pre-fabricated pontoon
developed by the British military at Christchurch in the Second
World War. We reached the Priory's east face, overlooking the
river.

"Look," she said, "top right." The newest grotesque was a
woman's face, wearing a surgical cap and face mask, the NHS
logo carved discreetly alongside it, the latest markings of a long
history.

I squinted at the golden form of the weathervane on the tower, glinting in the sunlight. "Is that a fish?" I asked.

"Yes, a salmon. I met someone in the fire brigade, and he said they'd come up sometimes to 'grease the salmon'. I was disappointed they didn't use lard." I thanked her for her time.

As I was walking along the graveyard's path towards the town, I heard a distinctive cry from the tower. The peregrines were about, pacing along a protruding drainpipe and calling. A group of people behind me complained that someone would soon have to clean up dead gulls, the peregrines' favoured prey.

The view from the tower must be quite something, but not everyone has appreciated it – Rose Moutray Read, writing in *Highways and Byways in Hampshire*, thought it "a most ineffective afterthought" although she was enthusiastic about the building as a whole ("exceedingly interesting"). Content to leave the tower to the birds, I made my way towards town. The twelfth century castle was now a jagged tooth on top of a mound which, aside from the gulls who had recently emptied a nearby wheelie bin, I had to myself. Oliver Cromwell decided that the castle's strategic position meant that he preferred to destroy it rather than risk it falling into Royalist hands.[19] By the river was the Norman House, a roofless rectangular building built around the time of the Norman conquest with one tall, perfectly preserved round chimney. It was reputedly visited on many occasions by King John, and now appreciated by a few visitors and nesting pigeons cooing from holes in the walls. Sitting between the Norman House and the castle was a bowling green; a sign warned me against cycling, roller-skating, skateboarding or walking my dog without a lead.

If Bournemouth, is young, Christchurch is old, in more ways than one. It has the highest proportion of people aged over 65 in Britain, but you can't escape death forever. Close to the Priory was a lonely section of ornately decorated wall; once a mausoleum for a Mrs Perkins, interred here in 1783. She was so scared of being buried alive that she instructed she should not be buried but placed above ground so that the pupils in the school which was then in the Priory's loft could hear her screams and release her. She also requested that her coffin not be screwed down and that the mausoleum be left unlocked so that she might escape her tomb on waking.[20] Closer to the Priory in a neat cemetery, ringed with benches for mourners, were some of Christchurch's more recent dead. Benches were everywhere, bearing names of the deceased. One carried an inscription on its brass plate: "Whisky and Cigars. Just What The Doctor Ordered". The dates revealed that Ken had lived into his 90s, although he might have been with us still had he eased up on the booze and posh fags.

My second coming at the Priory was more warmly received. The guides were generous with their time, eager to press a map into my hands and pleased I left a donation. The many ages of church architecture, Saxon and heavy Romanesque, arching Gothic and intricate Perpendicular had combined to give the interior an unexpected lightness, and on a sunny day, as light streamed through stained glass it was joyful. Moutray Read had been right – it was fascinating, a crash course in a thousand years and more of ecclesiastical architecture.

I was here for monuments. Towards the altar, behind the misericords where monks once sat in deliberate discomfort during prayer, was a beautiful memorial lit by warm light and carved delicately like the surface of a custard cream. This chantry was dedicated to the memory of Margaret Pole, Countess of Salisbury, who died in 1541. The Countess spent her long life perilously close to royalty, sometimes in favour, but frequently not. She held lands in her own right, and unusually for a woman in the sixteenth century, wielded real power. Arrested in 1539 for involvement in a Catholic uprising, almost certainly on evidence fabricated by Henry VIII's chief minister and fixer, Thomas Cromwell, she was detained for two and a half years, before being executed. Her death seems to have been bloody, and not long planned for. The king had new clothes made for her just two months before her death, no proper scaffold was built, and instead she was beheaded, and from the eye-witness account of Chapuys, the Holy Roman Emperor's ambassador, without skill. Chapuys and others could not believe an old woman would be executed – he guessed her age to be 90; in fact she was 67. By the time she died, Cromwell too had met his end at the hands of an executioner. Rose Moutray Read wrote that when the crypt at Christchurch was opened up it was found to be an ossuary, full of bones, later buried in the churchyard, but Margaret Pole's were not amongst them. Her remains were discovered at the Tower of London in 1867, whereupon Pope Leo XIII beatified her as a martyr.

At the west end a guide helped me locate a memorial commemorating the life of Percy Bysshe Shelley and Mary Wollstonecraft Shelley. Its siting here had been controversial, Percy was an atheist who had once eloped with a girl of sixteen who later drowned herself in London's Serpentine, before he too drowned in a boating accident off the Italian coast.[21] Most shocking for the faithful was that he was depicted, Christ-like in death, his bare left arm flung romantically over the knee of a woman gazing into his eyes and cradling his torso.

I left the church, checking for the remains of eviscerated gulls on the path. At the waterfront by the bandstand there were plentiful

supplies of birds for peregrines: ducks, pigeons, swans, milling amongst humans. I was at the confluence of the Hampshire Avon and the Dorset Stour as they mingled slowly into a wide channel, which had given the town its original name of Twynham – a place where rivers meet.[22] The benches were occupied by retirees eating ice creams, gazing contentedly upon the calm water. It was too early for an ice cream for me, but I sat at the end of the small quayside admiring the boats. I was at the site of another drowning, but unlike Percy Shelley's, no accident.

On March 28th 1935 Francis Rattenbury, a retired architect, died at his home in nearby Boscombe, leaving his second, much younger wife, Alma and young son, John. At the scene Police Constable Arthur Bagnell discovered that Rattenbury had been killed by a blow to the head from a mallet. Alma confessed to murder on the spot, but immediately changed her account, accusing instead the eighteen-year-old chauffeur and handyman, George Stoner, with whom she had been having an affair. Stoner was condemned to hang. But the story took a further, sadder, twist. The press accused Alma, twenty years older than George, of drunken nymphomania, of leading the younger man to an evil act; 300,000 people signed a petition to commute his sentence, claiming he had come under her 'undue influence'. A few days after the trial, her lover condemned and her reputation in ruins, she stood at the quayside in Christchurch, smoked a cigarette, and repeatedly stabbed herself before falling into the water. Her funeral was attended by 3,000 people, most of them women. In contrast her husband's funeral attracted a small number of mourners, perhaps a reflection of how he'd lived – he'd left his first wife, Florence, for Alma, in the course of the separation he had the heating and hot water cut off from the marital home.

Alma and Francis' son, John, was told that his parents had gone on holiday and only learnt of their fate a year later from a boy at his school. In time John too became an architect, working in Frank Lloyd Wright's studio – the celebrated architect's own life had in some senses prefigured the tragedies of his protégé. The designer of Fallingwater and the Guggenheim Museum left his first wife for the translator and feminist Mamah Borthwick. Five years later, in 1914, Mamah and six others were murdered by a servant in their home, Taliesin. In later life interviews John would say that Frank had taken him under his wing, sensing a connection between them. John Rattenbury was certain that Stoner was his father's killer, but remarkably bore him no ill will, thinking he was a "terrible victim of circumstance" who'd had a "terrible life".

George Stoner escaped the gallows, possibly owing to the petition to save him. On the outbreak of the Second World War he was released from prison and served in the army with distinction. He died in 2000, insisting that Alma had been the perpetrator of Francis' murder.[23] In a final twist, in 1977, while both George and John were still alive, Terence Rattigan's final play, *Cause Célèbre*, inspired by the case, was staged, later becoming a TV drama starring Helen Mirren as Alma and David Morrissey as George.

I needed a break from murders and drownings. I walked out of town, through streets of bungalows, front gardens paved over for parked Nissan Micras, and came finally to a bridge which crossed the River Stour. Beneath me was a small lozenge shaped island, accessible only to members of the boat club on the river's bank. The trees on the island were not yet in leaf and I could make out a large concrete structure sunk into the ground. In 1940, a German invasion very much a possibility, the land around Christchurch was designated as an anti-tank island. Coastal batteries and tank traps were built across the town, and as at Blandford Forum, bridges were mined, in case the invasion came.[24] This pillbox watched over the

Stour, others the railway. In the springtime sunshine it was just the background to a happy day on the water. Three older men happily messed about with the motor on their boat, and I looked happily on.

I crossed the bridge again, stopping briefly to watch a heron snatch a small fish from a muddy pond next to the river, which prompted an outbreak of applause from the few onlookers.

The location wasn't certain, but I knew what to look for – a piece of land in the shadow of 1960s high rise flats. My father was a ciné film enthusiast, always buying the latest equipment – cameras, outsize boom mikes, all carried around in large cases. This sometimes led to him being confused with a member of a TV crew by the public, who would later appear beaming widely on the four-minute-long segments of flickering film, ready for their fleeting moment of fame, replayed only to us. After dad died the rolls of film and heavy projector were locked away in an understairs cupboard. Eventually I had them converted to DVD. Years later, at mum's funeral, we set up a TV screen in the function room of the pub holding the wake and played the films. Chatting to guests, awkward in my rarely worn suit, I glimpsed a section from my childhood: a day at Tucktonia.

Tucktonia opened in 1976. The site had once been a golf course, but the owner, Harry Stiller, a former racing driver, had a grander plan. 'The Greatest Little Britain in the World' ran the slogan for Tucktonia, a model village writ large, featuring 200 buildings, from Buckingham Palace to a complete Cornish fishing village, Heathrow Airport to the Post Office Tower. There were motorways, railways and rivers. Time collided at Tucktonia – the timbered buildings that spanned old London Bridge featured and so did an oil refinery. It was huge and fantastic. Stiller threw himself into the project and its marketing – for the opening day he hired the comedian Arthur Askey, who agreed to do the job for £100 plus his train fare, and was happy to pose for photos, gazing up at the model of Big Ben, significantly taller than he was, ostentatiously checking his watch against its clock face. The grand opening had teething problems – miniature cars on the roads stopped and started, the model trains sometimes crashed, but still Tucktonia was a success, a local legend. In our childish enthusiasm we didn't notice the strange effect of scale revealed in the ciné film – the life-size blocks of flats just behind the site, dwarfing the tiny buildings.

But Tucktonia didn't last. The monsters appeared – bigger,

better, brasher theme parks: Alton Towers, Thorpe Park, Chessington World of Adventures. Finally, a decade after opening, Tucktonia, by then a little run-down, closed. Most of the buildings later burned in a warehouse fire. Buckingham Palace was relocated to another, more traditional model village in Wimborne, a few miles away.[25] Finally it moved to Great Yarmouth, where I understand you can see it still.[26]

I recognised the blocks of flats from the ciné film – they had had makeovers, but I was in the right place. Tucktonia's tiny buildings had been replaced by a small, quiet housing estate. I walked its neatly-kept roads. Nobody was around and nothing remained of The Greatest Little Britain in the World. The street-names reflected its golf course years: Fairways, Wentworth Drive. I had hoped for an Askew Avenue, at least. I crossed some open land to the Stour where I sat on the riverbank, ate a cheese sandwich and sent my brother a photo of the lost paradise. The Stour flowed silently; a coot flapped over to the cover of the reeds on the opposite bank, a lone paddle-boarder floated past. Fifty yards downriver a woman on the riverbank sat hunched over her puzzle magazine. It was a huge contrast to Tucktonia's colour and noise, preferable for the flats' residents, a contemplative spot.

I went east, to Purewell. Contemplation with a fervently religious bent brought a struggling novelist to this Christchurch suburb at the end of the nineteenth century. F.W. Rolfe, who wrote under the pseudonym Baron Corvo, came to the town first in 1889. Christchurch was then a haven for artists and writers, as seaside places often are. He dreamt of becoming a priest but never achieved his ambition; his best-known book, *Hadrian VII*, while occasionally popping up in 'Best Of' lists in literary magazines, remains obscure. The plot concerns an English Catholic priest who, through a series of coincidences, becomes Pope. Baron Corvo might have been forgotten altogether had it not been for a book about his life, *The Quest for Corvo*, by A.J.A. Symons. Subtitled *An Experiment in Biography*, the book was revolutionary, concerning itself as much with Symons' search for the enigmatic author as the life of the subject itself, a literary detective story which has itself become something of a cult.[27]

Tucked behind a street of Victorian houses in Purewell was a new Roman Catholic Church, but on the roadside was its predecessor, an unassuming smallish red-brick building. Rolfe became a member of the congregation here. He was also a photographer and amateur artist; in his biography Symons wrote that Corvo had created Italian Renaissance style frescoes of the archangel Michael at the church. To achieve this, models were photographed in appropriate poses, the archangel himself in a mid-air leap, after which Corvo made lantern slides of the images, projecting them onto the walls of the church and tracing their outlines. I've long harboured an interest in Rolfe and his alter ego – the wall paintings would be worth investigating.

It was not to be. The old church was now used as a food bank but was locked. I walked around the building looking for an alternative entrance but found none. Everything about Rolfe or Corvo is obscure, layered, little is straightforward. Restoration work on the old church carried out early in the twenty-first century heightened suspicion of the identity of the artist: the 'frescoes' described by Symons were discovered to be canvases which had been later stuck to the plaster. This was a technique used by Nathaniel Westlake, an artist who created similar designs in other churches, and some believe that the leaping Saint Michael was Westlake's work.[28] Rolfe may or may not have left an artistic trace at the Church of the Immaculate Conception, but he certainly left a reputation. In his relatively short stay he built up debts and ruffled feathers – during one botched property purchase the author sent a telegram to a solicitor instructing him to come to Christchurch immediately, where he would be met at the station by a "barouche with white horse" – a barouche being a carriage with a cover for the passenger. The solicitor, convinced that an important client was waiting, rushed to Christchurch to find only the usual station carriage drawn by what Symons' described as a "flea-bitten grey hack". Shortly afterwards Baron Corvo left town. He died in Venice in 1913, at the age of 53, still in penury, and living an erratic life with faint echoes of Thomas Mann's novel, *Death in Venice*, which had been published two years earlier.[29]

My miniature quest for Corvo fittingly frustrated, I went further east again. Catholic priests also played their part at Highcliffe Castle which sat above the beach. Gothic Revival is a definitively derivative style, snobbish, overly-elaborate and I'm a sucker for it. The castle's exterior didn't disappoint, shining pale stone, large windows, high octagonal chimneys, a long view across lawns towards the distant Isle of Wight. Rose Moutray Read was enthusiastic too, calling it a "fantastic modern building". Built mostly in the 1830s, it replaced the mansion High Cliff, which had boasted a laboratory, a room for natural history exhibits and a short-lived garden designed by Capability Brown. The new castle, owned by Lord Stuart de Rothesay, one-time ambassador to France, was a wedding-cake affair, spread out on flat lawns. Sparing no expense he brought stone from Portland and Purbeck but also French medieval masonry, lending the new castle an instant air of authenticity. Rothesay furnished it lavishly, creating a library, and filled it with expensive carpets, tapestries and curtains. Its centrepiece was a magnificent staircase in the main hall, which curved upwards in two graceful sections, meeting underneath a wide gothic arch, two palms meeting in prayer.

The lawn was busy with visitors, an outdoor café serving tea and ice cream, a wedding planner dressed entirely in grey was supervising a group of tree surgeons removing foliage from the window frame on the second floor, in preparation for the weekend. In the nineteenth and twentieth centuries the castle was a society hot spot, visited by Gladstone, Nancy Mitford, Kaiser Willhelm, and Dame Nellie Melba. For a few years Gordon Selfridge rented the castle, and was keen to buy it. Finally, in 1950, the castle was sold and became a children's home, advertised as 'Highcliffe Castle, Hants, Children's Homes and Schools For Health, Tuition and Holidays'. The thought of this made me shudder. Gothic architecture has more than a hint of nightmare about it, a shadow of the darker fairy tales. I couldn't imagine this as a happy place. Later I found out that the children's home closed after just a few years, together with its sister establishment at Lynton in Devon, following accusations of sexual assault.

For a few years the castle was occupied by the Claretian Fathers, an order of priests devoted to active missionary work, describing themselves as "people aflame with the love of God" (for 'people', read 'men'). In the 1960s a major fire led to a consortium acquiring the castle, with the intention of demolishing it in favour of beach huts. Shortly after permission for this was denied a second fire devastated the castle, leaving it a ruin but a useful home for doves. Finally the Council bought the shell and began the long process of restoration. I bought a ticket to see the interior.

In the first room I talked to a guide who told me the Council had decided not to recreate the building in its heyday, but instead to let it tell its own story, fire and ruination included. If I had hoped for book-lined rooms hung with tapestries and richly furnished with comfortable chairs, I could see the merit too in bare walls and scarring. Much of the internal structure of Highcliffe was gone, replaced by modern staircases and walkways. The interior's blond wood and glass had all the grace of a conference centre, and I wondered if limited funds had played a part in the Council's decision to leave the castle largely unrestored. I was the only visitor. But I was looking forward to the grand hall and its famous staircase.

I've spent nearly two decades enthralled by the idea of England's greatest folly, Fonthill Abbey, built by the eccentric novelist and collector, William Beckford, on a hill in Wiltshire and constructed with money earned by the labour of enslaved Africans on his sugar plantations. The abbey was monstrous, featuring a 300-foot-high tower, dominating the surrounding landscape. In 1825, two years after Beckford sold the 'abbey', the tower collapsed and the whole building became a ruin, leaving one small tower in the woodland. The entrance hall to Fonthill was huge; Beckford played further with the scale by employing a dwarf to open the enormous doors to very occasional visitors – Beckford was largely shunned by society having been discovered *in flagrante* with a young nobleman at Powderham Castle in Devon. Highcliffe was a sort of Fonthill in miniature, and the hallway in particular was thought to be redolent of the Abbey, which boasted an almost identical double staircase behind the dwarf-operated doors. I've visited Fonthill's ruins on occasion and tried to imagine the massive abbey, Highcliffe's grand hall would be the closest I could come to it.

I stepped inside the hallway. The room was long, narrow and high, as I had expected, white plastered walls as far as the second storey, but the brickwork above was now bare, although some of the decoration remained. The rug I had seen in photographs had been replaced by a carpet in corporate mauve. The paintings, tapestries and ornate wooden furniture was all gone. The grand double staircase was missing too, just a yawning black gothic hole above me. This was no casualty of fire – the Claretians, in their pious enthusiasm, had converted the hallway into a chapel and removed it.[30]

Slightly shocked at how shocked I was, I left as soon as I could, through a room laid out for the weekend wedding, stumbling past sprayed gold chairs.

Before Tucktonia opened, Hengistbury Head was a bank holiday weekend destination, a sandy, high, tussocky spit of land enclosing Christchurch harbour. As children we thought it impossibly large, a land bathed in dusty sunshine.

Hengistbury is a place under siege. In the nineteenth century mining eroded the land mass of the Head by around one third in just over a decade. Years later, Gordon Selfridge, unable to buy Highcliffe Castle, purchased Hengistbury Head instead, and shocked locals with his plans to build "the largest castle in the world", employing an architect to draw up panoramas of his dream which included four miles of ramparts, a tower the height of Fonthill's, a covered lake, terraces and 250 suites of rooms. Hengistbury Head was saved by the Wall Street Crash and Selfridge's already lavish life – in 1930 the Council bought the land from him, and the plans were abandoned.

I discovered that the two dips in the land that we used to charge over to reach Hengistbury's heights were in fact Iron Age defensive double ditches, now sensibly fenced off and nibbled by Cotswold Lions, a breed of sheep brought in to trim the grass. I was pleased to see that the 'land train', which dragged little coaches along the road across Hengistbury still ran in the summer months. This innocuous and colourful vehicle had once caused mayhem in Christchurch. It was an early move to conserve the Head, allowing the Council to ban cars, outraging owners of the huts on the far beaches who complained vociferously in letters to the local paper; the train was sabotaged shortly after its introduction in 1968, when tacks were scattered in its path, causing punctures.

The water in Christchurch harbour was distant across the marshland. A couple sat on a bench contemplating the view, and I hoped they were eating ice creams. The harbour is natural, a much smaller version of Poole's, but important nonetheless, partly because it gave easy access to smugglers, a business which provided a living to many in Christchurch. Beyond the harbour, tracks across Hampshire and Dorset provided routes for moving the contraband, as did the rivers Stour and Avon. In 1784 a naval ship surprised two smuggling vessels which were in the process of landing a cargo of tea and brandy at Christchurch. The ensuing three-hour battle, involving firearms and artillery, killed the captain of the naval ship, while most of the smugglers and their cargo simply melted into the land around the town. One man was hanged for his part in the Battle of Mudeford, his corpse hung for display in chains, but later cut down by sympathisers and given a burial.

Leaving the still waters behind me I drove away from the troubled Head to the residential streets in Southbourne where Christchurch fringes into Bournemouth – one was named for Gordon Selfridge, another was Rolls Drive. In July 1910 an air display was held in an airfield that once occupied this land – the first time that most of the spectators would have seen this new technology, seven years after the first heavier-than-air flight. One of the pilots was Charles Rolls, co-founder of Rolls Royce, and the first person to have made the return flight across the English Channel by plane, just one month earlier.

The tail on Rolls' modified version of the Wright brothers' 'flyer' failed in mid-air; he became the first Briton to die in an aeroplane crash. In the 1920s the airfield was abandoned in favour of bigger, better facilities elsewhere, so apart from Rolls Drive, all that's left is a small, circular memorial to Rolls, hidden in the sports fields of a school nearby.

It was now late afternoon. I headed to Christchurch's northerly edge and walked a sandy lane dotted with occasional houses through woodland towards Saint Catherine's Hill, once a hillfort, now a nature reserve. I clambered up a steep hillock, recently cleared of trees, and through a small gap in the gorse. From here Christchurch was laid out before me, the Solent shimmering and the Isle of Wight hazy. I was standing in the direct line of the Priory's tower and the western slope of Hengistbury Head, the site of Selfridge's unbuilt modern grotesque. From my vantage point I could imagine Christchurch as my own private Tucktonia.

There's a legend that the original site for the Priory was Saint Catherine's Hill, but having begun construction the builders would wake every day to find the stones they had laid had been transported to where it stands now, on the flat land where rivers meet. In Dorset these nocturnal shiftings were common – church stones moved at Lewcombe, Folke, Holnest and Winterborne Whitechurch, most of these nightly movements grouped in the north-west of the county. I picked up three, small, curiously shaped stones; were these part of the original chapel, somehow missed? I couldn't tell if the markings were shaped by nature or by chisel, but I slipped them into my pocket anyway, and brought them home. They're still on my desk, night after night, out of reach of any deity hoping to transport them along the smugglers' lanes and back across the old county line. Like Great Yarmouth's miniature Buckingham Palace, they're out of place, but seem happy to linger.

The *Shell Guide* was curtly dismissive: there was "not much else to do in Christchurch except to have a shrimp tea or to watch the alert trout by the water-combed weeds in the stream by the priory". My day had been packed with dead aviators, murder and suicide, burnt and unrealised castles, shifting churches, mysterious writers, smuggling, battles, a lost theme park, and I had annoyed a man of the cloth twice in less than five minutes – it was no wonder Christchurch's residents needed so many benches on which to recover, and possibly the whisky and cigars helped too.

Notes

1   Although the grand plans were never completed – see a painting of the proposed finished castle on the RIBA website www.ribapix.com/design-for-remodelling-brownsea-castle-brownsea-island-dorset-for-colonel-william-petrie-waugh-perspective_riba4063#

2   At the time this news story made headlines around the world. Good summaries can be found on the BBC news website, as can discussions of the degree to which Baden-Powell was a racist homophobe, although in summary we can conclude that whatever the positive consequences of his legacy, he was. The main objection to this viewpoint is the argument that we can't judge the past by our own standards. This is true, but opinions are a choice and not necessarily shaped by the age – being born in earlier centuries did not consign you to a certain set of beliefs. For examples see the lives and works of Robert Wedderburn, William Wilberforce, William Morris, Emmeline Pankhurst and Mary Wollstonecraft. For what it's worth I was an enthusiastic cub scout, especially proud of my badge for reading, but hated the Scouts, and left to join the local history society.

3   I'm being slightly flippant: usually west-country protests were well-planned. See an account of a protest in Poole in 1831 in *West Country Scum* by Dr. Leonard Baker, in issue one of *Romance, Revolution and Reform*, April 2019.

4   My edition, a reprint with additions by a later, un-named writer, from 1935, also makes reference to "steamers".

5   See Jarman's memoir, *Dancing Ledge*, Quartet, 1984, Vintage 2002, p 33. There's an example of one of Jarman's doors in the town museum.

6   For some excellent photos of potters at work in the early twentieth century, see *Discover Dorset: Pottery* by Penny Copland-Griffiths, The Dovecote Press, 1998.

7   For an extraordinary gallery of photos of the pottery's tiling work and especially on pubs see www.pooleimages.co.uk/carters-tiles

8   You might seek out the ITV series *Harry Redknapp's Sandbanks Summer*, in which the one-time manager of teams including West Ham, Tottenham Hotspur and AFC Bournemouth, together with his wife Sandra welcome "celebrity friends" to their home. It's as good as it sounds.

9   There was a failed bid to have Christchurch rejoin Hampshire before the creation of 'B.C.P.' in 2017.

10 Poor Hubert Worthington.

11 But he did create the town's sewage system, for which he was rewarded, after his death, with a bust on public display showing him seated on a toilet.

12 For more on the Somerset and Dorset railway, see the Shillingstone section of this book (North).

13 If this is your sort of thing IMDB has more information: www.imdb.com/title/tt3221544/

14 Percy Bysshe's heart is only "reputedly" buried with Mary – apparently the only organ in his body to resist the flames of cremation following his death by drowning off the coast of Sardinia, and in Hardy's case there was a rumour that his heart was eaten by a cat, just prior to its internment.

15 Her mother was of course the feminist Mary Wollstonecraft, her father the philosopher William Godwin. The Victorians didn't mind exporting their dead from the crowded capital, as evidenced by the Necropolis Railway.

16 They were really good.

17 Bournemouth is still well-provisioned with funicular railways – one on West Cliff and another, the Fisherman's Walk Cliff Lift at Southbourne, which has the distinction of being the world's shortest – see the Atlas Obscura website.

18 Rufus famously met his death in a hunting accident in the New Forest, a few miles away, the site marked by the Rufus Stone, although whether it was exactly the spot where he

was killed is uncertain.

19 At Corfe Castle too, the Parliamentarians destroyed the castle after a long siege.

20 I was informed of all this by a notice screwed to the wall, which referenced *The Smugglers of Christchurch* by E.R. Oakley as its source. For more mausoleum madness see the Holnest section of this book (West).

21 And for news of his heart, see the Bournemouth section of this book.

22 In Old English this was known as Tweoxneam.

23 For more on the case, which I was first directed to by a passing reference in the *Shell Guide to Hampshire* written when the case was fresh in the public's mind, see the British Newspaper Archive website: blog.britishnewspaperarchive.co.uk/2020/03/06/the-murder -of-francis-rattenbury/, and The Telegraph Online, November 19, 2007. An interview with John Rattenbury, who died in 2021, was published in The Times Online on November 29, 2007, when Rattigan's play was revived. More on the case can be found on the Murderpedia website. *The Herald* in Scotland also published an obituary for John, giving details of his career and how overshadowed it was by his parents' deaths.

24 See the Central section of this book.

25 For more on Wimborne and its model town, see the Central section of this book.

26 If you were unlucky enough to have never visited Tucktonia there are a number of videos on YouTube.

27 A.J.A. Symons (1900-1941) was the elder brother of the crime writer Julian Symons (1912-1994). To add further layers to this literary tangle Julian wrote a biography of his brother in 1950, and contributed the introduction to the 1955 edition of *The Quest for Corvo*.

28 Nikolaus Pevsner and David Lloyd took Symons' as his word, reproducing the technique described in *The Quest for Corvo* but adding that it was "typical of the man", employing "an element of cheating in the competence". The website devoted to the Catholic Buildings of England and Wales, Taking Stock, recounts the restoration work and its conclusions. But many years earlier the authors Dorothy Eagle and Hilary Carnell had already questioned the attribution, and pointed out that while Symons says the church is Saint Michael's it's actually dedicated to the Immaculate Conception and Saint Joseph. *The Oxford Literary Guide to the British Isles* by Dorothy Eagle and Hilary Carnell, Oxford University Press, 1977, pp 60-61.

29 His death notice in the *Star* newspaper in October 1913 included the sentence "Mr Rolfe resided for some years as Baron Corvo in Christchurch, Hampshire, where he was noted for outbursts of elaborate expenditure, alternating with an extreme ascetism."

30 For images of the hallway complete with staircase and a potted history of the Castle, see *England's Lost Houses* by Giles Worsley, Aurum Press, 2002, pp 178-181.

WEST

FROM WEST MILTON:
THE LAST AND LOST PLACE

Tucked deeply into the steep hills of West Dorset, the River Asker runs unobtrusively through the village of West Milton. All the roads that lead there are twisting lanes. I bumped down from Eggardon Hill in my car, taking a track with grass grown up its middle, where the land dropped steeply away to either side. Eggardon is ringed with legend: horses would sometimes refuse to cross it, the devil has been spotted hunting souls with a pack of dogs, cars stall mysteriously, and then re-start. My main concern was to stay on the road.

I had come for a walk with a 21st Century Yokel. Tom Cox is the author of several charming, funny, lightly psychedelic books about landscape and especially the West Country, the first of which is *21st Century Yokel*, but the easy looseness of his prose belies a deeply felt, unique and sometimes dark reckoning with the idea of place. There is no Merrie England in his books – his landscapes are undercut with magic and menace. He's also wonderful company, witty and sincere. We'd last seen one another at the Filly Loo, the midsummer celebrations at Ashmore, the highest village in Dorset, a few years before.[1] This time winter was clinging on through spring – we set off briskly.

Tom had written about West Milton in his book *Ring the Hill*. His first visit had been on the heels of Kenneth Allsop, the broadcaster who came to the village in the 1960s, and wrote *In the Country*[2] – a book about his love for the place, but also his despair at the increasing use of pesticides and his fierce conservation battles to save it, along with his neighbour, Brian Jackman, who still lives in the village. *In the Country* is a book divided between hope and despair – Allsop called the area around the village The Last Place, but in the end it was despair that won – Allsop took his own life in 1973.

We took the lane that led gently upwards through the village, and stopped to photograph the remains of the old church, now only a lonely tower, its nave gone, the stones re-used to build the primary school at Powerstock in the mid-nineteenth century. It reminded Tom of the ruin at Dartington and me of the church tower at Compton Abbas, where a seventeenth century firebrand cleric preached to the rebellious Dorset Clubmen.[3] Leaving the village we were soon in a sunken lane, a rutted track with ferns at either side and the first wild garlic, over us a canopy of still bare trees. One track met another, deeper still but barred with a red Highways Agency sign telling us that the road was closed. Holloways are the old lanes, trodden over time, but also sometimes boundary markings between old land holdings, existing only on soft sandstone, where repeated footfalls and carts slowly deepen the track. To walk a holloway is also to step back through time, their shaded darkness lends mystery too. They're a feature of West Dorset, and especially of the Marshwood Vale – further west and south than we were. In Geoffrey Household's muscular thriller, *Rogue Male,* originally published in 1939, the hero, having attempted to assassinate a European dictator, escapes eventually to West Dorset where he takes refuge in a sunken lane. Stalked, he burrows into the earth. Household doesn't name the dictator, but we can guess, and neither does he identify his holloway precisely. Later the writers Robert Macfarlane and Dan Richards, accompanied by the artist Stanley Donwood, came to the landscape around Chideock to lose themselves too, to research their book *Holloway,*[4] and were also deliberately vague about the location. Most readers have assumed that Household's lane is a composite,

not a single overgrown and sunken track but several. But one writer, Sara Hudston, has more recently proposed that it was based on a real location, and found an overgrown lane which seemed to have all the features and qualities which Household described.[5] A thorny mystery, but one which didn't trouble us, Tom and I being only very gently rogueish.

We pushed on into the light, and to sheep-nibbled, rounded hills, an empty place. In several hours we saw no-one else. We were talking so much I barely glanced at my map, so we got lost frequently, once crossing a field that we had crossed an hour before and recognising it only as we reached its far side. It was a landscape of itself, where the weather followed its own rules – warm sunshine rapidly followed by sleet. Others too have noted the landscape spook between these hills, its eerie silence. The land here may have inspired the sixteenth century Cunning Man John Walsh – a landscape in which he could see faeries, sprites, spirits[6]. Cunning Men were soothsayers or shamans[7], survivors of the pre-Christian age, they were in high demand in the time of magic. The received wisdom is that it was the industrial revolution which finally did for magic, as people moved to the cities. But Leonard Baker, a historian who has studied the rural traditions of Somerset and Dorset told me he believed that magic persisted, that people knew that finding the best Cunning Men would mean a trip to town.[8]

In North Poorton, an isolated settlement made up largely of a loose collection of farm buildings, Tom, who has a gift with animals, stroked the heads of lambs at a gate. We stepped inside the church. At the back of the nave, sitting slightly forlornly on the stone slabs was a small font, a poor relation to its gaudily decorated neighbour. The church was Victorian, its ruined predecessor from which the font was taken was marked on maps close by. Tom and I went in search of it, knowing only that it was just a few feet high, without obvious shape. It eluded us – we stood where we thought it must be, and it wasn't. A friend later said he had also never found it, a ghostly absence.

Several years ago, not long after we had moved to Dorset, I visited Mapperton House with Helen. The car park was full of coaches and cars, unlikely for an autumn day. Walking down the drive to the house we were surprised to find that the house, described glowingly in guidebooks as a glorious Jacobean manor, looked a bit of a shambles. The front garden was unkempt; between the gate posts, topped with large annoyed-looking stone eagles, straw was strewn. Opposite was a courtyard holding pens of animals. We stopped to admire the geese. A young man gently approached and asked us to keep out of the way: filming was about to re-commence. We had stumbled on to the set of *Far From the Madding Crowd*, which starred Carey Mulligan as Bathsheba, and where my friend Graham found brief employment as an extra, there being a general demand for men with beards who might lend a suitably rustic air to the crowd scenes.[9] It's a popular spot for film-makers, also drawing the producers of *Emma* (1996) and of the BBC serial *Tom Jones* (1997).[10]

Mapperton is best known for its Italianate gardens, laid out behind the house in a shallow river valley, where Gwyneth Paltrow practised archery and flirted, but I was more interested in an age before the house or garden. There's no village at Mapperton any longer, just scattered cottages on the estate. Villages empty for many reasons and over many years – we may be witnessing another slow depopulation of the countryside, but in Mapperton's case the desertion was definite and tragic. The churchyard was not consecrated – some have said the ground was too stony for burial – instead the nearby parish of Netherbury would take the bodies, carried along a Corpse Road – Dead Man's Lane – to Saint Mary's. When the Plague came in 1666 it devastated Mapperton. Refused burial in Netherbury, the dead were left at the parish boundary, a spot marked by a sycamore tree, known as the Posy Tree, and buried in a mass grave at South Warren Hill, which the A3066 respectfully skirts. Three hundred years later the tree, by then reduced to a hollow stump, was felled and later replaced with a new sapling; villagers were invited to a short ceremony and drank cider to mark its passing.

Tom and I didn't make it as far as Mapperton, instead getting lost in the dark woodland at Hooke Park, just to the south, following paths marked only by the narrow hoof-prints of deer. We might also have stumbled on wild boar, who have been rumoured to range across Powerstock Common towards the village of Toller Pocorum, Toller of the Pigs, appropriately enough. Some escaped from a farm once, three were shot by Luke Montagu, Lord Hinchingbrooke, of Mapperton, who still engages in the traditional sport of an aristocrat, despite describing himself as a "normal bloke".[11] Tom and I crossed a stream twice, quite unnecessarily, stumbled over trunks felled by the winter storms, and into open land, across the top of a steeply sloping hill, back where the ghosts could find us. Our chatter kept them at bay. I kept thinking of the day at Mapperton years before, the fake wisteria flowers hung around a barn for the sake of seasonal correctness, the herded sheep and geese, and Hardy's phrase: "Partly real, partly dream", to describe his Wessex. The film-set had been not quite real and not yet a dream, but this strange hidden landscape of hills and holloways, of cunning men and trees for the dead was both.[12]

WHITCHURCH CANONICORUM, ON THE PILGRIM PATH

"You're a long way from Uffington!"

A bearded man was carrying a long, coiled hosepipe through the graveyard of the church at Whitchurch Canonicorum. It was hot and the allotments nestled behind the church would need water. His cheery greeting was addressed to my T shirt, which bore the symbol of the stretched-out north Wiltshire chalk horse, galloping over its escarpment.[13] I replied that I couldn't yet buy a T shirt of the Cerne Abbas Giant.

The church tower rose high, square and certain, the crowded graveyard a hubbub below. The large parish church is known as the Cathedral of the Vale and dominates the rolling landscape of the Marshwood Vale. Virginia Astley, who I had come to meet, had been looking for some dead relatives in the graveyard, but had found none. We stepped inside the porch, and pushed the heavy church door open, that delicious moment of anticipation as one steps into an empty nave, a twist into the divine. It's a construction, a deliberate hushing, but it worked. It always works.

Church of England parish churches carry a weight of history deep in their walls, their stones speak of an understated religion. But the lack of decoration is a result of religious extremism, of sixteenth and seventeenth century altar breaking, of desecration.

But whatever the cause, inside the church the cool silence still descended, and my breath held. I had been told a little of what to expect by an enthusiast of Romanesque architecture, Alex Woodcock, a writer and academic turned stonemason, a sort of Jude the Obscure in reverse without the tragic end, but even his enthusiasm hadn't prepared me.[14]

The church, St Candida, is old, very old. It might have once been a minster, within it are tiles which may have come from a Roman villa, and it's been speculated that it could have been one of the very first monastic sites in Britain. The muscular Romanesque, all thick pillars and rounded arches is in harmonious conversation with the spiky, slender Gothic; as Alex told me, the Gothic here had a freedom, a sense that anything goes, before its language became the more rigid beauty that made Salisbury Cathedral. At Whitchurch there was a sense of playfulness, of space and air.

Virginia and her twin sister Alison had recently completed a project: Alison is an architect and church conservationist, Virginia is a poet and musician – together they had visited church porches throughout West Dorset, drawing and writing about these spaces, placed between the profane and sacred.

We soon found what we had come to see, a rarity, something somehow missed by the protestant reformers. On the north side of the church, hard against the wall was a stone structure resembling an altar. This was a shrine dedicated to Saint Wite or Saint Wita or Saint Candida. No-one really knows who she was. She may have been a hermit who lived on the cliffs and died in a Viking raid[15], or a Breton princess, two of whose children were also saints, or a Dorset-born saint who was martyred along with Saint Boniface in what is now part of the Netherlands. King Alfred might have founded the original church in her memory, or maybe he didn't.[16] She may not have existed. It may all have been a misunderstanding – an original whitewashed church, named after its colour, not a martyr after all.

Virginia and I approached the shrine with something approaching reverence, more reverence than Sir Thomas More had expressed in the early sixteenth century, when mocking the locals for leaving cheese and cake for the saint on her feast day of 1st June. At its base were three large oval holes, and within them were many handwritten notes. Saint Wite could cure the sick. The afflicted limb, or something belonging to the person who had fallen ill would be placed in one of these apertures, and a prayer said. The new notes told us that the prayers were coming still, for the newly unwell or the recently departed. Phantom or not, St Wite still exerts her pull.

How the shrine escaped the Reformation and its aftershocks is a mystery – saint's shrines in English parish churches are extremely rare.[17] Edward the Confessor's shrine remains in Westminster Abbey (he too had Dorset connections, having been elected at a council held in Gillingham), but Edward was a venerated king, too important to the Tudors and their sense of destiny to push aside, not an obscure, possibly mythical cliff-dwelling hermit. Maybe it was obscurity or remoteness which saved her shrine – this was a village that never became a town, despite its importance as a pilgrimage destination. Or it might have been the reverse – the locals feeling so strongly about her power that everyone simply kept quiet. And still she persists – Dorset's flag, a white cross edged with red on a yellow background, is known as St Wite's Cross. While we lingered others came – a young man carrying a tiny child who he took over to the shrine, another man about my age who sat on the flagstones in front of it and removed his straw hat. Later we saw him gathering dandelions and daisies in the graveyard, binding them into a posy.

Once we had established our walking route Virginia sensibly took control of my map and we pushed open the heavy iron gate to the rear of the churchyard, taking a path past the allotments. Guided to a nettle-free route by a friendly villager we found ourselves in freshly mown fields, and then to a low, damp pasture. We were a little way from St Wite's Spring which lies south of the village, the waters also thought to be curative, but Virginia is always happy to be around water, having written a book about a journey along the Thames[18], spending a summer working a lock along its course. She told me of its source, an innocuous and mostly dry field near Cirencester. We walked shady lanes and saw no-one else. We clambered over a gate where we found a patch free of cow pats for a picnic of cheese sandwiches, tea, apples and cherry cake. St Wite would have approved of the cake, but we left her no crumbs. We talked of our family and our pasts, how we'd fetched up in Dorset. Virginia is modest: I had to gently probe her to tell me a little of her previous career as a nearly pop star in the 1980s, leaving music school after a year because she had been offered a record deal, creating dream-pop albums and supporting The Teardrop Explodes on tour. She never wanted to be famous, or rather wanted only to be more famous than a cheating ex-boyfriend, which she achieved when she became the cover star of the NME in September 1983, wearing a cowboy's mask and clutching a small bouquet of flowers. She's pleased with those days: "I knew at the time it was good," she told me.

But when it ended, it was like a firebreak – she said it felt as if her music career had happened to someone else – her reminders these days come when one of her songs is played on BBC 6Music and she notices the receipts from her Bandcamp page the next day. She uses her time now to write, to study and play music.

Back at the church she pointed to the roof – during their porches project her sister had told her of 'diminishing courses': how the builders used a series of narrower tiles towards the top of a roof's pitch, ending finally in a 'farewell course', it was easier to carry smaller tiles higher, but also altered the perspective from below, creating a sense of height.[19] The porch at Whitchurch was topped instead by embattlements, St Wite defending herself against the Danes, the Protestants and the doubters.

My eye was drawn to the sturdy high, fifteenth century tower and its curious carving on the south side, a ship and an axe. Frederick Treves, who was clearly captivated by the church, thought that the tower may have been built by an adventurer who had made his fortune at sea. One, whom we might now more accurately term a pirate or, at best, colonialist, was Sir George Somers, who was shipwrecked on Bermuda in 1609 and later credited with its discovery. It's sometimes thought that his adventures on the island inspired Shakespeare to write *The Tempest*, itself often interpreted today as a critique of the nascent British Empire. Somers died of the pleasingly historical disease of 'surfeit of pig', too distant to be cured at the shrine at Whitchurch. He is buried in an unmarked grave at Whitchurch Canonicorum, but like Hardy and Percy Shelley, his heart lies separate from his body – in his case on Bermuda.[20] It was probably too fatty to easily transport.

St Wite has had something like the final say, overshadowing Somers. In 1900 the church shifted slightly, damaging what remained of her shrine. During repair works it was discovered that its top section contained a skeleton – the shrine was a grave too, and the remains were that of a woman around forty years old. The inscription found with it, when translated from the Latin, read: "Here Lies the Remains of St Wite."

LYME REGIS: A MORE ANCIENT DORSET

All routes to Lyme Regis are steep: the town sits on crumbling land to the west and east, a narrow river dribbles through its steep-sided valley. On a hot day in early July Helen and I walked into the town, pigeon-toed against the slope, where we found the side road of Long Entry, a dead end now, but it once extended over the dissolving hill of Black Venn to the nearby town of Charmouth. In 1725 the seventeen-year-old future novelist Henry Fielding, then at school at Eton, attempted to abduct his fifteen-year-old cousin, Sarah, with whom he believed himself in love. He used Long Entry as his escape route from Lyme with his hostage. His motivation might have been that Sarah was a wealthy heiress: in later life, while living at East Stour in the Blackmore Vale, he burned through his wife Charlotte's wealth in just a few years. After Charlotte's death, in a move that pre-figured Thomas Hardy's post-marital arrangements, he married his maid. Fielding's kidnap of a minor was easily thwarted, but summoned to appear before a tribunal he showed something of the arrogance that his school is associated with and refused, sending instead his valet and describing the jury as a panel of "fad and greasy citizens".

On the quayside nearly three hundred years later people around us were pulling pinging phones from pockets: this was the day before Prime Minister Johnson was finally forced to resign. The news was coming thick and fast, and excitedly relayed to friends and family along the harbour. Helen and I walked in the encroaching, syrupy heat, the beginnings of a drought, a harbinger of the Anthropocene's whirlwind. But the promenade was busy and candy-coloured beach huts faced the beach. Tourism dominates the town: Lyme was rescued from obscurity by the popularity of sea bathing in the eighteenth century. And although never as fashionable as Weymouth, the town made the most of it. Some of

the sixteenth and seventeenth century houses were given new
frontages in keeping with the Georgian style and for the first time,
as in many other seaside towns, new homes were built *facing* the sea,
giving them a view of what was previously to be respected or feared
but not enjoyed. The biggest asset lay in front of the town, and was
no longer to be hidden from.

At the end of the Promenade was Lyme Regis' most famous
feature – the Cobb – the stone harbour wall which snakes out into
the sea, encircling boats. In front of the RNLI giftshop was a group
of several imitation dogs, made from yellow wellington boots,
confusing the many real dogs which in the summer months were
not allowed on the beach. We passed a small blue wooden rowing
boat which had taken on water, the word BORIS painted unevenly
on its bow. We climbed the stone steps set into the Cobb, taking note
of the warning signs: DANGER UNGUARDED DROP,
CAUTION SLIPPERY SURFACE, STRICTLY NO ACCESS
IN HIGH WINDS.

The Cobb leans slightly towards the sea but was wide enough
to walk to its wavering end, where one man stood resolute, finding
a good spot for mobile coverage so he could nosily tell Joyce when
he'd be visiting. I'd been hoping for a more dramatic scene: Meryl
Streep turning to look directly into the camera, her cape around
her head, as on the poster for the 1981 film *The French
Lieutenant's Woman*, filmed here. The movie, based on John Fowles
novel and adapted for the screen by Harold Pinter,[21] is no
straightforward historical drama, but a film within a film, in which
present-day actors fall in love while filming a nineteenth century
romantic epic. At the Cobb's end were a series of huge
interlocking grey boulders piled up, reaching further into the sea,
like a collapsed game of Tetris. This was an approximation of the
original 'La Cobbe' as built in the thirteenth century, when
wooden piles were driven into the seabed to keep the structure in
place. Across the centuries storms washed it away many times,
each time it was rebuilt afresh. La Cobbe today is a nineteenth
century reconstruction.

We came down gingerly by a different set of steps, jaggedly
sticking from the harbour wall. Jane Austen, who visited the town in
1804 with her parents and attended a dance at the fashionable
Assembly Rooms which is now buried beneath a car park, used The
Cobb as a plot device, having Louisa Musgrove fall from it in
Persuasion. The Cobb has captivated others too – Frederick Treves

hailed it as "the chief glory and delight of Lyme" and the adventurous, practical, seventeenth-century traveller, Celia Fiennes described its importance, noting the "high and bleake" sea and the Cobb's shape like a "Halfe Moon". She had been told that the far promontory on the horizon to the west was the Lizard Point in Cornwall "a good distance", but actually her view would have been towards Brixham on the Devon coast. But she was right about the Cobb – it was critical to Lyme's survival, growing from a tiny village at Domesday to a reasonably sized port, despite raids from the French and the battering of storms. In the harbour today were few trawlers, and many boats for pleasure, reflecting the town's changing times.

Through a car park, and a boat park where masts rattled, Helen and I crunched our way across pebbles to a beach where the huts were bigger, pallets nailed to the doors as protection against the elements and thieves. This beach was largely unoccupied: seaside Lyme looks the other way but it was here that the world nearly turned.

The short reign of James II of England (VII of Scotland) is overshadowed by that of his elder brother, the flamboyant Charles II. James was an unpopular monarch, partly owing to his Catholicism, partly to his personality. In 1685, shortly after the accession, the Duke of Monmouth, one of Charles' illegitimate children, landed on this beach with a few dozen supporters and raised a local army with the aim of overthrowing James. His choice of town was careful – south-west England had been staunchly, if not universally, protestant in the Civil War, and were more likely to support Monmouth. Lyme had held out against a much larger royalist force. As Minette Walters, the crime writer and Dorset-dweller has written, the success of the resistance was owing in no small part to the women of the town who tended to the wounded, fought fires caused by the bombardment, reloaded guns and appeared on the defences dressed as men to make the defending forces look more numerous. In radical London a song inspired by their actions circulated: "the weaker vessels are the stronger grown".[22] Lyme's defenders might have then regretted the suffix Regis, granted to them by Edward I.

The Monmouth rebellion ended in disaster. For a few weeks the rebels wheeled around Dorset and Somerset, but finally, at the Battle of Sedgemoor, the better armed and trained troops of James delivered a crushing defeat. Fleeing towards Poole, Monmouth was captured near Horton, taken to London and executed. Revenge was infamously swift: Sedgemoor saw battlefield atrocities and the king dispatched his Chief Justice, George Jeffreys to the west: 150 men were sentenced to death, twelve were hanged on the beach where we now stood and 800 were transported. The response was so bloody that it earned Judge Jeffreys the sobriquet The Hanging Judge and added further to discontent – it was just three years before James II was deposed. William of Orange landed at Brixham, which Celia Fiennes later glimpsed on the far Devon shore, and he was invited to become joint monarch with Queen Mary. The 'Glorious Revolution' changed Britain, creating a bill of rights and wider religious toleration. Not everyone has seen Monmouth's rebellion as a turning point. Flicking to my *Highways and Byways* book, I found the section on Lyme Regis and Treves' description of the Duke as both "dreary" and "effeminate", although he gave no evidence for either adjective. Treves used similar language for the Monmouth rebels as he did for those other country refuseniks, The Clubmen, calling them "stupid yokels". Elsewhere, Cecil Cochrane, departing from his brief in his book *The Lost Roads of Wessex*, described Monmouth's misadventure as a "stupid, vain-glorious rising". We could find nothing amongst the pebbles and beach huts to commemorate the rebellion, beyond its name, Monmouth Beach, but Lyme Regis has not forgotten the doomed Duke. We found Monmouth Street, the Old Monmouth B&B and The Monmouth Pantry. The shadow of the king that might have been is still present in today's customs: the historian Leonard Baker, whom I met one spring day in a crowded coffee shop on the campus at Exeter University, told me that he believed that the tradition of West Country carnivals began as a protestant commemoration of the rebellion.

In the busy bookshop the manager, Michelle, told me about the shop's changing appearance. For the filming of *The French Lieutenant's Woman*, a whole new frontage was made, to blend better with the set, like the older houses given a Georgian sprucing up in the sea-bathing craze. Fittingly, for a film set in two time zones, the bookshop's new fascia remained in place long after the film was made, removed only when it had become dilapidated and probably dangerous, nearly thirty years later.

Helen was drawn back to the beach but in search of more Fowles I climbed the steep hill from the town centre. By a car park was a building behind iron gates, a fondant fancy pink confection, richly decorated and assured of its own prettiness. It faced away from the sea, intimating construction before sea-bathing, but the rear gardens gave panoramic views to the town and bay. This was Belmont House, built at the end of the eighteenth century. Originally it was the home of Eleanor Coade, the pioneering businesswoman behind Coade Stone, which was used for manufacturing garden ornaments and neoclassical flourishes employed by architects such as Robert Adam and Sir John Soane. Belmont was decorated with her work, an advertising billboard for her business. Much later Belmont was John Fowles' home; after his death in 2005 the building became the property of the Landmark Trust, which rescues and protects significant buildings, turning them into prestigious holiday homes. The restoration was complex and protracted, Fowles' widow was furious that the building's appearance deteriorated during the process and complained vociferously to the local press. Lyme attracts strong, independent women. Belmont House today looked perfect, unflappable.

I turned down Sherborne Lane, first built in the eighth century when the dramatically named Saxon King, Cynewulf granted the area to Sherborne Abbey. Local folklore described the devil driving a hearse bearing the corpse of a Civil War Royalist turning into the lane, galloping into hell. Sherborne Lane was hot, but otherwise did not remind me much of the underworld, lined with ridiculously pretty houses, front gardens spilling hollyhocks. The lane met the Lym, Lyme's narrow river, and a network of back streets. The town's layout had not pleased Frederick Treves. He wrote that the main street "wavers to and fro like a drunken man", that the "lanes were in disorder" and that altogether the "unmethodical seaport" was "very undecided… a place of wandering and unrealised ideas" but also "drab". Treves' mood would have benefited from an ice cream. I joined Helen on the beach and we chose exotic ices from a shop on Hollis' Promenade, watching the gulls whirl and loop above us, eyeing their targets, preferring pasties and chips, savoury over sweet. One neatly picked a sandwich from a wrapper in someone's handbag, and as Helen observed, everything became very Daphne du Maurier. Helen paddled in the sea, I shuffled my bottom into the pebbles.

In the height of the sea-bathing craze Lyme attracted

opprobrium. In 1818 the cartoonist and satirist George Cruikshank produced a print showing bathing machines on the beach, naked women splashing in the sea, a top-hatted man sitting on a nearby rock gazing on the scene through a telescope. Cruikshank called the sketch 'Hydromania! Or a Touch of the Sub Lyme and Beautiful'. He was being imaginative – naturism was never a feature of Lyme's life, but the point was made. When the short-lived railway came, much later than elsewhere in 1903, it suddenly brought an influx of new visitors, up to 2,000 every day; these newcomers weren't the middle-class frequenters of the Assembly Rooms where Austen had danced, but to the horror of some residents, working-class people. The railway closed in 1965, but just across the border in Devon the massive Cannington Viaduct which carried the passengers into town, remains. The station buildings were re-located to Hampshire for use on the Watercress Line.

Lyme isn't all that it seems. The town may once have extended into the sea further than it does now and even its beaches are imported. In recent years sand, shingle and even cliffs have been shipped in from France, Norway and the Isle of Wight, as coastal erosion has nibbled the town, while dredging keeps the harbour clear. The whole west end of Marine Parade was rebuilt after a landslip in 1962. The illusion is maintained. Given the dependence on tourism, it's just as well. In the back streets around the Lym almost all the houses bore plaques advertising them as holiday homes – the town's year-long and less wealthy population live further up the hill in more recent, less picturesque housing. The poor have sometimes had a hard time in Lyme – nineteenth century doctors worried about outbreaks of epidemics in the town, sometimes only extinguished by occasional fires.

Helen dusted some imported sand from her feet and we walked east along the harbour wall and up the hill. The elegant form of the whitewashed Marine Theatre shyly poked its nose out above the sea defences. This may have been the site of an argument that led to murder.

The largest ever increase in Dorset's population was during the 1940s: thousands of American soldiers were stationed in the county in preparation for the invasion of Nazi-occupied Europe. Their camps, vehicles and uniforms were everywhere, and their impact on a predominantly rural county was massive.

On the whole the glamorous, gum-chewing incomers were welcome, but Dorset people were puzzled and occasionally

outraged by the treatment of Black soldiers, their regiments segregated and often relegated to more menial duties. One west country farmer commented: "I love the Americans, but I don't like the white ones they've brought with them." The Black GIs[23] built hospitals and airfields, guarded facilities and were notable for their politeness and kindness. Some even asked their wives back home in the States to send food parcels and clothes to Dorset children they had befriended.

While there were examples of racial prejudice in a county which had little recent experience of outsiders, generally the Black soldiers met with an acceptance they didn't find at home. Some formed attachments to local women, a number of children resulted, left without fathers after the mobilisation that saw the army depart for Normandy and the wider war.

But sometimes the segregation, tacitly approved by the British Government and enabled by an Act of Parliament that allowed US military law to operate in the camps, led to trouble. In Dorset towns running battles between Black and White soldiers sometimes erupted.

One story that circulated around Lyme was that at the Marine Theatre a Black soldier tried to buy a Zippo lighter, an item usually the preserve of White people; an altercation became a fight, the soldier was stabbed and killed with a bayonet by one of his compatriots. There's no official record of the murder; similar unverified accounts of the killings of Black GIs cropped up in other West Country towns, but there were credible eye-witness accounts, and it's been suggested that these incidents were covered up by the authorities to avoid negative news stories at a time of national crisis. In any case the multiple rumours of these killings indicate how entrenched and visible the racial divisions between the White and Black GIs were to Dorset people.

Helen and I climbed the hill. St Michael's church was sunk slightly into the hillside – buildings cling on in Lyme. In the neat churchyard, the grass browning in the dry summer we found a gravestone, a simple slab:

Under the text, I noticed that about half the stone was empty of words.

Dorset makes much of its 'Jurassic Coast' which has attracted fossil collectors for centuries, first as inexplicable curiosities, and then, after Darwin, as a key part of our deep past. Lyme Regis has fossil shops and I found one stall, tucked away in a garden, selling polished prehistoric treasures. Even the lampposts along the Promenade had ammonite motifs on which gulls perched.

We were standing at the gravestone of the pioneering palaeontologist Mary Anning. Born at the turn of the nineteenth century, her father taught her fossil collecting but he died young. Her family in desperate straits, Mary sold her finds to help pay for their needs. When she was twelve she unearthed a skeleton over five metres long – later named Icthyosaurus, or fish lizard, although it was neither fish nor lizard. This was a marine reptile over 200 million years old, now named Icthyosaurus Anningae. In her early twenties she discovered a skeleton of a Plesiosaurus, ('near to reptile'). So strange was this find that it was accused of being a fake and only accepted after a special meeting of the Geological Society of London, to which Mary was not invited; women were not admitted for another eighty years. In 1828 she found the skeleton of a large, winged creature – a Pterodactyl, the largest ever flying animal. Impoverished and barely recognised in her lifetime, an artist friend Henry De La Beche created a scene of the strange animals in the sea, attacking and devouring one another amongst ammonites. He called the work, itself a pioneering example of paleoart, *A More Ancient Dorset* and sold prints to raise money for Mary.

She did not live long – breast cancer claimed her before she was fifty, and slowly the world forgot, the memory only sticking to language in the tongue twister 'she sells sea shells on the seashore'. Only more recently has her extraordinary contribution been recognised – *Ammonite*, a film released in 2020, starred Kate Winslet as Mary, and gave her an undocumented love affair with a woman.

But if the world had forgotten, Lyme did not. In the church was a stained-glass window devoted to her. Her grave had recently been re-leaded. Opposite the church was Anning Road. Most spectacularly, below the churchyard on the seafront was a new statue, unveiled only two months before our visit. The sculpture was extraordinary – a life-size Mary striding purposefully, hammer in hand, ammonites carved into her skirts, her dog Tray at her heels. The work, by Denise Dutton and funded by the Mary Anning Rocks campaign, was unexpectedly moving, and Helen and I

stopped for a minute to take it in. The statue had taken time to find its rightful place, prompted by a local teenager, Evie Swire, asking her mother why there was no permanent monument to the palaeontologist. But now Anning was back, the deep-time explorer returned home.

It was busy around us, people and dogs. We overheard a snatch of a conversation from one family group who had clearly been discussing physics.

"I just can't get my head around light years." I looked again at Anning's shining but blank eyes – she would have understood light years better than all of us.

As we turned away it struck me that more than any other town in Dorset, Lyme exists in several time-zones simultaneously, as ancient as an Icthysaurus, as modern as the statue of its discoverer, mostly at ease with itself and its past, but watchful for the future waves rolling in against the Cobb.

BEAMINSTER

Three weeks after visiting Lyme, the heatwave bit again. Beaminster, a tiny town sunk into a valley a few miles north of Bridport, was bleached – the tall hollyhocks growing in dusty cracks outside houses, were wilting, the yellowed stone buildings that usually remind me of a Cotswold town was taking on an Andalucian aspect. Beaminster was running its annual scarecrow festival: Bob the Builder flopped outside the ironmonger's, Queen Elizabeth II smiled out from the greengrocer's.

Beaminster is more than a village, a little less than a town, centred around a market square where there's no market, and surrounded by the shops that bigger towns have often lost: baker, butcher and a bookshop. I met Louisa Adjoa Parker in the bookshop – it's run by the independent publisher Little Toller Books, for whom I work – we publish books in the room upstairs and sell them downstairs, along with an increasingly wide range of other books.

Louisa is thoughtful and sensitive, someone who makes others feel immediately comfortable. Of English and Ghanian heritage she was born in Yorkshire but has spent most of her life in England's south-west. A troubled childhood marked by racism and abuse led to still more troubled teenage years, especially when, as she put it over coffee and pastries in a nearby café, she discovered "drugs and boys." A low point came after she was sacked from a job for petty theft and spent several months living under a tarpaulin in the Forest of Dean. She was saved, she told me, by two things: the first was a confrontation with an ex-partner in a pub; the sudden realisation that he could no longer threaten her, he was simply a troubled and pathetic man. The second was education – taking A-Levels and then a degree at Exeter University. In one class a tutor talked about Black History in England's south-west. Louisa was stunned.

"Honestly, I was in my early thirties, and I suddenly realised I wasn't the first Black person here."

Louisa became a poet, memoirist, a social historian and activist, documenting the hitherto unexplored histories of Dorset as experienced by Black people. It's made her passionate about understanding and explaining the roots of racism – empire and its attendant evil: slavery.

"It all comes down to colonialism. Without Empire there would be no need to see other races as inferior." The slave trade was, as Louisa has explained in her books, triangular. Ships set off from England with cargo to sell in exchange for people in Africa. Africans would be shipped to the Caribbean (the journey known euphemistically as the 'middle passage') and finally goods, especially sugar, transported back to Britain. We associate this trade with cities such as Bristol or Liverpool, but even Dorset's relatively small ports were part of this business. For Louisa, who lived in Lyme Regis for nearly twenty years, a life by the sea summoned mixed emotions and a reflection on the experience of her ancestors. Often Dorset's manor houses and grand estates, the landscapes we cherish, are a legacy of slavery, and while some institutions like the National Trust have done work to address this difficult history, others have been less forthcoming. Dorset landowners benefited directly, and hugely. George II was irritated when he met a sugar trader from Weymouth who was reputedly richer than he was.

"Sugar, sugar eh?" said the monarch. "All that sugar!"

Dorset's most visible example of the slave trade's legacy is Charborough Park, five miles from Poole, parkland guarded by three miles of high wall, studded with gateways upon which stone animals perch, including a five-legged stag. On a hill in the estate, visible for miles around is a folly tower, the model, possibly, for Hardy's *Two in a Tower*. The park is home to the Drax family, the current inhabitant being Richard Plunkett-Ernle-Erle-Drax, the

Conservative MP for South Dorset. It was his ancestors who invested in Caribbean sugar plantations in the seventeenth century, owning, buying and selling enslaved Africans. The Drax estate is estimated to be the joint largest in Dorset.[24] The estate still holds land in the Caribbean and at the time of writing has not responded to calls for reparations[25] – Louisa joined a march to protest this injustice to the gates of the Park during the annual Tolpuddle Festival. Nobody came from behind the long wall to meet the protestors.

Plantation owners brought Black enslaved servants to Dorset, some of whom were left bequests in their masters' wills, and who lived the remainder of their lives in southern England. Their stories are embedded in folklore. Four miles west of Beaminster is Bettiscombe Manor, home to Dorset's most famous ghost story – the Screaming Skull. One story has the skull as a Black servant screaming down the years, distressed at his exile. Louisa pointed out that forensic work on the skull had ruled this out, but that the story exists is a sign of the impact of these strangers and their plight on Dorset people.

Louisa, especially in her younger life and especially in poorer seaside towns, experienced appalling racism, rarer she thinks these days, although she thought she heard someone shout the N word at her from a car recently. White people may have taken exception to the treatment of Black American soldiers by their white compatriots during World War Two, but as Louisa said, that may have been because they were transient and useful, off to help fight the Nazis.

Black faces, Louisa reflected, are much more common in the TV dramas she loves these days but pointed out that the first two series of *Broadchurch*, which was filmed at West Bay, featured few Black characters, until Lenny Henry appeared in the third series. "He worked in a garage, in real life he'd probably have been called 'Black Jim'" she said.[26] Over a second cup of coffee Louisa told me that sometimes colour-blind casting ignores the truth about history and the way Black people have been treated in rural areas. "Sometimes television feels like a metropolitan producer's idea of Black people in the countryside." Louisa and her husband have found some amusement in spotting 'blacksessories' in TV dramas, Black people without speaking roles, standing around looking glamourous and gorgeous at parties.

We stepped into Beaminster's quiet lanes for a short walk through its shady footpaths. The River Brit is a stream here, close to its source and was still full, despite the drought, and we made our way to the church, whose golden tower and shining cockerel weathervane is a beacon in the folded valley. We were surprised to find Dawn French sitting in the porch, another scarecrow, in her Reverend Geraldine Granger guise. Inside the church was cool, beautiful corbels gazed down at us from the wooden ceiling. We found a grand marble memorial for a powdered-wigged worthy, visibly upset cherubs on either side, another of a toga-wearing man sitting on a bath-shaped plinth as if he was taking a long soak, being read to by a similarly-attired woman. Both monuments were for the Strodes of Parnham, the nearby manor house which was gutted by fire in 2017, a blaze which took days to extinguish and was thought to be started by the then owner, who later committed suicide. The new owner whose career as a music promoter has probably not helped him, attracted local controversy when he announced plans to make the house an entertainment venue, including turning part of the building into a "Batman House". Louisa and I wondered if the new occupants of Parnham House would one day command extravagant memorials in their local church.

I picked up a leaflet that told me that the mound the church stood on was once a sacred spot, but made no mention of Beaminster's most grisly legend. Following the Monmouth rebellion and the terrible judgements handed out by Judge Jeffreys in his ultimately futile attempt to shore up James II's reign, the corpses of those who were hanged were sometimes put on public display, at Beaminster they hung from the church tower, whose bells now chime musically every quarter of an hour.[27] But terror and grief were elsewhere visible in St Mary's: a memorial for Henry Samways and five of his children who succumbed it is thought from anthrax, brought in with the sheep wool which made the town rich. The vestry, out of view, was converted from an ossuary, where old bones were kept once space in the churchyard was used up.

That Beaminster, hot and sleepy, might have conjured such devils and distress, was improbable and true. Louisa, always busy, had to leave, so I drove on a few minutes up the road to an engineering marvel. The Horn Hill tunnel was a long, narrow bore into the hillside, faced by hamstone. It was opened in 1832, one of the country's first road tunnels, decades before the motor car, allowing easier access to the towns of Chard and Crewkerne than the high road over the hills. It closed for refurbishment in 2009, but in July 2012 a landslip engulfed the tunnel, killing two people travelling through it, their bodies only discovered days later in their car. The tunnel remained closed for years, proving its original worth – while it was closed Beaminster's trade suffered. It has reopened now, still a magnificent achievement, a route to Dorset's western border with Somerset, a way to leave the valley behind.

BRIDPORT: THE POOR MAN'S FRIEND

I sat in a corner of the small café with my cappuccino and tried to ignore the Elephant in the Room which was, more accurately, the Elephant on the Wall – a large mural featuring both a pachyderm and a young woman in a cocktail dress overshadowed me. But I have a rule of thumb: the worse the art on the walls, the friendlier the service, and I was right on this occasion – I tried to leave a tip and was told not to.

Bridport's layout is simple, on the surface. Two wide Georgian streets, meeting at right angles, remarkably harmonious and pleasingly busy. The streets' right angles reflect its history and one dominating industry. Walking through the back alleys and side streets I could glimpse long, narrow, back gardens. These were the original ropewalks, where the strands were laid out long and straight, before being woven together. By the eighteenth century, thousands of people were employed in the rope business, and Bridport became famous for the industry. Gruesomely, if someone was hanged it was said they had been stabbed with a Bridport dagger. The trade declined only when the Royal Navy developed its own ropewalks, such as at Chatham in Kent. The nooses are long gone, but rope-making is still part of Bridport's living: the nets used at the Wimbledon Lawn Tennis Championships are made locally, and Bridport rope was used for exploration further afield – plastic and textile versions finding their way on to the space shuttle.

Bridport has found a life beyond rope: it was full of independent shops and busy market stalls. There were two branches of an independent record shop, one had a life-size Davie Bowie waxwork painted with Ziggy lightning strike make-up, sitting in a chair and wearing a space suit. There were four bookshops, two for new books, two for second-hand. The opening hours notice for Wild and Homeless Books encapsulated Bridport's unforced workaday bohemianism. On Mondays the shop would be open "by about 10,

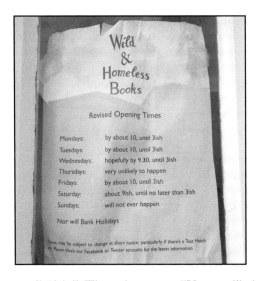

until 3ish.", Thursdays were "Very unlikely to happen". I was there during the advertised hours for Wednesday – the shop was shut. In the bookshop next door the energetic owner, Antonia, was completing her stock order for the forthcoming Literary Festival, a highlight of the town's calendar, but when I asked her what I should look for in Bridport she immediately abandoned her spreadsheet, led me out of the shop, down a small alley and into a hidden garden. This quiet spot, herbaceous borders around an oval lawn, was run by volunteers, one of whom, secateurs in hand, came over to explain how they had cleared the space and uncovered the stone path that ran around the edge of the garden, bringing the space to new life. An iron artwork spread out gracefully into the shape of lungs, an appropriate symbol for the garden.

A little to the south was the church. The graves were old, and mostly illegible, but the church was full. Food was piled up, cereal boxes and cans. In secluded corners hushed and serious conversations were taking place. A young woman, sitting in a pew and tapping at her laptop, explained that the church was regularly used as a food bank, as a Citizens Advice Bureau and by charities advising on getting into work. The services were well-used, quiet efficiency and compassion filling the space with sad and important work.

A flipside of the Bridport spirit is its subversiveness. I found this in an antiques market in the old Victorian industrial area, between terraces, car parks and rubble. A large painted wooden board on the street announced an exhibition of works by Billy Mumford. In a large back room I found the greatest and most varied collection of art imaginable, some on the wall, some leaning against other works. Pieces by Picasso and Rembrandt, Leonarda da Vinci, Modigliani. Each one was signed and each was a forgery, or more accurately, a copy.

As I was looking through the paintings, the owner of the market came into the room, a confident man of middle age, a buzz cut and neat beard, carrying plastic umbrellas under one arm. He was delighted to tell me more about the collection. Billy Mumford was an extraordinarily prolific forger, a career which began when he was thrown out of St Martin's School of Art, its director telling him "I've met many artists with a drink problem Billy, but never a drinker with an art problem." Mumford specialised in twentieth century artists but made it a rule not to forge work by anyone still living. Eventually his sheer productivity caught up with him – so many works by individual artists appearing in auction rooms that suspicions were raised and finally, in 2011, he was sentenced to two years in prison, where he taught art to fellow prisoners. Even this did not entirely end his underworld career, the owner hinted, and somehow more of his work made it to market. The prison warders were sanguine, being chiefly concerned with stopping goods coming into prison and much less worried about what found its way beyond the gates.

Mumford is now a reformed character, using his criminal past to great effect, holding events where he discusses his life for a paying audience, and now sells his work exclusively to the antiques market, and is sometimes commissioned by clients keen to have a work on their walls by a well-known artist.

Methodism was not universally well-received in Dorset,[28] in Bridport one congregation of the new religion was even pelted with stones and dead rats by the inhabitants. But once adopted by the progressive middle classes it became an important reforming movement. For years its most prominent local figure was Dr Roberts, born in nearby West Bay in 1766 and whose interest in medicine led him to open a Bridport pharmacy in 1788, carrying out procedures which included tooth extraction, somewhat beyond what we'd expect from a branch of Boots today. Putting the poor and needy first he gave medical advice without charge and during a cholera epidemic printed a pamphlet on healthy living, distributing it throughout the town.

Nevertheless his lack of formal medical training raised eyebrows, so he enrolled as a student at Guy's and St Thomas' hospitals in London, gaining a medical diploma and licenses to practice as a surgeon and pharmacist in 1797. His potions and pills were popular, if unconventional: those made from spiders and cobwebs might treat flatulence; horseradish was just the thing for sprains, bruises and flatulence; senna and coriander would resolve constipation, although I hope with not too much flatulence, or you might reach for the cobwebs again. Dr Roberts' life was not especially long, dying at the age of sixty-nine[29], but his legacy was.

In Alan Garner's strange, magical novel *Treacle Walker*, shortlisted for the 2022 Booker Prize, the titular character gives the hero, Joe, a small pot of ointment: Beach and Barnicott's 'Poor Man's Friend' a lotion which recurs throughout the book – eventually curing Joe's lazy eye and unlocking a series of parallel mirror worlds.[30] 'Poor Man's Friend' was no invention of the novelist, who has plenty of imagination to spare, but was originally prepared by Dr Roberts, and sold in small white pots engraved with blue text. When Roberts' health declined he passed his business to his apprentices, Beach and Barnicott, who continued to market the mysterious ointment passing on its secret to their successors until 1946. In the 1970s a pharmacist bought Dr Roberts' old shop and discovered a recipe for Poor Man's Friend – mostly lard and beeswax, bergamot and lavender, a mixture which might have effectively treated some minor skin complaints as it also contained zinc oxide. It was unlikely to cure impaired vision or to open up colourful new worlds – for that you need lysergic acid diethylamide, or *Treacle Walker* itself.

A series of the pots were on display upstairs in Bridport's charming museum, which was otherwise understandably dominated by rope. One of the attendants pointed out to me where Roberts' pharmacy had been, the lettering crisp over dark grey paint: "Beach and Barnicott, Successors to the late Dr. Roberts, Bridport". Finally, although the name lived on, the building became a restaurant: the member of staff told me that while it had atmosphere she could wait 45 minutes for a coffee, longer for spiders and cobwebs. I found it boarded-up, and now according to the estate agents sign, a Rare Freehold Business Opportunity.

Poor Man's Friend was Bridport's spirit bottled – an eccentric tincture invented and embraced by the town for the care of its citizens, exemplified today in the community activities in the church, the cheerful market stalls, the hidden garden, the harmless fake paintings and gentle bohemianism.

WEST BAY

When Frederick Treves was writing *Highways and Byways in Dorset* a railway ran to Bridport, a town he described as loveable, and then on to West Bay. I hate to agree too much with Treves, but as I walked around the small harbour settlement his assessment of West Bay seemed accurate – the buildings were "arranged with no more method than if they had been emptied out of a dice box." Terraces of houses started and stopped again without warning, the road layout twisted and changed its mind. It was a paved place with no discernible heart, not its marina, nor its harbour wall. Tourists slipped about, a little lost. I gave myself purpose by buying hot chips soaked in vinegar from a stall and was warned by the young woman serving me not to let gulls steal my lunch; I might be fined by the council for feeding them. Guarding the chips preciously I stepped through the grey place towards the sea and found a bench to look out across the bay, from Portland to Lyme Regis.

This directionless place is the fault of the railway and its leaving. When it steamed here first in 1884 as a spur from Bridport, the Great Western Railway had grand plans to transform the working harbour into a destination for holidaymakers. But they needed to inject some glamour into the workaday port, then known as Bridport Haven, Bridport Creek or most commonly Bridport Harbour, so they decided on a name change and fell upon West Bay, removing the everyday, and promising much. The harbour had never developed into the town it thought it might become – while it provided the means to export Bridport's rope the harbour was too small, and a sand bar presented a hazard to shipping. In 1820 the artist J.M.W. Turner had produced an etching of a ship in high seas just off the coast, pitching violently.[31]

The railway track was laid, but tourism was not the answer – the line closed to passengers in 1930, and in 1962 to goods trains too. In 1967, Barbara Castle, then Minister for Transport, refused to allow closure of the line that ran from Maiden Newton to Bridport on the grounds that it would cause hardship, but finally it too closed in 1975.[32] The station buildings at West Bay had since been rescued and I found a restaurant operating out of a single passenger carriage on a short section of track next to the platform. West Bay had its destination changed for it, and it showed.

If it's now known for anything it's as a set for TV. The ITV series *Broadchurch* had its coastal scenes filmed here, David Tennant and Olivia Coleman searching for a child killer in a small community and occasionally looking mournfully out to sea. In the late 1990s it was also the setting for the mercifully short-lived BBC series *Harbour Lights*, starring Nick Berry, returning to his home-town to become the harbourmaster.[33] More impressively it was on the beach at West Bay where Leonard Rossiter discarded his clothes and ran into the sea in the title sequence of David Nobbs' comedy *The Fall and Rise of Reginal Perrin*, the not-quite suicide running from the direction of Burton Bradstock.

West Bay is, in its heart, Bridport Harbour still. The piled-up oyster pots were mobbed by starlings, the tang of sea was for the trawlers not the bathers, and the bench I was sitting on had a small brass plaque bearing the name of a shipwright who had died in 2003. A small group of teenagers on a geography field trip milled around and were amused that they had been asked to take photographs of the groynes, the breakwaters made of boulders. But once they had snapped their rock-pics they dissipated and faded into the wafting groups of tourists slowly making their way out along the harbour wall, finding their own rhythm of drift in the greyness.

HOLNEST

Dorset's north-west country has its own character, distinct from the eastern Blackmore Vale: more wooded, more secretive, a land of long looping lanes and scattered villages. Holnest, lying south of Sherborne along an A-road, was a hard to pinpoint place on the map, not quite here, and not quite there. But I found the beautiful, isolated church, cowering at the back of its large and curiously empty graveyard. The building was a patchwork – the earliest part thirteenth century, with a tower added later, a porch later still. Gorgeous box pews lined the nave: I pushed one of the wooden doors open and sat down, just to know how it might have felt to worship privately. Above each pew were wrought iron candle holders. I wrote enthusiastically in the visitors' book and considered buying a fridge magnet of the church (£2.50).

The church, dedicated like many to Saint Mary, has survived insults, threats and literal obscurity. Its congregation diminished through plague and depopulation. The Victorian restoration was sensitive, unusually, but still, by the outbreak of the Second World War it was in a sorry state, made worse by thefts of lead from its roof, and the church was closed for worship in 1939. In 1957 it was proposed that the church be demolished. The community mounted spirited resistance and enlisted the support of the charity Friends of Friendless Churches, founded that same year by Ivor Bulmer-Thomas, and supported by luminaries including John Betjeman, John Piper, Roy Jenkins and T.S. Eliot.[34] The church re-opened in 1968, commemorated with a small crab apple tree in the churchyard. But the battle was far from over. In the 1990s the Council decided that land adjacent to the church would be perfect for a new landfill site, importing rubbish from around Europe. It was only the discovery of a colony of great crested newts that halted the application, reflected in the defiant sundial above the church door, which bore a stone newt, crawling over the words HOLNEST PARISH 2000 A.D.

The footpath which led from the iron gates of the churchyard took a strange route, turning at two seemingly unnecessary right angles on its way to the church door and its guardian newt. The reason was the greatest insult suffered so far by the church. John Sawbridge Erle-Drax (1800-1887) was a Tory MP who controlled the 'pocket borough' of Wareham with few voters and fewer still prepared to voice their opposition to him, and who reportedly spoke only once in his Commons' career, when he asked the Speaker if a window could be opened. This may be legend only, but he made no speeches in the House in a long career.[35] This shouldn't be put down to shyness. Even in the sacred environment of St Mary's was a notice which referred to Erle-Drax's "overweening idea of his own importance".[36] He was also obsessed with his own death, and held rehearsals for his funeral, occasionally shouting at his pallbearers if he felt their demeanour to be less than perfectly fitting for the occasion. He had constructed in the graveyard of Holnest church a mausoleum, made only for himself. An extraordinary edifice, it was designed in a style that might pass as Byzantine, but with a few twists, notably a letterbox so he could have *The Times* delivered to him after death, daily. Maybe he wanted to read his own obituary.

It would be fun, I thought, to read Frederick Treves description of the mausoleum *in situ*, so I pulled *Highways and Byways in Dorset* from my rucksack and found the appropriate page. He was in blistering form.

It is almost as large as the humble church, which is overshadowed by its vulgarity. Its general appearance at a distance is that of a pumping station. On nearer inspection it proves to be a gaudy building, in the Byzantine style, made up of grey and yellow stone, worried by much carving and enlivened by highly polished granite pillars.

What was most shocking was the scale, the mausoleum would have almost entirely blocked the view of the church from the road. But maintaining the monstrosity proved expensive, and with neither the church able to pay, or Erle-Drax's family willing to pay, in 1935 it was demolished, and a relatively modest slab installed to commemorate him in its place. The photographs of the mausoleum prove Treves to be a reliable witness. Topped by a huge, curved roof, it would have been a viscerally ugly sight.[37] The mausoleum was the reason the footpath took such an unusual route to the church – leading straight to Drax's tomb and then slipping round one side. The grass was damp and had grown in the warm autumn, but still I could make out the footprint of the old building. The script on Erle-Drax's tomb was illegible, smudgy under moss, but I could read the names of those also buried in the graveyard, who would have been in his literal shadow: Smart, Moger, Covan, Cooper, Jesty, Bugg, Wells, Gould, Philip, Bird.

YETMINSTER AND RYME INTRINSECA

Ryme Intrinseca has Dorset's most poetic name, too whimsical for T.S. Eliot whose ashes are interred just over the border with Somerset at East Coker[38] but not for a fellow-founder of the Friends of Friendless Churches, John Betjeman, who employed it in his poem 'Dorset'.[39] Frederick Treves may have had a rather obvious sort of premonition – his passing reference to Ryme Intrinseca in *Highways and Byways* was that it was "surely worthy of the consideration of the Poet Laureate as the spot for an official residence."[40] I found neither Ryme Intrinseca nor its near neighbour Yetminster to be whimsical, both attractive stone-built villages, neat and reserved. Ryme Intrinseca's nod to oddity was that its slightly chilly church is dedicated to Saint Hippolytus, an obscure third century martyr whose claim to fame was that he was the first anti-pope, having set himself up in opposition to Pope Urban I. He is also the patron saint of prison officers and horses, the latter an unusual choice given that the means of his martyrdom was that he was dragged by wild horses.

The junctions in the lanes around Yetminster and Ryme Intrinseca appeared to have an unusually large number of white fingerposts – the distinctive road signs which are a feature of the

Dorset countryside. Of the 700 or so which remain, repeatedly repaired by enthusiastic volunteers, four have red-painted finials – it is thought at least one of these was to help prison guards find their way when taking prisoners from Dorchester to the docks at Portsmouth for transportation, should Saint Hippolytus' guidance fail.

One fingerpost in this corner of Dorset was used on the cover of the 1972 album, *Dorset is Beautiful*, by the local folk group The Yetties, whose four members, one of whom is dressed as if he's just back from a morning working at a building society, stand on a verge around a signpost. The band's prodigious decades-spanning output was part of a small musical trend, 'Scrumpy and Western'. The most famous example of the genre was the surprisingly popular comedy band The Wurzels, who also recorded a version of the album's title song. The style tended towards the humorous and celebratory, and avoided the darker twists associated with the folk music and folk-inspired pop of more recent decades. The Yetties' music is not for everyone, and I confess it's not for me, being rather too full of earthy male innuendo, but the band was likeable and defiantly Dorset – the group resisted encouragement to move to London knowing it would separate them from the source of their inspiration. They were also popular, appearing often on TV in the 1970s and '80s while on radio their version of the song 'Barwick Green' was used as the theme tune for the omnibus edition of the long running drama *The Archers*.[41]

The Blackmore Vale is cow country, Hardy's "Vale of Little Dairies". In the churchyard at Holnest I had seen a headstone for Betty Geraldine Jesty (1918-2004) and her husband Frederick Walter Jesty (1917-1997). Old Dorset surnames like Samways and Mogridge are common, families who have become bound to the county, but Jesty has a special significance, not just in Dorset, but for the world. Benjamin Jesty was a dairy farmer from Yetminster who noticed that the dairy maids he employed didn't contract smallpox, an illness that killed one third of those who contracted it. Making the connection between the women's work and their immunity, in 1774 Jesty took some pus from lesions on a cow's udder, and using a needle, scraped it into the arms of his wife and sons (but not, I note, his own arm). His wife fell ill, and though she recovered, the wider community were unsettled by his strange tactics. But his sons didn't contract smallpox, despite attempts to infect them. Twenty years later this small study caught the attention of Edward Jenner who scaled it up and began a vaccination campaign. Two centuries later, in 1980, smallpox was declared eradicated throughout the world.[42]

BATCOMBE

The low-lying land of the north-west ends with a wooded ridge, a climb into the Cretaceous.[43] I approached Batcombe driving down a steep and winding narrow lane and parked on an innocuous verge a quarter of a mile from the church. Almost everyone I met while researching this book was kind, curious, helpful, friendly and interested. So those who were not (hello Red-Faced Clergyman of Christchurch, hello again Woman who Tried to Run Me Over in Gillingham) stand out in the memory. As I walked back along the lane to the church a woman emerged from her house, remonstrating with me angrily for parking on land that was not hers, nor blocking her gates. I tried to explain but moved the car anyway.

The church sat dramatically in the lea of the hill which stooped menacingly above. Frederick Treves wrote that the villagers abandoned the place to "escape the boredom of unutterable solitude", although I expect that plague, changing land ownership and farming practices would also have played their part. The church itself was set back from the land, undramatic, square-towered and topped with four pinnacles. I was here for legend. A local squire, known as Conjuror Minterne, galloping home on his way to dismiss a servant who he somehow knew had broken into his study and was examining the only book in the room, jumped from the hill above, clearing the church completely, except that his horse's hoof clipped one of the pinnacles, knocking it to the ground. The squire, John Minterne, might have died in 1592 or 1716, according to Treves, who was fascinated by the story, and he might be buried in the church's wall, like Ettricke's sarcophagus in Wimborne[44]. Or he might not. Supernatural powers had prevented the pinnacle from being replaced, but in the intervening centuries these malign forces had clearly waned, all four being proudly in place. The magic in the landscape was in no way diminished; in the shadow of the hill it was no wonder that the few remaining residents of Batcombe were wary of men arriving unexpectedly on their home patch.

Notes

1   Ashmore has a circular pond which dries up rarely, even in drought, but if it did a feast was held. This tradition seems to have morphed into the Filly Loo – not an ancient festival but invented in the mid-1950s. It's an extraordinary night, in which dancers holding aloft antler horns make their way from each end of the village to the sound of a drum beat and a single tin whistle. The crowd watches in silence and photography is not permitted.

2   *In the Country* by Kenneth Allsop, published originally in 1972, republished by Little Toller in 2012 in the Nature Classics series. The book was originally a series of articles for the *Daily Mail*.

3   For more on The Clubmen, west-country rebels who rejected both sides in the English Civil War, see the Hambledon Hill section of this book (North).

4   Robert Macfarlane had first visited the holloways in the company of his friend Roger Deakin, who died in 2005. Macfarlane also wrote the Introduction to the recent edition of *Rogue Male*. Stanley Donwood is best known, perhaps, for his artwork for Radiohead's albums, although his work often explores the sense of the eerie in the landscape. His densely shaded work perfectly captures the atmosphere of a holloway, its history and mystery.

5   See Sara Hudston's article in the *Guardian* Country Diary, 4th April 2022. www.theguardian.com/environment/2022/apr/04/country-diary-a-secret-hideaway-and-a-mystery-solved

6   For a full description of Walsh and his subsequent interrogation see *Folklore of Dorset* by Fran and Geoff Doel, History Press, 2007.

7   Cunning is derived from the Anglo-Saxon word for 'to know'.

8   Dr Leonard Baker has written widely on rural protest, folk traditions and how important the idea of 'place' was to those seeking to defend their rights and customs, especially during the Enclosure Acts.

9   Graham, being slightly mischievous, attempted to insert a couple of chronological errors, slipping into scenes where he could not be, having appeared seconds earlier an impossible distance away.

10 For an outdated article on Dorset in the movies and on TV see the BBC Dorset webpages from 2004: www.bbc.co.uk/dorset/content/articles/2004/11/23/film_locations_feature. shtml. A fuller list was more recently compiled by Ed Roberts: www.stayindorset.co.uk/ handbook/dorset-film-locations?fbclid=IwAR1NVunFS2IbW6SMzpzAaFlp8U2NkxfZ42P wFlHCHNq9Unv9gSgqLWETgrc

11 See an interview with the family, the very model of a modern aristocratic set-up: www.greatbritishlife.co.uk/people/luke-and-julie-montagu-the-duo-taking-up-the-reins-70 14462

12 Jos Smith wrote an essay for *The Clearing* on this subject – he too had been at the set, and wrote about Hardy's Partly Real, Partly Dream country. His piece on the way we see the countryside is well worth reading: www.littletoller.co.uk/the-clearing/jos-smith-a-partly -real-partly-imagined-country/. Another essay, by Georgina Gardner, also on *The Clearing* reflected on the significance of the Posy Tree in a time of a new pandemic: www.littletoller. co.uk/the-clearing/dead-mans-lane-by-georgina-gardner/

13 The T shirt is a close match for the sleeve of the album *The English Settlement* by XTC, an album I very much like, but it's not the only reason I like the T shirt.

14 See Alex's memoir and exploration into the Romanesque in England's south-west: *King of Dust*, Little Toller Books, 2019.

15 Sarah Hudston has written about St Wite on her website: sarahudston.co.uk/st-wite/

16 King Alfred referred to it in his will as "aet hwitancyrccan".

17 "An exceptional rarity" say John Newman and Nikolaus Pevsner in *Buildings of England, Dorset*.

18 *The English River* by Virginia Astley, Bloodaxe, 2018.

19 For more on the traditions of roof tiling see www.chippingcampdenhistory.org.uk/ content/history/buildings_and_other_landmarks/traditional_cotswold_roofs (thanks to Virginia Astley for providing further information).

20 See the Bournemouth section of this book.

21 The film, directed by Karel Reisz, the music by Carl Davis, was nominated for five Oscars.

22 See the Dorset History Centre blog: news.dorsetcouncil.gov.uk/dorset-history-centre-blog/2021/03/22/the-siege-of-lyme-regis/

23 GI was a term applied to American soldiers whose kit bore the words Government Issue.

24 See Guy Shrubsole's post on the Who Owns England website: whoownsengland.org /2020/01/04/the-ten-landowners-who-own-one-sixth-of-dorset/

25 For more detail on Drax, his landholdings both in Dorset and in the Caribbean see *The Guardian*, 18 July 2021 https://www.theguardian.com/world/2021/jul/18/protesters -demand-wealthy-mp-pays-up-for-familys-slave-trade-past.

26 See the article in *The Guardian* for Lenny Henry's involvement, 23 May, 2016 www. theguardian.com/media/2016/may/23/lenny-henry-joins-broadchurch-previously-saying-dr ama-too-white-itv

27 Although both the sources I found made use of a 'carrion' analogy, making me doubt the truth of this story.

28 See the Stalbridge section of this book (North) for John Wesley's reception.

29 For more information on Dr Roberts see the display in Bridport Museum and also this website devoted to ointment pots (although note that the headline on the page confuses Bridport with Plymouth) www.ointmentpots.com/victorian/drroberts

30 Another important plot device in the novel is the appearance of Stoneage Kit The Ancient Brit, a character from a real but long gone comic, *Knockout*.

31 The harbour town has provided inspiration for many artists possibly because it's still a working place. They have included Turner, David Inshaw, Nicholas Hely Hutchinson, Marzia Colonna and Walter Tyndale. There's a flourishing gallery in West Bay: Sladers Yard.

32 See the excellent website Disused Stations: www.disused-stations.org.uk/b/bridport_

west_bay/

33 If you really must find out more, IMDB has information: www.imdb.com/title
    /tt0165028/locations?ref_=tt_dt_loc

34 An amazing organisation, run on a shoestring, which rescues redundant churches and
    keeps them open: Read more about them: friendsoffriendlesschurches.org.uk
    /story/our-founding-story/

35 Historic Hansard reports no contributions from the MP. By contrast Disraeli made 3532,
    Gladstone made 5945 and Palmerston 4313.

36 Erle-Drax's descendant is the Tory MP Richard Plunkett-Ernle-Erle-Drax, first elected in
    2010. See the Beaminster section of this book for more.

37 See the photo in Discover Dorset, *The Blackmore Vale* by Hilary Townsend, p 72, and on
    Somerset Live www.somersetlive.co.uk/news/heatwave-reveals-location-incredible-lost-
    1802732.

38 One of the poems in Eliot's *Four Quartets* is *East Coker*, a meditation on the cyclical nature
    of life, death, nature and creativity.

39 And see the section on Sherborne in this book (North).

40 Betjeman's poem appears in a collection published in 1937, thirty-five years before he
    became Poet Laureate.

41 See The Yetties website, theyetties.com and for an interview with a member of the band
    see *Dorset Life*, May 2016.

42 Shortly after the programme of vaccination began a cartoon by James Gillray, 'Cow Pock
    or the Wonderful Effects of the New Inoculation' appeared, which showed the recently
    vaccinated sprouting cow's heads from their limbs. The conspiracist Anti-Vax movement
    was born already. Benjamin Jesty is buried at Worth Matravers on the Purbeck coast, and
    it's well worth a visit, if only because the village is home to the Greatest Pub in the World,
    The Square and Compass.

43 See *Geology and Scenery of Dorset* by Eric Bird, Ex Libris Press, 1995, map on page 16. This
    high land is also where most of the archaeological finds in Dorset have been made, from
    the Dorset Cursus to the stone circles around The Valley of the Stones.

44 See the Wimborne Minster section of this book (Central).

CENTRAL

DORCHESTER'S DARK ROOMS

Dorchester: the heart of Dorset, in a way. County Hall loomed above me, red brick and sprawling. The confident building was completed in the 1950s but I was standing in a grassy bowl amongst an older group of buildings, walls reduced to their footings and low rubble. The Roman House was unearthed during the construction of the new civic buildings, whose design was altered to make allowance for their older companions. A site of some importance, then and now, power drawn to the same place, millennia apart.

My attention was drawn by a small group of people in the ruins. They were of all ages and marked out by their dress.

"Would you like to wear a robot's head?" asked a child, holding out for me a carboard box with a square hole cut in its front.

I slid it on.

"You can keep it," said the child.

"I'll get too hot if I wear this all day but thank you." I handed it back.

Two adults approached, a young man and woman, also wearing cardboard. I complimented them on their attire. They explained that they were Counter Tourists, subverting the heritage industry through unconventional ways of engaging with historic places. Liberty and Andy had dressed in a cardboard toga and as the Black Knight from *Monty Python and the Holy Grail* ("it's only a flesh wound!"). They had spent the morning admiring a car park, would

shortly march up the hill to Poundbury. That week Liberty had taken a group to St Catherine's Chapel above Chesil Beach where the folk tradition was that women would gather there to pray that they might meet their future husbands. In contrast Liberty led a rendition of Beyoncé's 'All the Single Ladies'. Recently Andy had led a walk to Birmingham's Spaghetti Junction to celebrate its fiftieth anniversary.[1]

"Sometimes," said Andy, "we make eye contact with statues." I admired their dedication and felt like an amateur. They gathered their group and set off for their march.

In his appealingly eccentric book *The Lost Roads of Wessex*, Cecil Cochrane described Dorchester as having a "Shangri-La remoteness" and the quiet Victorian terraces close to the town centre had that air. But mostly Dorchester is, and always has been, about bustle. Daniel Defoe wrote that there were 600,000 sheep grazing within six miles of the town, which brought money and status.[2] In 1832, before the railway came, ninety-six coaches stopped at Dorchester every week, connecting Shangri-La to London, Bristol, Southampton and Exeter.

I walked around the prison's curved walls, passing a ginger cat lolling on a drain cover. The prison closed in 2014 and when I visited was shortly to be redeveloped as apartments, but my way was still barred by a high metal gate and fence, topped with rolls of barbed wire. This was the spot where, in 1856, the last woman to be publicly executed in Dorset was hanged. Martha Brown had murdered her husband with an axe after suffering domestic abuse, which included being whipped. One eyewitness to the hanging was a sixteen-year-old Thomas Hardy, who later wrote he was ashamed that he had gone, the experience finding its literary expression in Tess's end.

Robert Wedderburn, a mixed-race Unitarian minister and radical, whose father had been a plantation owner and his mother enslaved, had in 1819 been imprisoned at Dorchester. Wedderburn arrived in England at the age of sixteen and soon became involved in debating and politics. Having written that Jesus Christ was a radical reformer he was sentenced to two years on charges of seditious blasphemy. On his release he went on to publish the hugely influential book *The Horrors of Slavery*, hastening its end.[3]

This silently violent place was shrouded in shade; the shadow of conflict cropped up again on High East Street. One building with the words PALE ALE BREWERY inscribed over an arch was an old pub. This had been the Three Mariners, once famous for Saturday night singalongs. It closed in 1971, after which it had a spell as the British Legion, and for a time in the 1980s as Cunards Nightclub. But a century and a half earlier, in 1829, a 'Christmas Frolic' turned sour when soldiers and townspeople turned on each other, the military using swords and bayonets while the civilians made weapons out of whatever was to hand, including pokers and pitchforks. The local newspaper recorded its surprise that no-one had been killed.

Dorchester's nineteenth century was marked by rebellion, a drive for reform. The political establishment and a long line of local Tory MPs resisted change, believing that since England had already had the 1688 revolution, which replaced one monarch with another, there was little need for future reform. This was underpinned by some disgust for their constituents, and brutal tactics. At a bad-tempered hustings in 1831, the long-serving MP, Henry Bankes, whispered to his servant that once the election was over he wanted nothing more to do with this "West Country scum", a remark overheard by his Whig opponents who repeated it to the outraged 12,000 spectators. Bankes was forced to leave the scene hastily. For the first time in Dorset's history, the county elected two Whig MPs.[4]

Territory matters in Dorchester – in the nineteenth century two villages clashed violently over the movement of 'boundstones' which marked the border between two pieces of common land, while in the 1940s tensions between the Black and White American troops, segregated even at leisure, erupted when one group moved into the perceived territory of the other, the fight being broken up by the US Military Police.

Before executions were moved to the prison, hangings took place at Gallows Hill; to mark this sad crossroads at the end of Icen Way the artist Elisabeth Frink made a sculpture: two life-size figures gazing blank-eyed at a third, pacing towards them: the hangman or death. I looked into the eyes of one of the figures in sincere imitation of a Counter Tourist.

"Mummy, why is that man doing that?" asked a child.

"Because he wants to." The woman ushered her son away, across the road to safety.

It was hot and I sat on a bench. A woman approached, her friendly dachshund in tow, and asked if she could sit next to me.

The dog's name was Baxter, I didn't ask the woman's name. Baxter, I heard, suffered from dry ears, so had oil applied to them every day. The woman asked me why I was here, and suggested I visit the oldest, and once poorest suburb of Dorchester, Fordington.

At The Green it was clear that Fordington was now gentrified – a delicatessen, a café which had put out tables under trees, cutlery in old Lyle's Golden Syrup tins. Left at the One Stop took me past a road called Little Britain and to the river, over which Himalayan Balsam was staking its claim. In these quiet streets, deadened further by the heatwave, were disused factories, cleaned up, remnants of an industrial past. In the small yard behind the Dinosaur Museum a fibreglass Triceratops and Tyrannosaurus Rex faced-off, safely behind railings. They'd be no match for 'Dippy', the Diplodocus skeleton, who, on his or her extended tour from the Natural History Museum, had recently stopped off at the nearby Dorset Museum, drawing thousands of visitors.

The busy pedestrianised main street still supported independent shops and cafés, although one brave experiment had failed. When the retail chain Woolworths went bust in 2008, the manager of the Dorchester branch re-opened it under a new name, first Wellworths, and then when the owners of the Woolworths trademark objected to the similarity, to Wellchester. Apparently successful, eventually the landlord's head was turned by a better offer – the premises was now a Poundland.

In a side street I found another statue, this one of The Dorset Shepherd. He was looking to his left, doubtless worried about the 600,000 sheep he had to watch over. I couldn't make eye contact with him, or the poet William Barnes outside a church, nor Hardy, sitting brooding in a chair by the car park, facing away from the home he designed for himself on the other side of town.

I drove up the hill to Poundbury, Dorchester's newest, loudest neighbour. Amongst the Range Rovers and Audis, my little Fiat was dusty and out of place. Poundbury is King Charles' vision. Publicly upset with modernist architecture he used the hilltop as his model town, and had it built from scratch, a beacon of traditional hope in the sea of concrete brutalism which he so detests.

Poundbury is big, really big. Once it was a quaint Dorset new-build vernacular village, but its later buildings have transformed it into a brazen, royalist Greco-Roman, Palladian pastiche. I passed a huge statue to the late Queen's mother. The Carpet Company ('The Flooring Experts') occupied an imitation of the Acropolis, but with more underlay. Poundbury is Bridgerton, ersatz Georgian high-camp, a stuccoed Jacob Rees-Mogg having undergone a Queer Eye makeover.[5] The layout was deliberately twee – buildings jutting into the streets as in a medieval market town, but here only for effect or for traffic calming. There was no discernible centre and no heart. There has been a genuine attempt to accommodate social housing, usually only a convenient and temporary developer's ploy, but I could see

no-one on the streets, and the shops were Waitrose, bridal shops, mysterious investment companies, a branch of the Dorset-based deli Olives et Al. The Spar was rebranded as Poundbury Village Stores. I drove to the edge of the still expanding experimental town, where the buildings were breezeblocks before receiving their set dressing, their railings or miniature castellations. Below me was Dorchester proper, the red brick buildings of twentieth century social housing glaring up with a mixture of defiance and disbelief.

Poundbury is papering over the cracks, addressing the concerns of the late 1980s, when young fogeys worried about the social effects of modern architecture, before *Grand Designs* and middle-class enthusiasm for clean lines and white kitchens. But Poundbury does matter – new housing estates everywhere in England nod to it by juxtaposing architectural styles from every century except this one, or the even the one before.

But still I couldn't shake the feeling that for all its solidity, towers, balconies, and heavy-handed royal allusions, Poundbury was ephemeral and impermanent. Ancient, muddled and sometimes violent Dorchester was unimpressed with its influential, carbuncular hilltop neighbour, and for the most part, ignored it, while Maiden Castle, to the south, turned its massive head away towards the coast.[6]

WINTERBORNE CAME

> Let other v'ok meäke money vaster
> > In the aïr o' dark-room'd towns,
> I don't dread a peevish meäster;
> > Though noo man do heed my frowns,
> I be free to go abrode,
> Or teäke ageän my hwomeward road
> To where, vor me, the apple tree
> Do leän down low in Linden Lea.
> > > *Linden Lea*, William Barnes

Both Thomas Hardy and William Barnes ended their long lives near Dorchester, Hardy in 1928, Barnes in 1896. Hardy may be much better known and dominates Dorset's culture, but Barnes' influence is growing. A poet of the Dorset dialect, he set out, as Edward Thomas wrote, to "make himself the mouthpiece of the Dorset carters, cowmen, mowers and harvesters." He was born at Bagber, in the Blackmore Vale, but for the last twenty years of his life was rector at the village of Winterborne Came, from where he would walk most days to Dorchester. Ralph Vaughan Williams set some of his poetry to music, W.H. Auden said he could not enjoy Shelley, who had strong Dorset connections, at least in death,[7] but was delighted by every line of Barnes. Most recently the two-times Mercury Prize-winning musician PJ Harvey, who grew up in Dorset, published *Orlam*, a book of poetry in the Dorset dialect, following a year in the life of a girl on the cusp of adulthood. The book has poems in both the dialect and a modern English translation: the darker the text of the translation on the page, the farther it has travelled from its original. For this great piece of art, in which time collapses across the centuries, Harvey used Barnes' *Glossary of the Dorset Dialect.*

Winterborne Came lay down a long and unsignposted single-track lane, a shaded hamlet. The village was a strange, half-abandoned place, dominated by its large and somewhat forbidding Palladian House, both the church and Barnes' grave hard to find. It felt as if it were slowly slipping the same way as its ghostly neighbour, Winterborne Faringdon, of which just one church wall remained standing in a field. Both villages were in decline as early as the sixteenth century. One of Barnes' predecessors was unhappy that he was unable to collect the tithes which gave him his living –

the sheep kept moving and the owners were hard to tax. I walked around for a few minutes, wondering if I should feel a connection to the poet, and realised belatedly that I was missing the point of Barnes, and of the hamlet itself. It wasn't supposed to be a place for pilgrimage, somewhere to buy a William Barnes tea towel. For a poet of the people, one unconcerned with greatness, this hard-to-reach place seemed appropriate, and best left to its sleep.

HERRISON HOSPITAL, CHARLTON DOWN

In the sixth form at school, I and one other student opted to spend our Wednesday afternoons doing 'community service' instead of sport, an escape from the horrors of the rugby field. We were sent to the local 'mental hospital'. Without checks as to our suitability we were presented to a roomful of women and asked to entertain them. We copied the crossword from a newspaper onto the blackboard, read out the clues and waited for answers. These women were of all ages, unvisited, often heavily drugged and lost, some asleep or half asleep. They had what we would now call complex needs, which seemed mostly unmet, and all we could do was pass their time. Something called Care in the Community was coming, and no-one knew what it meant beyond a slogan and a hope.

Dorset's County Asylum was the Herrison Hospital, founded in 1832 on the downs north of Dorchester. At its peak it housed nearly a thousand patients in a huge facility. Without sensible diagnoses, anti-psychotic drugs, therapy or counselling, all the Victorians knew was to keep people from harming themselves or others, and out of sight.

The hospital was in decline for many years: in 1979 only two hundred patients remained at Herrison, and finally it closed in 1992. I'd seen a video made in 1996 of the hospital derelict, papers in rotting carboard boxes, peeling patterned wallpaper, an empty canteen, a menu of cottage pie, beef curry, cauliflower cheese, a salad bar.

It was easy to find the hospital, its buildings sprawling and unmistakeably Victorian. Herrison Hospital had been converted into apartments, its red brick jet-washed and bleached. A tower looked like it had been built to watch for escapees. It retained an institutional sadness, a blankness. I couldn't imagine stepping into the place without the sniff of cleaning fluids, and a sense of lost promise. Most of it was off limits, but I could walk onto the sloping grass that constituted the gardens. Under trees at the end of the grounds was a double line of gravestones: one stone was for a nurse who had died in 1880, another for a cook. If the gravestones marked also burial spots for the patients I couldn't tell, but their spirit circulated still. In the twentieth century those treated here were increasingly looked after with compassion and better understanding. I hoped those still living had found lives beyond Charlton Down, were able to speak of their sadness, and find recovery in Dorset's towns, villages or hamlets.

BLANDFORD AND ITS BASTARDS

I stood on the stone bridge that crossed the River Stour between Blandford Forum and Blandford St Mary, and was buffeted by passing lorries and vans. On the opposite side of the bridge was The Cliff, the steeply-shelving woodland below which the river snaked, behind me the water meadows and the brewery. It was still a busy place but before the bypass came in the 1980s, the bridge really mattered.

The rural uprisings of the early 1830s engulfed Blandford – one pamphlet distributed in the town proclaimed: "if we do not have reform, soon we will have Revolution."[8] Thousands of rioters destroyed documents, paraded the streets playing drums and horns, and carried suspected Tories out of town across the bridge. I found, screwed to the bridge, mottled with age, a sign warning those who damaged the bridge that they may be transported for life to Australia, in the years when even membership of a trade union could earn you the same fate, as at Tolpuddle.[9] Later, in the Second World War the bridge was mined against the Panzer tanks which never came.

It was close to this spot that Roger Deakin slipped into the water and floated downstream, recounted in his book about swimming Britain's rivers and coastlines, *Waterlog*. Although this was a spring afternoon, I was in no mood for a dip, and was wary of Blandford's frightful monster – the Blandford Bomber, or Blandford Fly.

The fly is famous for delivering painful bites and from time to time crops up in national newspapers, attracting headlines like "Bite Fright" (*The Sun*, naturally), and others accuse Blandford of being its original source. Blandfordians have come up with their own stories: the fly had become caked in mud on the boots of soldiers returning from Africa to Blandford Camp, or that one had escaped from a laboratory at Bryanston School. Neither is true – the Blandford Fly has lived for thousands of years in the slow-flowing waters of southern English rivers, occasionally breaking out beyond its usual zones.

But the rumours told me something about the town: it's dominated by two institutions on the hills either side of it – the Army Camp, home to the Royal Signals Museum, and Bryanston, the large public school, in woodland above The Cliff. The fly might have been both useful and a curse to the town – one campaigner thought it was a blight to have the name of the town attached to it, as it might keep tourists away, others have turned it to their advantage – the Hall and Woodhouse Brewery, based in the town, has a beer named after it.

Blandford town bridge escaped the threat of dynamite but across the meadows I found the remnants of a bridge which *was* destroyed decades later, the long railway bridge left when the Somerset and Dorset Railway closed. For years the viaduct remained, a spot favoured by children for diving into the river, but in the late 1970s demolition was decided upon. Raffle tickets were sold – the winning ticket holder would push the button that would blow the dynamited bridge. The winner was Joyce Stevens, and a large crowd gathered to see her reduce the structure to rubble.

Two arches of the bridge remained, nudging up to the Stour, looking like a small-scale version of the Maxentius Basilica in Rome's Forum. Blandford is fond of explaining its past – everywhere I went I found Interpretation Boards screwed onto pieces of the town's history, leaving little to the imagination. Under the arches was a profusion of dense text, images of photographs, maps and plans of the history of the railway, in turn being photographed by a man with a long-lensed camera.

I walked to the town's centre. There's nothing Roman about Blandford Forum, despite its arches and a leaflet advertising local tradespeople featuring a photograph of a man dressed as Party Shop Roman Centurion, breastplate and all. The town was first mentioned as a borough in the fourteenth century, its original name being Chipping Blandford, renamed to lend it grandeur.

Its newish name suits it. I stepped into the main square and into the eighteenth century. The brick-fronted buildings had a Georgian unfussy sense of purpose. The square had the eerie emptiness of the end of a market day, unsold clothes being folded into plastic boxes. Blandford Forum produced the Victorian artist Alfred Stevens, but the town's square was best rendered by Rena Gardiner, whose oil painting of Blandford's market day in 1966 is full of life, the square enclosed by its grand buildings under a restless blue sky. The church of St Peter and St Paul was built on the footprint of its predecessor and has attracted much praise from various writers: "a noble and imminently interesting building", "exceptionally fine", "light, sophisticated and rather un-churchy".[10] The voice of dissent was provided by Frederick Treves in his Dorset book, thundering that it was "ugly and tolerable only from a distance". I had to leave others to squabble about it amongst themselves – the church was mostly invisible, covered in scaffolding and plastic sheeting for restoration. The tower and upturned pepper-pot cupola poked through the modesty-veil of the cladding.

Next to the church, facing the square, was a small neo-classical porch, the date 1760 carved beneath the roof. Blandford's need to explain itself was no recent phenomenon – on the back wall were several stones inscribed with text. The most recent was from 1899 explaining that this drinking fountain had once been a water pump. The pump deserved its prominence because fire forged Blandford.

Towns were hardly immune to burning in medieval and early modern England, but Blandford got unlucky. There were fires in 1564 and 1677, again in 1713. But the big one was on 4th June 1731, ripping through almost all the town's buildings. It melted pewter in homes, and lead on the church roof. In 1666 fire had quashed the most recent outbreak of plague in London; in Blandford the fire hastened the end of smallpox, for the time being[11]. But the flames killed people in Blandford – at least nine women and three men. The records of deaths haven't survived, but in the months that followed there were more burials than usual.

Fire was Blandford's bad luck and its accidental town planner, but the town delights in its Bastards, its nominated saviours. Set into the pavement outside the Corn Exchange I found a slab inscribed with the words:

Recipe for Regeneration
Take one careless tallow chandler and
Two ingenious Bastards

The tallow chandler was the equivalent of Pudding Lane's baker –
blamed for the fire, rather than attributing it to thatch and timber.
The Bastards were the brothers William and John.

Down a passage leading from the square was the town's
museum, stuffed with exhibits and scarily life-sized dolls, enacting
the domestic routines of previous ages. Upstairs was a
counter-factual model of the town in the 1940s, showing German
tanks crossing the Stour by the bridge, approaching tiny rolls of
barbed wire and a caption glued to the green-painted grass: "We
Would Have Blown It Up". Downstairs the friendly assistant
showed me another diorama housed in glass, recreating the
afternoon of the fire. To demonstrate its ferocity she pushed a
button which lit some of the buildings with a dim red glow from
small lamps – I liked it very much. She mentioned the Bastards and
we both sniggered.

William and John were architects and builders in Blandford. They set about rebuilding, mostly following the older layout, although we don't quite know what the town was before, so complete was the devastation. The intrepid traveller Celia Fiennes, sweeping through thirty years before the fire thought it a "pretty neate Country town", but didn't linger long enough to tell us more. It was William and John whose work gave us Blandford's centre, sniffed at by Frederick Treves who described it as "prim". Treves was more appreciative that Blandford had no outskirts, that one could step straight from the centre to the fields, but this was a sign of nineteenth century decline, when the town's population fell. There are suburbs now, rings of housing which have spread out since Treves' time; a new estate was growing to the south on land where the railway once ran.

I wondered if the town's fondness for plaques, interpretation boards or inscribed paving slabs stemmed from a need to record history in case the next disaster snuffs out the stories. When Wareham burned thirty years after Blandford's fire the town sent bacon, cheese, bread and money, a mark of solidarity and memory.

In the museum were images of portraits of the two Bastard brothers side by side. John had jowls, William's jawline set with confidence and determination. Recent restoration to the original paintings revealed that William had what looked like a black eye. The brothers had planned the new church to have a spire, but lack of funds prevented it. Instead the church ended up with its small wooden cupola, designed by another architect, causing much offence to the Bastards. There is speculation that William's black eye was a result of a brawl, but it could instead have been symbolic, a mark of an ambition unfulfilled.

In the side streets Blandford was less a product of the mid-eighteenth century and more like the mid-twentieth century, a jewellers with a serif-heavy font above the windows, a shop called Beds Beds Beds Beds Beds, which I think sold beds, a 'traditional tea shop' attached to the Fashion Museum. Opposite Sleek and Chic Hair Design, whose building once housed *The Blandford Express*, a short-lived nineteenth century newspaper which promoted abstinence (in a town noted for its brewing, this was always ambitious), I found a more modern spot for lunch. I ate beetroot humous with sourdough and the proprietor told me that they "do Facebook, Instagram, all that stuff". I noted that they were shortly to open at weekends too.

In the quiet side streets. I overheard a young man telling his mother that he had it on good authority from TikTok that Boris Johnson would shortly be forced to resign as Prime Minister; she questioned the reliability of the source, but accepted her son's reassurances.[12] I stopped outside an extraordinary house, its deep red brick, a stone roof, ornate chimneys and arched porch all marked it out as quite unlike its neighbours. This house was built in the mid-seventeenth century. Did other houses in Blandford look like this fire survivor? Did England's new buildings around the time of its revolutions have this confidence? The small round plaque from the Blandford Civil Society thought that it showed "German Influence". A streetlamp poked incongruously from the first floor to splash sodium over the night-time pavement.

I crossed the bridge by the old railway station, now a car park. I had read a strange story that a Blandford worthy had recorded a dream in which a monster attacked him, breathing fire and smoke, people watching him from its body, 150 years before the railway tore through what had been his garden, but this premonition had something both too obvious and too insubstantial about it, and Blandford's Nostradamus recorded no useful visions of towns on fire or bridges exploding. Would the residents of the new estate be woken by retrospective nightmares of thundering trains rushing through their sitting rooms?

Down a narrow alley between modern housing and Blandford's fire station, behind which two members of the crew were washing a fire engine, preparedness for emergencies being especially important here, was Blandford's oldest building. St Leonard's Chapel was a small flint and stone building, its walls leaning precariously, buttressed by recent red brick, in a tiny patch of grass. It was originally part of a larger complex, a hospital designed to treat and isolate sufferers of leprosy away from centres of population. While taking a closer look at the exterior a young man poked his head out from the doorway and gave me a thumbs up when I told him I was interested in the chapel. The building was still in public service, now used by Dorset Council's Countryside Rangers.

Once, too reliant on my bike's sat-nav, I laboured up the long hill leaving Blandford Forum, hoping to reach the Tarrant Valley. At the top a soldier stepped from a sentry box and blocked my way, wearing a smile and carrying a rifle. I was at the gates of Blandford Camp. The sentry congratulated me on the climb and sent me back. While stationed at the camp Rupert Brooke wrote his patriotic poem 'The Solider', foretelling a likely death in a corner of "some foreign field" which would be transformed thereafter into a piece of England. In fact, while Brooke avoided Blandford Fly, he died of sepsis from an infected mosquito bite while on the way to the disastrous Dardanelles campaign, which claimed the lives of almost the whole division. The camp's recent history has some drama too: in 1952 three soldiers doing national service stationed here were accused of fighting after Lights Out, their successful defence being that they were in fact barricading their room against the angry ghost of a woman who had been murdered at the camp before the Second World War, although I could find no evidence of the original crime. In December 2000 a woman working in the Semaphore Arms at the camp decided to avoid her shift the next day by planting a fake bomb, which led to a thousand people being evacuated from their homes while it was investigated. While the tragedy of the Dardanelles is recorded with a monument for the fallen, the more recent stories have, unlike the town at the camp's feet, been unrecorded on local signage.

TARRANT CRAWFORD

Tarrant Crawford, a few miles from Blandford, is an unmarked place where the Tarrant River slowly disgorges into the Stour. At the end of a long winding lane, under trees where a few late daffodils were fading and bluebells were sprouting, was a fishpond where the Tarrant had been dammed, beyond was an ancient roofless tithe barn. In a graveyard of broken headstones and plastic flowers was St Mary's, stone and flint. I was unprepared for what I found inside the church: the walls were covered in beautiful, faded, intricate wall-paintings dating from the fourteenth century, saints and knights with skinny legs in armour. I found a crucifixion scene, and another of three dancing skeletons.[13]

The church is on the site of one of the wealthiest Cistercian abbeys in England and is also the burial place of a Scottish Queen, Joanna, daughter of King John, supposedly in a gold coffin.[14] The abbey buildings had all vanished, some of the stone probably re-used in the construction of the nearby farm. The Romans had avoided Blandford Forum but they had been here, remains of their building materials were discovered and some of them were probably incorporated into the abbey. I wrote in the visitor's book, as had many others, noting the peace they found here. I could have spent as long in here as in any cathedral, soaking it in under the barrel-vaulted ceiling, but I was disturbed by two young men, builders I guessed from the plaster dust on their trousers, who also fell silent as they came in. I slipped away from the old place, returning to my car, my head full of skeletons and fire, lepers and bastards, soldiers and flies. Blandford over-explained itself, Tarrant Crawford left matters hanging.

TARRANT RUSHTON

A few summers ago I accompanied the cyclist and writer Jack Thurston on a day's ride in Dorset, while he was researching his book *Lost Lanes West*.[15] His series of books aims to help cyclists slip through the countryside unmolested by traffic and in doing so, recover some of the history left in the margins. Sitting outside a pub at lunchtime, poring over maps and plotting quiet routes across the county, he remembered once visiting the isolated hamlet of Tarrant Rushton.

I thought I knew the Tarrant valley and its villages well. At Tarrant Gunville the seventeenth century baroque architect Vanbrugh designed a huge and now largely vanished mansion, Eastbury Park[16]. Eastbury had a short life, being mostly demolished only eighty years after its completion, leaving behind a couple of good ghost stories and a reputation for political intrigue. Tarrant Monkton had been the home of the artist Rena Gardiner and was also where I tortured my guitar teacher's ears every week for a few years before he sensibly moved to Scotland. And at Tarrant Crawford I had found a lonely church, the only remnant of a once important monastery. But Tarrant Rushton had escaped my notice.

Across a narrow bridge Jack and I cycled through the hamlet, tucked into a steep hill above the valley, the winding lane becoming a concrete track. Jack, strong, lean and fast, snaked up the slope while I trundled behind, wheezing like a traction engine at the Great Dorset Steam Fair. We emerged onto a wide plateau, sown with crops encircled by a cracked road. In the distance I could make out a large barn. This was the site of Tarrant Rushton Airfield, built in the hurry of war in 1942, the barn being a repurposed hangar. We made our bumpy way along the perimeter track, until finally we reached the southern end of a runway, now reduced to a long and narrow straight track through the field, the crop crowding in.

Before my provisional licence came through I took driving lessons on a disused airfield in the New Forest, wrestling with the heavy steering of our family's Ford Cortina while my dad sat in the passenger seat, wincing at my unsteady progress. We were used to these overgrown ruins of a global war, but Tarrant Rushton's history was extraordinary. A base for bombers and gliders, dropping supplies and troops into the European theatre of war, it was especially notable for its role in D-Day, for the Arnhem

Operation and in the lesser-known Operation Varsity which established bridgeheads across the Rhine. We pedalled up the long runway but I found it impossible to imagine this empty field as a hive of human activity, a place where nearly 3,000 men and women were stationed.

Later I came across transcripts of the airfield's Operations Logbooks online. I'm grateful for local history books and webpages in the dustiest corners of the internet, but they lean towards the dry and technical, to have sucked out the humanity, leaving neat parcels of vacuum-packed facts. As I downloaded the documents I readied myself for pages of tedious detail, from which I hoped to extract a few slices of life. I couldn't have been more wrong. Crowded together in these pages, painstakingly transcribed by an unknown enthusiast, was the epic and the banal, the tragic, the inconsequential and dramatic, sometimes leavened with dry wit, revealing a hidden world, detailing every day from the establishment of the airfield until its mothballing in 1946. I was riveted.

The pages were unedited and raw, recording events as they happened, written only to serve as an operational history and without knowing how their war would end. Short summaries of the weather ended each day's report. The logbooks recorded the visit by General Dwight Eisenhower a few weeks before D-Day, during which he addressed flight crews, the account of this momentous occasion followed with "Weather: early fog becoming fine." Or, more tragically: "Stirling aircraft crashed in the vicinity of Tarrant Hinton. Crew of Six killed. Weather fair to cloudy."

But there was news too of hundreds of people crammed into the Corn Exchange at Blandford Forum for dances, lectures from the secret service on how to evade capture if shot down and how to respond to interrogation ("If you talk, you kill"). There were records of the popularity of various sporting activities – squash was hampered, so the transcripts told me, by a shortage of balls, while a five-a-side football tournament in December 1944 was cancelled owing to 'Christmas Spirits'. Occasionally details of the loss of life recognised a need to record suffering and heroism, overcoming the logbooks' tendency to brevity. I read how Flying Officer Anderson died after his bomber crashed in woodland south-west of Paris, reported by his crew who had been rescued by the French Resistance and returned to England weeks later.

Entertainment played a vital role in the lives of the people stationed here, especially as the war wore on, with personal appearances by actors Barry K. Barnes and Diana Churchill[17], and a recital by the famed pianist Shulamith Shafir[18]. A dining hall was converted into a cinema – in July 1945 screenings included Frank Capra's *It Happened One Night* and Powell and Pressburger's *A Canterbury Tale*. *Sex Hygiene,* an information film, was shown for all male personnel, while the women on the base were treated to a lecture on 'Moral Welfare', revealing a nice line in double standards. In the documents I found just two reported cases of gonorrhoea, so somehow the message hit home.

The reports of VE Day, and later VJ Day, were remarkably muted – no parties or parades through Blandford, but what struck me was the education programme, with classes including Maths, French, German, Economics, General Science, History, Woodwork and Domestic Science. Periodicals and newspapers were supplied. These men and women had fought fascism and won, had recently elected a reforming Labour Government and were keen to be educated in preparation for their new world.

I returned to Tarrant Rushton alone. Coming back was distinctly eerie, knowing that this had been no quiet wartime backwater, but teeming with life. I also wanted to find physical signs of its post-war afterlife. In August 1946, the planes and remaining personnel were relocated to other airfields. This was always part of the plan – the logbooks had mentioned several visits from a Mr Guyatt, a horticultural advisor, who came to consider possible cultivation of the site beyond the perimeter road, even in the hectic weeks leading up to D-Day. I imagined this enigmatic figure, in baggy tweeds with a pipe stuck into a top pocket, poking around the soil, while Halifax bombers lumbered along the runways behind him.

But the peace didn't last. In 1948 the airfield became a base for flight refuelling and played a major part in the Berlin airlift. A decade later a new world order embedded itself at Tarrant Rushton: for seven years the airfield was a dispersal point for bombers armed with nuclear warheads. The runways were strengthened to accommodate the V Bombers and their payload. These planes had waited for their signal, crouching on hard-standing areas on the edge of the perimeter road, which I found to be broken concrete bays, anonymous crumbling relics of the Cold War.

Beyond where the squat control tower had stood at the eastern end of the airfield was the main entrance, now a simple five bar gate. The old hangar was full of retired double-decker Routemaster

buses, their purpose unclear. Nearby was a brass plaque screwed onto a rough slab of stone, commemorating those who were based here, unveiled in June 1982, two years after the airfield's last closure and the return of the land to agriculture, Mr. Guyatt's final victory. The austere memorial stone was incapable of reflecting the struggles, ambitions and pain of the servicemen and women who lived here. But it was surrounded by little offerings of flowers and plastic poppies in vases and jars. These gifts, together with the logbooks, were a more fitting testament to those who worked, fought, studied, danced and sometimes died while stationed on the hill above the Tarrant valley.

IMITATIONS OF WIMBORNE

Anthony Ettricke was a half and half man. Antiquary and judge, he swore that he would neither be buried in a churchyard nor a church, so he ended up as The Man in the Wall. I found his brightly painted sarcophagus emblazoned with his heraldic shields in a niche in the wall of the Minster at Wimborne, not in the church exactly, nor out. He was obsessed with the supposedly magical properties of the year 1691, a year that if turned upside down would also read 1691, and became convinced this would be the year of his death, even having it etched on his tomb. Unfortunately he survived until 1703. Crouching I could see that some crude attempts had been made at altering the date, although I wondered if in the intervening years, there might have been some restoration to reveal the original date. After all, it's a good story.

Wimborne Minster is a curious, compelling building in a compact, attractive town. Almost every writer I had come across loved Wimborne, its architecture and atmosphere, with the exception of Frederick Treves, who laid into it with some ferocity, writing that it was "characterless", "commonplace", that it was "successfully mediocre" and that it "looks its best when viewed from a distance." But he allowed that the Minster was magnificent. From the outside my impression of the building was long, low, two-towered, made from two shades of stone, as if a child had got hold of a LEGO set with two colours: grey and brown.

Inside, it was a different story altogether, a deeply impressive building from the ages. There's a vague association with the Roman, but the real origin of the Minster is Saxon, when it was founded by Cuthburh, a sister to King Ine of Wessex, as a monastery for both sexes, strictly segregated. The site was well chosen, where the Rivers Allen and Stour met, and the monastery prospered. Cuthburh's tomb was one of the most venerated in Saxon England and

Wimborne attracted many religious relics:

1. Piece of the true cross (one)
2. Straw from Jesus' manger (some)
3. Earth from aforementioned manger (a handful)
4. Hairs of Jesus' beard (quantity unknown)
5. Thigh bone of Saint Agatha (portion thereof)
6. Tooth of Saint Philip (one)
7. Thomas à Becket's hair shirt (one, previously worn)
8. Thomas à Becket's blood (some drops)
9. Cuthburh's head (condition unknown)

The author of the *King's England* books, Arthur Mee, never more than a paragraph or two away from patriotic whimsy, wrote in his 1939 *Dorset* book about King Alfred and Wimborne: "We must think of him on this very spot with a prayer in his heart that he might be a true King of England." This would take some imagination: almost all the Saxon church is gone. Alfred's sworn enemies, the Danes, destroyed the monastery in 1013 and strangely, all the relics are now lost.

The Minster was rebuilt. The collision of the Romanesque and Gothic created a glorious chaos; the wooden roof was painted brightly, as was the astronomical clock under the west tower. Wimborne avoided taking sides in the Civil War somehow, and so the Minster escaped war's depredations, but fifty years later the spire fell down anyway.

The Minster's chief glory is its chained library, above the vestry. It was donated by a principal of an Oxford college in the late seventeenth century, for use by the town's citizens, which seems like a noble endeavour, although the citizens were clearly not to be trusted or the volumes would not have been shackled. Some of the books were important and valuable – the oldest was *The Direction of Souls*, dating from 1343. Wimborne's general population weren't the major hazard for the library – a copy of Sir Walter Raleigh's *History of the World* was damaged by burning, probably while under repair, and later patched up. All this was invisible – every time I have visited the Minster the library has been closed, despite the donor's original intention. You can't be too careful. Instead a wide-screen television played a DVD explaining its hidden treasures.

An organist was bashing out a discordant, distracting tune, like the crescendo to a Hammer House of Horror movie, suitable for Ettricke's tomb, less so for the lone woman in a woolly hat kneeling in silent prayer at an altar rail in a side chapel, shopping trolley at her side.

Outside the town was busy, café tables spread across part of the main square. The town had a sense of being prosperous without ostentation, modern Wimborne at ease with itself. This impression concealed a lively past: in 1910 the square was the scene of the declaration of three parliamentary results in January, June and December, marred by violence, intimidation, and accusations of bribery. But while the Wimborne men were arguing amongst themselves, eight years before any other of her sex were permitted, one Eleanor Dixon cast her ballot and had her vote counted: an accident of the electoral register, but one that was honoured.[19]

Wimborne's history is long and storied, but there's one corner of the town that is forever the 1950s. Just a short walk from the town centre was Wimborne Model Town. I had to pay to get past the turnstile which, given that the *real* Wimborne is close, free to enter and much bigger, might be thought strange. But the volunteer who sold me the ticket was friendly and knowledgeable, told me the best way to walk round the tiny town and thrust leaflets into my hand.

Wimborne Model Town was conceived in what appears to have been a post-war boom in miniaturisation, at least in southern England, joining many other tiny towns and villages. Was this an overly literal result of a sense of Britain's declining status on the world stage, or an attempt at control, of keeping everything where

you could see it? Wimborne's model town was built in the early
1950s, and it's stayed that way. Initially hugely popular it also drew
snobbery – the *Shell Guide* called it "grotesque", but like other
visitor attractions in the 1970s and 80s it suffered at the hands of
the new generation of theme parks which offered a whole day's
entertainment.[20] It closed in 1983, but a group of volunteers
rescued the buildings and found a new site for it, where it re-opened
in 1991.

It was great. Wimborne was made perfectly small, the street
layout identical to its authentic self. I took some pleasure in
retracing my steps in miniature. The stone was a little too grey, the
illusion broken by an occasional real-world pigeon or child, but it
was beautifully done. The volunteer had said that they had recently
been complimented on the accuracy of the model by a visiting
surveyor. The Minster, despite being one tenth the size of its
inspiration, appeared to tower over me more than the original had.
Peeking inside I could see a sparsely attended wedding taking place,
the piped organ music soft and sweet, in contrast to the thundering
from the real Minster. There was a bookshop, although not where
Wimborne's bookshop is now; the full-size version is named
Gulliver's, not after Jonathan Swift's adventurer, but for Isaac
Gulliver, the smuggler who ran a contraband racket all over Dorset,
before following every gangster's dream and retiring into
respectable obscurity[21] – I'd found a slab commemorating him in
the Minster tower. But still I enjoyed my Lilliputian wandering –
some of the model town's windows were lit and I could look in on
small domestic scenes. Above a replica of a branch of the defunct

fishmonger's MacFisheries was a candlelit dining table, a doll lolling drunkenly in the corner, making me an uncomfortable voyeur.

The model town had its own model town. Had it been accurately placed the smaller model would have been, I thought, somewhere in the perimeter hedge of the larger model, but the mis-location was all to the good – otherwise this new, smaller model would eventually have its own model, and so on. The new version was 3D printed and slightly disappointing; it was too easily overwhelmed by autumn leaf-fall and I couldn't walk its tiny streets like a giant. But thrillingly, from one vantage point I could just see all three sets of the Minster towers, small to large, close and far away.

THE LAST OF CANFORD

Getting a grip on my usual scale I walked out of town and crossed the sluggishly meandering Stour. The signs ahead welcomed me to the Borough of Poole, but I plunged off, following a footpath along the riverside, passing a grand-looking gatehouse. The path was shady and quiet, and the traffic noise began to recede. Suddenly and startlingly a lonely, ornate stone bridge arched over, half lost in bramble and buddleia. I climbed the steps to its left and found that the path over it led nowhere. This was the 'Lady Wimborne Bridge', constructed to carry the railway to Wimborne, and possibly designed by Charles Barry who also remodelled the stately pile of Canford Magna at the same time. It's sometimes been thought that

the bridge was a symbol of the power of the aristocracy in the nineteenth century who could even dictate the design of bridges running over their land, but it was more likely a compromise – the landed gentry making the best of a bad job by constructing a carriage-drive in which the bridge might, in a certain light and provided no dirty steam locomotive was running across it at the time, enhance the landscape. The railway is long gone, and so are the aristocrats, here at least.

I could tell I was approaching a public school – all the signs were there: two teenage girls in hockey tops talking into their fingers, their bikes at the riverbank, grossly strain-faced boys rowing past at speed, the boathouse, the Private Property signs.

The footpath led over a very narrow footbridge which bounced with each step, taking me to the far riverbank safely out of sight of the school which was hidden by high trees. Glimpses of the tower gave an impression of Molesworth's St Custards,[22] but Canford is no minor public school. Its pupils have included the novelist Alan Hollinghurst, the osteopath at the centre of the Profumo affair, Stephen Ward, and the film-maker Derek Jarman.[23] In the last part of *Jubilee,* Jarman's 1978 punk-rock movie, some of the cast leave war-torn London for a Dorset run by a totalitarian regime where the border guard shouts that "Jews, Negroes and Homosexuals" are banned. In the closing scene, as it fades to black, Elizabeth I, played by Jenny Runacre, accompanied by her court astronomer John Dee (Richard O'Brien), walks along the coast close to the quarries at Winspit.[24] Jarman would have known the Purbeck cliffs from his Dorset schooldays – he called his memoir *Dancing Ledge,*[25] the name of a flat area of rock about two miles from Winspit where a tidal pool was dynamited to create a safe place for school-children to swim.

Canford School, screened from view as it was, was still obviously wealthy. Some of this opulence comes from an unlikely source. In the nineteenth century, before the school, Canford Manor's owner Sir John Guest, who had the house remodelled and the extravagant railway bridge built, was given an ancient Iraqi frieze, dating from around 860 BCE. It had been excavated from the palace of the Assyrian king Ashurnasirpal II by a British archaeologist, and Guest incorporated it into a wall in his newly renovated English home. For many years it was assumed to be a copy and the school paid it little attention, even allowing a dartboard to be hung nearby. But when auctioned at Christie's in 1994, it fetched over £7 million. The buyer was an obscure Japanese art collector, the school spent the money on 'sports facilities'.

Jarman, always an eagle-eyed and curious cultural shoplifter would have found this piece of colonialism noteworthy, Hollinghurst would too – but I thought that Stephen Ward, much-maligned though he was and hounded to death, might simply have pocketed some of the cash himself.

CERNE ABBAS: THE MYSTERY OF THE GIANT

David's lallies[26] were on display, even though it was mid-September. My friend is Scottish, and the southern warmth had clearly overwhelmed him, his legs drawing admiring glances in Cerne Abbas. Helen and I were more demurely dressed, but anonymity is not David's way.

Cerne sits almost exactly in the middle of Dorset, in the shadow of the line of hills that divides the county between the flatter north and more rolling south, an unashamedly pretty town with an appealing mix of architecture. Beyond St Mary's church we found a metal gate which led us to a private garden, in the middle of which was a lone gatehouse. This was the sole recognisable remnant of the Benedictine abbey. Setting off to explore it we were accosted by a woman, striding over from the large house. She was the owner of the gardens and what's left of the abbey, and she was in fine form.

"Hello, hello! I just wanted to come over and say how welcome you are here, and please DO take photographs. All I ask is that you pop some change in the honesty box at the gate if you enjoy yourselves."

We told her had done so already.

"Marvellous, marvellous. I'm very pleased with myself today. Look at this."

She did a neat twirl on the gravel, showing off her black double-breasted jacket, buttoned up, a few stray dog hairs on its back.

"I had this when I was a Navy Wren, forty years ago, and I can still get it on. Now, let me take your photograph."

She took Helen's camera, held it unsteadily and took a remarkably good photograph of us, but cut off David's legs.

The gatehouse was three storeys high, latticed windows above, little sections of crumbling stone wall clinging to it, hinting at the wider vanished abbey. Inside the archway was a spyhole for the monks to keep an eye on those who came and went. Beyond the adjacent graveyard was St Augustine's Well. It was undeniably convenient that Augustine of Canterbury[27] was rumoured to have visited and created the spring after meeting a group of thirsty shepherds, helping to drum up pilgrim trade. The trees surrounding the spring were hung with ribbons and messages for those who had died recently, its significance to local people undimmed. Beyond the graveyard all that remained of the once pre-dominant abbey was a series of irregular earthworks.

Why devoted monks,[28] dedicated to a Christian God, would permit an enormous chalk figure of a man with an outsized erect penis and wielding a club to remain on the hillside immediately above the abbey is a mystery. We trudged up the steep slope through woodland to the famous Giant, fenced off by the National Trust. From the hillside we could make out the deep-cut gullies of his body, but not the overall shape which would be much better seen from the viewpoint across the valley. Still, he was impressive. In his *Dorset* book Arthur Mee described him in detail: "He equals thirty tall men, standing one on the other, each of his fingers measures seven feet, and the club in his hand is forty yards long" but managed to omit any mention of his member, calling the Giant "very ugly". Sir Frederick Treves had also avoided the intimate but noted the figure had of late been neglected. Even as late as the Second World War he was a controversial figure – a letter to a local paper claimed the Giant was "a disgrace and should be destroyed". This wasn't a universal view – the writer Eardley Knollys, in a letter to his lover written around the same time, reported with some relish that he had "strolled up and down his cock".

A tendency to look the other way might have led, quite inadvertently, to his most notable feature gaining length. The Victorians, fearing for the morals of the townspeople, allowed the Giant to grass over, and when the Edwardians cleaned him up it appears they mistook his belly-button for the end of the phallus and therefore extended it. We laboured up the slope and around the figure, watching a hen harrier hover over us, barely a wing beat in the wind.

But what is the Giant? Where did he spring from, and when? Speculations are rife. He might be a figure of Hercules[29] and Romano-British, or he might be older still. This deep history theory is appealing – women wanting to become pregnant, including one of my friends, have taken to sitting on the end of the Giant's penis in the hope that ancient Gods might intervene. In 1958 the 6th Marquess of Bath and his wife Vivian visited and 10 months later gave birth to a daughter, Lady Silvie Cerne Thynne.

It remains unexplained that no-one, not an abbot or local lord, a pilgrim or a traveller, mentioned him in writing before 1694, when the parish wardens reported that three shillings was paid to repair "ye Giant". And it's not as if the place had been short of visitors. As the historian Katherine Barker[30] pointed out to me, John Leland, Henry VIII's antiquarian, no slouch when it came to recording the kingdom, and who visited Cerne Abbas, failed to mention Ye Giant in his extensive writings.[31]

Another theory emerged – that the figure was a seventeenth century caricature – its target being Oliver Cromwell, rampaging malevolently through the countryside, and explaining the giant's late arrival in the written record. From the breezy hillside we could see that this was no artful representation of a revered icon, but instead a monster. The spirit of resistance to the armies of both sides in the English Civil War was alive in Dorset, epitomised by the rise of The Clubmen – and the Giant might have been a potent symbol.[32]

In 1996 Katherine Barker held a day of debate in Cerne Abbas to settle the matter: the audience were asked to vote before and after the debate on the Giant's age. She spoke in favour of the seventeenth century theory. "At the start of the day," she told me, "he was overwhelmingly ancient. At the end of the day he was still ancient, but only just."

Both David and Helen are kind about my obsession with Dorset but decided that a few hours in a Cerne Abbas pub would beat my proposal of a longer walk so I pressed on alone, snatching a handful of blackberries from a bush for sustenance, and setting off north.

The National Trust owns the hillside around the Giant, but the wider landscape is Digby land, their family seat being at Minterne Magna. They've allowed some playfulness on the hill near the Giant – in 1997 Katherine Barker persuaded Lord Digby to use the land adjacent as a site for her students to build a temporary Giantess, a companion for the Giant, which they taped out on the ground, a neat riposte to his aggressive masculinity. Ten years later permission was given again, this time to use the hillside as a huge advertising board to promote the *Simpsons Movie*. Homer Simpson was painted alongside the older figure, preparing to hurl a doughnut at the Giant's erection. Ann Bryn-Evans, the district manager for the Pagan Federation, was most upset at the indignity visited on the chalk figure and promised some "rain magic" to wash away the biodegradable paint from which Homer was made.[33]

The Digby family house looked impressive and ancient, but in fact was built only in 1904. I muddled my way down the hill past the house, until I reached the road and St Andrew's church, full of outsized memorials to the Churchill and Marlborough families, and it all felt a long way from Springfield.

Crossing the road I sat by the side of a track to eat a squashed cheese sandwich before walking south along the Wessex Ridgeway with only a few late swallows and a clattering tractor in a nearby field for company. For much of the walk back the Giant dominated the valley, peeking out through woodland or rounded hilltops, brandishing his club, his expression one of perpetual surprise.

Finally, regaining the main road and passing the Casterbridge Care Home,[34] once Cerne Abbas' workhouse, demonstrating how large the town had been, and how needy its poor, I came to the little car park at the top of Duck Street, the best place to see the Giant. A few people were reading the information signs, a couple vaped on a nearby bench and gazed at the Giant's muscular form. Helen and David, refreshed, joined me.

In 2020 archaeologists undertook soil sampling work, scooping out the deposits of chalk around the Giant's feet and elbows to find the earliest samples. The lead archaeologist Martin Papworth spoke to me on the phone about the process and the results. Like Katherine Barker, he had been an advocate of the seventeenth century. To his astonishment he discovered he was wrong, but so too were those who argued for an older Giant. The oldest sediments revealed that the Giant was Saxon, probably created around the year 800 CE. Martin thought that the Giant had simply faded away without regular scouring, but that one winter's day centuries later, as the low sunlight struck the hill, his form became briefly and dimly visible. Standing in the car park, Helen, David and I considered what this moment of revelation would have been like, when two seventeenth century farm workers first saw the figure:

> Seth: Here, Reuben, take a look at Trendle Hill[35], why don't you?
> Reuben: God's Teeth! What is it?
> Seth: Well, it looks like a massive cock, don't it?

Even given this new research, the debate rumbles on. Katherine told me she was unsure, still favouring the seventeenth century. And controversy follows him still – in 2015 Eco Comics were forced to re-issue a cartoon featuring the giant, wearing a large pair of pants after objections to his nudity. I wondered if he could have been many things – a Saxon figure, inspired by Hercules, lost and found, given a new significance as Cromwell, looking again for purpose on his hillside. Maybe artists had it right. Eric Ravilious painted the Giant in 1940, a mystical echo of his painting of that other chalk figure, The Long Man of Wilmington, but starker, as well as starkers, on his hillside, all energy, all life. Jeremy Deller, the Turner Prize-winning artist who has explored the countryside in the context of 1990s rave culture, rendered the figure in dazzling acid-pink neon.

The controversy about his origin only makes him more powerful – let him be a Cromwellian lampoon, a symbol of our rebellion, a Roman God out of place, a Saxon mystery, mystical figure or raver. Let him grass over and grow back again. He can be whatever Dorset needs him to be, but most of all, let him be ours.

For centuries the town decayed, missing out on the railway, which was routed through the next valley, but today Cerne is a

thriving large village. Residents know the Giant is important for reasons beyond the mystical. The landlord of the New Inn[36] told me the chalk figure was the reason that people came here; we found a shop opposite the pub selling aprons with the Giant's figure on – for an extra £2, you can buy a pair of multicoloured shorts to cover his manhood to avoid offending dinner guests or readers of American comics. We decided against the purchase, although it would have set off David's lallies very well.

WITH ELISABETH FRINK AND NEIL ON BULBARROW

I had not seen my oldest friend Neil since the day of my mother's funeral, six years previously, and as we clambered from his car with his ancient dog at the church in Woolland, we had much to talk about. Neil was fundamentally unchanged – grey now and bearded, but the same voice as I remembered from our teenage years, connecting me immediately to a past I had tucked away. We began to climb a long and steep narrow lane, which shimmered with unexpected rain.

Bulbarrow, named for its barrows and burial mounds, is part of the spine of chalk hills extending towards Purbeck. It was once a beacon, nearby Rawlsbury Camp is an Iron Age hillfort, but more recently the Christians got here too – erecting a large wooden cross overlooking the Dorsetshire Gap, where a dip in the hills allows the cyclist or walker to pass from north to south without effort.[37]

Neil had recently and finally sold the business he had spent his working life nurturing: he and his wife, Kate, were on the brink of moving house, and had successfully narrowed down their search area to most of the British Isles. They wanted to move from South East England's commuter belt, a place they felt no real connection with.

At the top of Bulbarrow, puffing slightly from the climb, we stopped. Guidebooks exhort us to 'take in' the view and suddenly the idea of letting the land below seep into us was completely appropriate. As the morning mist cleared, the sense of space and peace silenced us. A jay, that most charismatic corvid, flapped over to a small oak copse. We were not the first to find something special in Bulbarrow's unexpected majesty. Frederick Treves, overcome by the view more than a century ago described it in detail:

> For miles there stretches a waving valley of green fields, with trees in lines, in knolls, in avenues, in dots; a red roof, the glitter of a trout stream, the trail of a white road, and at the end, blue-grey hills so far away that they seem to be made of a sea mist.

Its appeal wasn't limited to long-dead Edwardian writers, but extended also to John Peel's indie-rock darlings, Half Man Half Biscuit, who in their song 'Third Camera Main Track Four Minutes' sang in their Wirral-inflected deadpan:

> Oh, he shouldn't have gone to Cuba
> He should have just gone down to Dorset
> With its wonderful Bulbarrow hill[38]

I once cycled up the long road running from Winterborne Stickland to Bulbarrow's peak,[39] and was made more breathless still by the startling view. As I gazed out, my legs still wobbly, I was approached by a man, probably in his seventies. He had spent his adult life in Essex, but a Dorset accent was strong in his throat. He was returning for what he hinted was a final time. His eyes misty with recollection and emotion he told me that he'd come up here as a boy, riding pillion on a friend's motorbike – "oh, that lad," he said, his voice falling, making me wonder if the friendship was something more. Bulbarrow is a good place to come with a friend.

Neil is a military history enthusiast: on one occasion, on a walk near army ranges, he once came across a spent shell ("just a 25 pounder") which he stuffed in his rucksack and now sits on his desk. We walked under two huge masts, which dominated the landscape across the Vale. The site was no longer military, but these sentinels had wooden predecessors, built in 1942 as part of a network of stations, guiding bombers to their targets. A little further along the lane, now overgrown with brambles, were redbrick ruins, remnants of the wider base.[40]

A footpath which led into open country on the south side of the hill opened a new landscape of flint-studded stubble fields, a deep coomb slicing into the earth. A farmer, skilfully gathering in his sheep from behind the wheel of a 4x4, redirected us to the footpath from which we had strayed. The contrast between the land here and the Vale to the north was striking. John Aubrey, the seventeenth century writer and antiquary had divided southern England into two types: chalk and cheese. Chalk dwellers were shepherds: hardworking and strong, but he wrote that those in the "dirty clayey country" where "they only milk the cowes and make cheese...their persons are generally plump and feggy." Aubrey went to school, briefly, in nearby Blandford Forum, so he may have had some

first-hand experience of Dorset's relative body shapes. This open, empty land reminded Neil of a trip to the battlefield of Waterloo. He described standing there, his amazement at its scale.

"You can see it all from one single vantage point – the whole battlefield," he said. "It was so small but that's where the history of Europe was decided."

Dodging nothing more deadly than sheep we descended the deep coomb and picked our way through lumpy ground of thistle and bramble. The Ancient Dog, a German Pointer of equable temperament, had recently had surgery on her back legs, leaving her with a Charlie Chaplin waddle, and could no longer hop even small obstacles so the series of stiles we met were overcome by Neil gently lifting and dropping her over, or managed with an ungainly pass-the-dog game between us. It was with relief that we recovered the higher road and the drop through the ferny holloway of Baker's Folly towards the Blackmore Vale, back to the cows and the clay, and Treves' happy valley.

Ibberton, right on the junction of clay and chalk, clung to the hillside – its church, dedicated to St Eustace, patron saint of hunters, was abandoned following landslips in the nineteenth century but was restored in the twentieth, although its walls still bow. We walked back to Woolland along the road and encountered the remains of a morning's hunt – stray riders trotting, followers starting cars in improvised muddy laybys. In part it was country sports which brought an artist here in the 1970s.

Alex Csáky was a Hungarian businessman who had spent his

schooldays in the English countryside, at Clayesmore School, and decided to return to enjoy country pursuits. In the mid-1970s he and his wife, the sculptor Elisabeth Frink, bought Woolland House. Frink too was keen to return to Dorset, having spent time in childhood at Bovington Camp. The original eighteenth century house in Woolland had been knocked down in the 1960s, leaving only the stable block, which was derelict on their arrival. Here Frink was to spend the rest of her life, working first in the old schoolhouse opposite the church and then later in a studio built at Woolland House[41].

If the empty chalk-scapes to the south of Bulbarrow had reminded Neil of Waterloo and the great strategic battles for Europe, here under the hill, above the tangled chessboard of fields to the north, Frink battled with the human pain of war. Her childhood memories included seeing planes on fire returning from missions near her Suffolk home, and once, at school in Devon, she had been strafed by a German fighter. Her elemental work of animals and men was often informed by war and its threat, and by the death camp at Belsen, from which she created new myths and fables. Although sometimes at odds with the fashions of pop-art and European modernism, she counted amongst her friends Francis Bacon and Lucien Freud. Quentin Crisp sat for her, George Melly collected her work and today she is regarded as one of the most important British artists of the twentieth century.[42]

Neil and I and the Ancient Dog passed the gateway to her house, before entering the small church nearby. Unmistakeably Victorian, with dark stained glass of weeping saints around the polygonal apse, it was made from materials from an earlier church on the same site, and designed by Sir George Gilbert Scott, responsible also for the Albert Memorial and St Pancras Station. He held back from his full-blown vampiric excess in this parish church, so modest that no saint bears its name. Scott also designed, along with his son, who was also named George, the church at Cattistock in West Dorset. Tragically the younger George, troubled and plagued by alcoholism, died in his father's creation, St Pancras Hotel, in 1897.

We emerged into the autumn light, the air now clear, and bundled the Ancient Dog into the boot of Neil's estate car, pulling away from the steep slopes of Bulbarrow, where the abandoned military installation mouldered into the hilltop and a sculptor made her living and her reputation from the shadow of war.

BINGHAM'S MELCOMBE, MELCOMBE HORSEY, MELCOMBE BINGHAM

Spreading out the Ordnance Survey map across the roof of my car parked in the village of Ansty I could see some village names in Dorset's heart written in the Gothic script that signified absence: phantom settlements. I was keen to find them or what remained of them. Walking across a cattle-churned field and through beech woodland I came to a wide avenue of trees leading to the grand, isolated house at Bingham's Melcombe. The sign on the gate was clear – I was welcome to walk the avenue but should keep away from the gardens and house, definitely still privately owned. I marvelled anyway at the huge evergreen hedge which overhung the bowling green on the other side of the precariously leaning wall, a scene reminiscent of David Inshaw's painting *The Badminton Game*.

At the front of the house was the small square-towered church of St Andrew's. I'd arrived in time to find the fag end of a funeral, a few dark-clad mourners straggling from the house to their cars. The graveyard had another forbidding sign: 'No Dogs' but this applied only to canines still with us. The shady burial area in the churchyard set aside for beloved pets (bending down I read one tombstone: "Hugo 1948-1960, and in memory of his friend Treasure") made me wonder if this was a private chapel for the big house; actually it was the orphan of an earlier settlement. Beyond a freshly-dug grave heaped with flowers I clambered onto the churchyard's compost heap and peeked over the hedge – beneath the lumpy field beyond, lit with low sun, lay the medieval village of Bingham's Melcombe, abandoned sometime before the end of the fifteenth century. The trees dotted across the site cast shadows like sentries but there was little to see here – the best view would be from above; the work of recreating Bingham's Melcombe lay mostly in the imagination.[43] Vanishings were not confined to the village. The Bingham family lived in the house for six centuries before selling up in 1980, one notable family member being the 7th Earl, better known as Lord Lucan.

Leaving the lost village behind, crossing a small bridge by the fishpond, I walked a track that led into a steep holloway, hart's tongue ferns licking at the chalky path. My day was dry, in wet weather this would soon run with slippery rivulets. As I reached the top, another solitary walker, no dog in tow, walked past me, red raincoat zipped up, ignoring me precisely. I followed him before he slipped over a gate heading north towards the village of Hilton, putting ground between us and soon out of sight. I came down to the watery hamlet of Aller, where brooks ran under the road and ponds abounded. I passed a caravan, painted wittily in half-timbering, and a group of chickens pecking at a huge pumpkin left out for them.

It was growing darker by the minute. Constantly calculating and recalculating the time I pressed on into a wide valley west of Ansty. Frederick Treves, in a dour mood, described the land here as "work-a-day, austere, and bare, seamed by the plough and scraped

by the harrow, a haunt of the wind-driven sea-gull in winter, a sober, puritan country." He was right, I felt exposed, visible. Suddenly, across a field of bare stalks in the gathering gloom I saw the man again, his red anorak stark against a copse – he couldn't have walked here so soon, but there he was, the Other Man, ahead still and striding.[44] At the end of a long private track I came across an assemblage of farm buildings, empty but clearly still in use, a bull watching me from his solitary field, a single house with a chapel incorporated into its structure. The field opposite was lumped and bumped, another lost village – Melcombe Horsey. The two settlements – Horsey and Bingham's – were linked from Domesday onwards, impossible to disentangle in documents, and both abandoned at around the same time. Not far from here was the Dorsetshire Gap, where five ancient trackways meet, but going on would invite only darkness. There was spook in this gloom, broken by four teenage girls, riding ponies, laughing and taking selfies, their humanity shaking me from nervy retrospection.

I retreated through modern Melcombe Bingham, a village very much alive and a collection of the ages, the thatched and the bungalowed, one of the latter named 'Shangri-La', after the mystical, fictional valley. It was tempting to sneer but having walked the new puritan landscape to the west, I found comfort in these familiars.

MILTON ABBAS

Visit Milton Abbas, the rural idyll… Longing to stay in a chocolate box hideaway, nestled in beautiful countryside with a welcoming pub on the doorstep? *Visit Dorset website*

It was a hot year, a ladybird summer, and as I cycled down the road from Bulbarrow into Hilton from Treves' puritan landscape I rode straight into a hovering cloud of the little insects, tiny jewels on the wing. Several attached themselves to my jersey, hitching for half a mile or so. The narrow road swept left and right, demanding my concentration but when I did look up I immediately pulled sharply on my brakes, astonished. Ahead of me, in this wide valley, was half a cathedral. Crouched next to it obsequiously was a long, low stately home. And around these two uncomfortably juxtaposed buildings was nothing except level lawn. It was hugely impressive, horribly arrogant. Arthur Mee, author of the *King's England* books, had a near-fainting fit of ecstatic aesthetic pleasure here which went on for several interminable sentences ("enthroned like a joy for ever on the green lawns"[45]), but even allowing for his liberal use of the thesaurus, I could see he had a point.

Meet anyone from outside Dorset who has a passing knowledge of the county and within a few minutes they'll tell you that Dorset has no motorways. Why this statistic is worthy of note is baffling. You may as well point out that Leicestershire is a bit light on coastline. It's much more interesting that Dorset has no cathedrals any more. That's been outsourced to Salisbury, in Wiltshire. But the county did have abbeys: rich and powerful – Shaftesbury, Cerne, Sherborne and the building before me: Milton Abbas.

Milton Abbas was founded by the Saxon king Athelstan in the

tenth century, having apparently had a dream here about defeating the Danes in battle. The building burnt in the fourteenth century and was rebuilt, mostly. Our medieval forebears never got round to the Nave so at the time of the Dissolution, there were few monks and the impressive but strangely truncated building. At the tail end of the eighteenth century Joseph Damer, 1st Baron Milton, a Whig MP for Weymouth, had his new home built adjoining the old abbey building. The landscape, the woods, the long views were all stage-managed, created by Capability Brown at Damer's behest.[46] The landscape was huge but also strangely familiar, a needling at my memory.

My childhood Sunday evenings were dominated by television serials adapted from best-selling or classic novels. I associate them still with that end of the weekend torpor, of lingering vague headaches. One programme which my mother especially enjoyed was *To Serve Them All My Days*, partly because she had taken a fancy to the lead actor, John Duttine. Based on R.F. Delderfield's novel, the lead character, played by Duttine, returns from the First World War to teach at a public school. He's a fish out of water, a young Welsh socialist damaged by his experience in the trenches, working in the epitome of the English class system. He falls in love a few times, there's triumph, tragedy, and a gloriously beautiful set. In one episode an aged teacher falls slowly asleep and dies while watching a game of cricket on a summer's day in a deckchair in the shade. The series was filmed at Milton Abbey, itself a public school by then, and its beauty was one of the chief attractions of the series, Duttine aside.[47] But it wasn't always so peaceful here.

Abbeys were both economic and spiritual centres, and in the centuries after Athelstan a town grew up around the building. Damer found his new mansion surrounded by houses, trade and people, although this cannot have been much of a surprise. Once described by Horace Walpole as "the most arrogant and proud of men", he took exception to the sight, sound and smells of the press of humanity and so simply had the town demolished, drowning some of it in his new ornamental lake.

I left my bike by the roadside, finding a footpath that led into steep wooded hillside and soon, in a clearing, came across a low chapel, St Catherine's, from which, far below was the abbey building, perfectly aligned. The chapel was connected to the lawn around the old abbey by a huge turf staircase, stomping across a bridge over the road to a set of locked iron gates.

Back on my bike I found the new village of Milton Abbas just half a mile away in a narrow coomb, above Damer's ornamental lake. From the bottom of the hill the village was the essence of the Picturesque. On each side of its single road were deep, uniform lawns, a series of identical white, thatched cottages, every front door placed symmetrically in the centre. The church, St James,[48] sat complacently in the middle of one row of the cottages, while the Hambro Arms kept a respectful distance further up the road. An idealised village, tucked away in a sleepy green English fold, safe and timeless.

When Damer knocked down the old town, he had his architect construct the new village out of sight and earshot of his grand home. This was no philanthropic venture to give the poor better homes – it's possible that he made new homes for his estate workers only and many of the old townspeople were forced to leave. It was a sham too – each neat square house contained two cottages, and some are thought to have housed more than thirty people. These days it's been settled by the middle classes, but even now seems a little unsatisfactory, property agents reporting that the houses come on to the market more often than you might imagine.[49] I cycled up the hill, past the pub where summer drinkers were enjoying the view and after the perfect village fizzled out and the trees crowded over, turned left. Here, unphotographed and left out of magazine supplements was the real Milton Abbas, a collection of post-war houses, a playground and recycling bins. There was no room for any of these necessities in Damer's vision, but unremarkable though it was, it served its residents better than the superficial prettiness of the village below, just as the original town once had. Give me the new Milton Abbas, the Shangri-Las of Melcombe Bingham, or leave us with the haunted fields of the deserted villages, but spare us the follies of aristocrats.

Notes

1 For more on Counter Tourism see Phil Smith's book *The Counter Tourism Handbook*. Andy and Liberty make video diaries of their work, which can be found at videostrolls.com/

2 This is a lot of sheep: today there are around 30 million sheep in the whole of the UK.

3 For more on Wedderburn's life see *Dorset's Hidden Histories* by Louisa Adjoa Parker, DEED, 2007, pp 44-45, and this article in the *Church Times* on the legacy of slavery: www.churchtimes.co.uk/articles/2021/3-december/features/features/faith-and-identity-sketches-of-heavenly-things. One of Wedderburn's direct descendants was the Labour peer Bill Wedderburn.

4 Dorset has tended to return Conservative MPs, especially recently. An exception was 1945

when north Dorset elected a Liberal, but only because the Labour Party did not field a candidate.

5   I know this reference is peak 2022 but I can only work with the culture I have to hand.

6   For a more balanced view of Poundbury and a spirited defence of it by its charming architect, see *The Guardian*, 27 October 2016 www.theguardian.com/artanddesign/2016/oct/27/poundbury-prince-charles-village-dorset-disneyland-growing-community

7   See the Christchurch section of this book.

8   The 1834 Great Reform Act largely settled this, for a few years.

9   There are a number of these signs dotted across the county's bridges, signed by "The court, T Fooks". Dorset is not the only county to have these signs – there are a few in Wiltshire I hear – but most of them are here. I can only surmise that the rural rebellion in a county where the labourers were paid so poorly was especially feared by the ruling classes.

10 *Buildings of England, Dorset* by John Newman and Nikolaus Pevsner, Penguin, 1972, Yale, 2002, p 96; *Dorset the Complete Guide* by Jo Draper, Dovecote Press, 1986, 1996; *Dorset, a Shell Guide* by Michael Pitt-Rivers, Faber and Faber, 1965, 1966, p 46.

11 Luckily Dorset also had Benjamin Jesty. See the Yetminster section of this book (West).

12 TikTok was right – see the Lyme Regis section of this book for local news of his later downfall (West).

13 For more on the church see the Churches' Conservation Trust website: www.visit churches.org.uk/visit/church-listing/st-mary-tarrant-crawford.html

14 Frederick Treves notes that this is her burial place, but neglects to mention the gold coffin, which is probably no more than a rumour, perpetuated by me.

15 Get a copy today.

16 His other works include Castle Howard and Blenheim Palace. Today he'd be called a Maximalist.

17 Although she had the same name as the Prime Minister's daughter, this Diana Churchill was a theatre and film actress with a long career, her last role being in an episode of the New Avengers in 1971.

18 She gave many such performances during the war.

19 See *Lost Dorset, The Towns* by David Burnett, The Dovecote Press, 2021, p 210. This excellent book, together with its companion volume covering the villages and countryside, is comprised of many postcards taken from the collection owned by Barry Cuff. On this page the photograph taken in the January election shows many people and cars crowded into Wimborne's square to hear the result read from the balcony of the Kings Head Hotel.

20 For a dramatic example see the section on Tucktonia in the East section of this book.

21 See the smuggling.co.uk website and the South section of this book for more on Isaac's antics.

22 See the excellent series of books by Geoffrey Willans and illustrated by Ronald Searle which follows the misadventures of Nigel Molesworth at a minor public skool, as any fule no.

23 Both Jarman and Ward have a link to Pet Shop Boys, the greatest duo in the history of pop. Jarman directed their 1989 tour, as he recounts in his later diaries *Modern Nature*. Pet Shop Boys also composed the song 'Nothing Has Been Proved', sung by Dusty Springfield, the title track to the film *Scandal* (1989), detailing the Profumo Affair, and Ward's suicide.

24 The whole film can be found on YouTube. The cast includes Adam Ant, the late punk priestess Jordan, The Slits and Toyah Wilcox. The script of the last minutes of the film is in his memoir *Dancing Ledge* ending with the words COME AWAY.

25 *Dancing Ledge* by Derek Jarman. Its foreword, titled 'A Footnote to my Past', written three years before his death, is still affecting today: "I would…survive Margaret Thatcher. I did.

Now I have my sights set on the millennium and a world where we are all equal before the law."

26 Polari for legs. Polari is the underground language used by gay men to escape the notice of the police when homosexual acts were still illegal, and popularised by the characters Julian and Sandy in the 1960s radio comedy *Round the Horne*. David regularly uses "lallies" in place of legs, just for fun.

27 Not to be confused with St Augustine of Hippo, author of *City of God*. More on the evangelist who brought Christianity to much of England on the English Heritage website: www.english-heritage.org.uk/visit/places/st-augustines-abbey/history-and-stories/who-was-st-augustine/

28 Possibly not all were that devout. Henry VIII's dissolution of the monasteries was enabled here by accusations of immorality against the final Abbot, Thomas Corton. See *Cerne Abbas* by A.O. Gibbons, Longmans of Dorchester, 1962, pp 51-52.

29 A fascinating article on the myths of Hercules in Dorset can be found at: the-past.com /feature/the-giants-story-revisited-identifying-the-cerne-abbas-hill-figure-as-the-choice-of -hercules/

30 See The Shire Rack section of this book (North).

31 Leland is largely forgotten although he's sometimes known as the Father of Modern History and crops up often in the Highways and Byways books for whom this corner of history remained relevant. The big problem with Leland is that we don't have all his work so drawing any definite conclusions is problematic. Flatteringly Katherine Barker compared my Dorset wanderings to Leland. He went mad and died young.

32 See the chapter on Hambledon Hill in this book (North).

33 Reported in *The Guardian* 17 July 2007. That Pagans have a 'district manager' is remarkably British. They also seem nice, progressive and thoughtful: www.paganfed.org/category /meet-the-team/

34 Casterbridge is Hardy's name for Dorchester. Like most of Hardy's novels, *The Mayor of Casterbridge* is a tragedy, this one involving the drunken sale of a wife and daughter, and a life of regret. Welcome to the Care Home – enjoy your stay.

35 Trendle Hill is named after the earthwork just above the Giant, where the village once assembled their maypole, and still do, each May Day dawn. It's an excellent, if chilly start to the day – the pubs in the village open early to compensate.

36 Not that new – seventeenth century. The town once had seventeen inns, now just three.

37 See the Knowlton section of this book (North) for more on Christians imposing themselves on the landscape.

38 Find the song on their album *Trouble Over Bridgwater,* (Probe Plus, 2000) and for the lyrics see the sprawling and all-encompassing Half Man Half Biscuit lyrics project website halfmanhalfbiscuit.uk/trouble-over-bridgwater/third-track-main-camera-four-minutes/

39 At the time of writing Google Maps designates Bulbarrow as a Mountain Peak, which is pushing it a bit.

40 More on 'Gee' Stations and their uses can be found on the Secret Bases website, itself hard to find and navigate, but a treasure trove nonetheless: www.secret-bases. co.uk/wiki/Gee_(navigation)

41 Two studios were created at Woolland, but Frink only lived to work in one of them, which was later dismantled and reconstructed in Wiltshire, the other remains at Woolland.

42 A snappy biography of Frink can be found on Christie's website www.christies.com/ features/Collecting-Guide-Elisabeth-Frink-9909-1.aspx) and more on her place in the canon here www.hauserwirth.com/resources/2678-elisabeth-frink- transformation

43 The house, by all accounts, is a wonder, centuries of domestic architecture beautifully preserved; the lost village too, is documented superbly by *An Inventory of the Historical Monuments in Dorset*, Volume 3, Central, HMSO, 1970, pages 161-175, and digitised at

British History Online www.british-history.ac.uk/rchme/dorset/vol3/pp161-175. See also *Lost Villages* by Linda Viner, Dovecote Press, 2002, p 52. The cover has an excellent colour aerial photograph of Bingham's Melcombe.

44 In Edward Thomas' *In Pursuit of Spring,* the author meets another traveller, whom he names The Other Man, at various points in the journey. It's usually assumed to be Thomas' alter ego. My Other Man was very real, I hope.

45 Mee goes on "…enshrined in a landscape that could hardly be surpassed for beauty" and of the village: "the church stands like a monument of the centuries in as rare a piece of country as even an Englishman need wish to see." Englishmen must therefore have a higher standard of "rare country" than other nationalities, but he remains silent on the opinions of Englishwomen. *The King's England, Dorset* by Arthur Mee, Hodder and Stoughton, Revised edition 1967, p 108.

46 The local history group website is exceptionally detailed: miltonabbashistorygroup.com/

47 *To Serve Them All My Days* was adapted by Andrew Davies for the BBC and it was broadcast in thirteen episodes in 1980-1.

48 Probably designed by the ever-busy James Wyatt around 1786, later extended: historicengland.org.uk/listing/the-list/list-entry/1118560

49 They talk it up though, of course www.dorset.live/news/property/milton-abbas-houses-sale-more-5830666

WORKS CONSULTED

Adjoa Parker, Louisa, *Dorset's Hidden Histories – Beginning to Explore Four Hundred Years of the Presence of Black People in Dorset*, DEED, 2007.

Adjoa Parker, Louisa, 1944: *We Were Here: African-American GIs in Dorset*, DEED, 2013.

Allsop, Kenneth, *In the Country*, Hamish Hamilton, 1972, Little Toller Books, 2012.

Amory, Mark, *Lord Berners: The Last Eccentric*, Chatto & Windus 1998, Pimlico 1999.

Baker, Leonard, *Spaces, Places, Custom and Protest in Rural Somerset and Dorset, c. 1780-1867*, PhD thesis, University of Bristol, 2019.

Barker, Katherine, et al, *The Dorset County Boundary Survey*.

Barnes, William, *Selected Poems*, selected by Andrew Motion, Faber and Faber, 2007.

Bickley, Francis, *Where Dorset Meets Devon*, Constable and Co., 1911.

Bird, Eric, *Geology and Scenery of Dorset*, Ex-Libris Press, 1995.

Bond, Lilian, *Tyneham, A Lost Heritage*, 1956, new edition The Dovecote Press, 2012.

Burnett, David, *Dorset Shipwrecks*, The Dovecote Press, 1982.

Burnett, David, *Lost Dorset, The Towns*, The Dovecote Press, 2021.

Burnett, David, *Lost Dorset, The Villages and Countryside*, The Dovecote Press, 2018.

Cochrane, C., *The Lost Roads of Wessex*, David and Charles, 1969, Pan Books, 1972.

Cope, Julian, *The Modern Antiquarian, A Pre-Millenium Odyssey Through Megalithic Britain*, Thorsons, 1998.

Copland-Griffiths, Penny, *Discover Dorset: Pottery*, The Dovecote Press, 1998.

Cox, Benjamin, *The Great Fire of Blandford Forum, 1731*, Blandford Forum Museum Trust, 1987.

Cox, Tom, *Ring the Hill*, Unbound, 2019.

Crocker, Peter, *Around Gillingham, The Second Selection*, Nonsuch Publishing Ltd, 1992, new edition 2007.

Deakin, Roger, *Waterlog, A Swimmer's Journey through Britain*, Chatto and Windus, 1999, Vintage Books, 2000.

Doel, Fran & Doel, Geoff, *Folklore of Dorset*, The History Press, 2007, 2017.

Draper, Jo, *Dorset, The Complete Guide,* The Dovecote Press, 1986, revised edition, 1996.

Draper, Jo, *Discover Dorset: Regency, Riot and Reform,* The Dovecote Press, 2000.

Eagle, Dorothy & Carnell, Hilary, *The Oxford Literary Guide to the British Isles,* Oxford University Press, 1977.

Edwards, Anne-Marie, *Waterside Walks in Dorset,* Countryside Books, 2000.

Eliot, T.S., *The Complete Poems and Plays,* Faber and Faber, 1969, 2004.

Everett-Heath, John, *Concise Dictionary of World Place Names,* Oxford University Press, 2018 (online).

Fenwick, Simon, *The Crichel Boys, Scenes from England's Last Literary Salon,* Little Brown, 2021.

Fiennes, Peter, *Footnotes: A Journey Round Britain in the Company of Great Writers,* Oneworld Publications, 2019.

Fowles, John, *A Short History of Lyme Regis,* The Dovecote Press, 1982.

Gale, John, *Prehistoric Dorset,* Tempus Publishing, 2003.

Gardiner, Juliet, *The Thirties, An Intimate History,* Harper Press, 2010.

Garner, Alan, *Treacle Walker,* Fourth Estate, 2021, 2022.

Good, Ronald, *The Lost Villages of Dorset,* The Dovecote Press, 1979, 1987.

Hardy, Thomas, *Jude the Obscure, Return of the Native, The Mayor of Casterbridge, Tess of the D'Urbevilles, Two on a Tower, Collected Poetry.*

Harris, Alexandra, *Romantic Moderns: English Writers, Artists and the Imagination, from Virginia Woolf to John Piper,* Thames and Hudson, 2010, paperback, 2015.

Harrison, J.F.C., *The Common People, A History from the Norman Conquest to the Present,* Flamingo, 1984.

Harvey, PJ *Orlam,* Picador, 2022.

Harte, Jeremy, *Discover Dorset, Legends,* The Dovecote Press, 1998.

Hawkins, Desmond, *Discover Dorset, Cranborne Chase,* The Dovecote Press, 1998, 2018.

Headley, Gwyn & Meulenkamp, Wim, *Follies, Grottoes and Garden Buildings,* Aurum Press, 1986, 1999.

Hill, Christopher, *The World Turned Upside Down, Radical Ideas in the English Revolution,* Maurice Temple, 1972, Penguin Books, 1975.

Hinton, David A., *Discover Dorset, Saxons and Vikings*, The Dovecote Press, 1998.

Hodgson, Louise, *Secret Places of West Dorset*, Roving Press, 2011.

Holt, Jonathan, *Discover Dorset, Follies*, The Dovecote Press, 2000.

Hoskins, W.G., *The Making of the English Landscape*, Hodder and Stoughton, 1955, Little Toller Books, 2013.

Household, Geoffrey, *Rogue Male*, Chatto and Windus, 1939, Orion Books, 2013.

James, Jude, *Discover Dorset, The Victorians*, The Dovecote Press, 1998.

Jenkins, Simon, *England's Thousand Best Churches*, Allen Lane, 1999, Penguin Books, 2000.

Jarman, Derek, *Dancing Ledge*, Quartet, 1984, Vintage, 2002.

Jarman, Derek, *Modern Nature*, Century, 1991, Vintage, 2018.

Ingrams, Richard & Piper, John, *Piper's Places: John Piper in England and Wales*, Chatto and Windus, 1983.

Lees-Milne, James, *William Beckford*, Compton Russell, 1976, Century, 1990.

Light, Vivienne, *Circles and Tangents, Art in the Shadow of Cranborne Chase*, Canterton Books, 2011.

Lloyd, David, *Around Gillingham*, Nonsuch Publishing Ltd, 1998, new edition, 2006.

Lloyd, David, *Gillingham Through Time*, Amberley Publishing, 2014.

Mabey, Richard, *Flora Britannica*, Sinclair Stevenson 1996, Chatto and Windus, 1997.

Macfarlane, Robert, Donwood, Stanley, Richards, Dan, *Holloway*, Quive-Smith Editions, 2012, Faber and Faber, 2013.

Mackellar, Landis & Hart, Bradley, *Captain George Henry Lane-Fox Pitt-Rivers and the origins of the IUSSP*, California State University, 2014.

McCall, Fiona, *Church and People in Interregnum Britain*, University of London Press, 2021.

Marwick, Arthur (general editor), *Illustrated Dictionary of British History*, Thames and Hudson, 1980.

Matthews, Rupert, *Haunted Places of Dorset: On the Trail of the Supernatural*, Countryside Books, 2006.

Mee, Arthur, *The King's England, Dorset*, Hodder and Stoughton, 1939, revised 1967.

Mendelson, Charlotte, *Almost English*, Mantle, 2013.

Mercer, Roger, *Hambledon Hill, an Overview of its Past* (online resource, linked to Shroton Parish Council website).

Morris, Richard, *Churches in the Landscape*, J.M. Dent and Sons, 1989.

Morris, Stuart, *Discover Dorset: Portland*, The Dovecote Press, 1998.

Moutray Read, D.H., *Highways and Byways in Hampshire*, Macmillan and Co, 1908, 1928.

Mwyn, Rhys, *Real Gwynedd*, Seren, 2021.

Myers, A.R., *England in the Late Middle Ages*, Penguin Books, 1952, revised 1976.

Newman, John & Pevsner, Nikolaus, *The Buildings of England, Dorset*, Penguin Books, 1972, Yale Books, 2002.

Newman, Paul, *Lost Gods of Albion, The Chalk Hill-Figures of Britain*, Robert Hale, 1987, Sutton Publishing, 1997.

Ollard, Richard, *Dorset*, Pimlico, 1995.

Rackham, Oliver, *The Ash Tree*, Little Toller Books, 2015.

Pevsner, Nikolaus & Lloyd, David, *The Buildings of England, Hampshire*, Penguin Books, 1967.

Pierce, Hazel, *The Life, Career and Political Significance of Margaret Pole, Countess of Salisbury 1743-1541*, Bangor University, 1997.

Pitt Rivers, Michael, *Dorset, a Shell Guide*, Faber and Faber, 1935, revised 1966.

Porter, John, *Discover Dorset: Towns*, The Dovecote Press, 2008.

Rayner, John, *Hampshire, a Shell Guide*, Faber and Faber, 1937.

Sharpe, J.A., *Crime in Early Modern England 1550-1750*, Longman, 1984.

Stainer, Peter, *Discover Dorset, The Industrial Past*, The Dovecote Press, 1998.

Stonehouse, Ann F., Locke, Tim and Duff, Stephen, *50 Walks in Dorset*, Automobile Association, 2002, 2009.

Symons, A.J.A., *The Quest for Corvo, An Experiment in Biography*, Cassell and Company, 1934, 1955.

Taylor, Christopher, *The Making of the English Landscape: Dorset*, The Dovecote Press, 1970, paperback edition 2004.

Taylor, Marion, *West Bay, a Visual Journey from Bridport Harbour to West Bay*, Studio 6, 2021.

Thomas, Edward, *In Pursuit of Spring*, Thomas Nelson, 1914, Little Toller Books, 2016.

Thurston, Jack, *Lost Lanes West, 36 Glorious Bike Rides in the West Country*, Wild Things, 2018.

Townsend, Hilary, *Discover Dorset, The Blackmore Vale*, The

Dovecote Press, 2004.

Treves, Frederick, *Highways and Byways in Dorset*, Macmillan and Co., 1906, revised 1935.

Vale, V. & Vale, P., *The Parish Book of Cerne Abbas*, Halsgrove, 2000.

Various authors, *Dorset Mysteries*, Bossiney Books, 1989, 1992.

Viner, Linda, *Discover Dorset: Lost Villages*, The Dovecote Press, 2002.

Viner, David, *Discover Dorset, Roads, Tracks and Turnpikes*, The Dovecote Press, 2007.

Weinreb, Ben & Hibbert, Christopher, *The London Encyclopaedia*, Macmillan and Co, 1983

Woodcock, Alex, *King of Dust*, Little Toller Books, 2019.

Wright, Patrick, *The Village That Died for England, Tyneham and the Legend of Churchill's Pledge*, Jonathan Cape, 1995, revised edition Repeater Books, 2021.

Warren, Adrian & Sasitorn, Dae, *England, an Aerial View*, Last Refuge, 2004.

Worsley, Giles, *England's Lost Houses*, Aurum Press, 2002.

Periodicals

Air Power Review, Volume 7, Number 1, April 2004.

Operations Record Book, R.A.F. Station, Tarrant Rushton, 1943-1946.

Romance, Revolution and Reform Issue 1, Baker, Leonard, *West Country Scum: National Politics, Local Ritual and Space in the English South-West, c 1820-1832*. Issue 1 April 2019.

History Workshop Journal, Issue 87, Baker, Leonard, *Human and Animal Trespass as Protest: Space and Continuity in Rural Somerset and Dorset*, 2019.

Websites

BBC

British History Online (including the Inventory of Historical Monuments in Dorset, originally published by HMRC in 1975)

British Listed Buildings

British Newspaper Archive

Caught by the River

Churches Conservation Trust

Clubmen 1645

CPRE Dorset
Cranborne Chase AONB (and *Chalkeboard* blog)
Daily Mail
Daily Telegraph
Dorset Area of Outstanding Natural Beauty
Dorset Echo
Dorset Explorer (explorer.geowessex.com)
Dorset Historic Towns survey (on Dorset Council website)
Dorset History Centre (on Dorset Council website)
Dorset Life
Dorset-Hampshire Airfields
English Heritage
Folly Flaneuse
Friends of Friendless Churches.
Historic England
Historic Hansard
Megalithic Portal
National Archives
National Trust
Natural History Museum
Open Domesday
Oxford Dictionary of National Biography
Poole Images (for Poole Pottery)
Royal Academy
Sara Hudston's blog
Secret Bases
Survey of English Place Names (Nottingham University)
Tess of the Vale
The Clearing (Little Toller Books)
The Guardian
The Independent
The New Yorker
The Tate
The Thomas Hardy Society
This is Alfred
Vision of Britain website (for Celia Fiennes travel diaries).
West Country Voices
Who Owns England?

Music and Recordings
Andy Wilkinson, *Hambledon Hill*
Flanders and Swann, *Slow Train* (1963)
Gordon Haskell, *Hambledon Hill* (1990)
Half Man, Half Biscuit, *Trouble over Bridgwater* (2000)
Hawkeye and Hoe, *Hambledon Hill*
PJ Harvey: *Let England Shake* (2011)
The Yetties, *Dorset is Beautiful*, (1972)
Tim Souster, *Hambledon Hill* (1985)
Vaughan Williams, *Linden Lea* (1902)
Virginia Astley: *From Gardens Where We Feel Secure* (1983)

Films and TV
Abroad Again: Father to the Man (2007)
Blade Runner (1982)
*Far from the Madding Cro*wd (1967 and 2015)
Jubilee (1978)
Lawrence of Arabia (1962)
Old Country, Jack Hargreaves (1984)
The Betjeman Collection: Betjeman Revisited – Sherborne (1962)
The French Lieutenant's Woman (1981)
To Serve Them All My Days (1980)

THE PHOTOGRAPHS

ACKNOWLEDGEMENTS

Writing a book about a county with a rich recorded history presents its own challenges: inevitably I leant on what had gone before, but I was especially grateful for the many friends and collaborators, old and new, who helped me see Dorset in a new light.

Firstly I must thank my patient, encouraging and empathetic editor, Peter Finch. Peter wrote some of the early *Real* books and has edited the remainder, but his enthusiasm remains undimmed. An excellent sign was his proposal that we meet for a walk on a Dorset hillfort, and later go to the pub, made more auspicious by his later writing a poem in which he compared me, for the first and doubtless only time, to Clint Eastwood, riding across a dusty plain. At Seren, Mick Felton, Sarah Johnson, Simon Hicks, Natalia Elliot, and Jamie Hill were careful and expert guides.

My long-time friend Mike Parker (also the author of *Real Powys*) has for many years been an unofficial mentor, without his encouragement I'm sure I would never have written a word. My wonderful colleagues and friends at Little Toller, Gracie Cooper, Adrian Cooper and Graham Shackleton gave much support and listened to me endlessly talking about a book that they weren't even to publish. In the wider Toller family Nick Robins and Martin Maudsley were always on hand with a tip or to point me towards some previously unknown piece of Dorset arcana, and Martin gave a whole day of his time to accompany me in the search for standing stones. David Burnett of the amazing Dovecote Press generously gave me a large selection of books from his library, enriching *Real Dorset* enormously. Dorset is lucky to have David, who has published books on the county for more than forty years.

Many people accompanied me, corporeally or figuratively, on my journeys across Dorset: Jack Thurston, Katherine Barker, Kieron Smith, John Porter, Martin Papworth, the team at Cranborne Chase AONB, Neil Turner and the ancient dog, Joe Hickish, David Fox, Malcolm Anderson, Paul Cheney, Patrick Wright, Tim Dee, David Flockhart, Horatio Clare, Pamela Petro, Simon Moreton, Jeff Young, Alex Woodcock, Baz Nichols, Leonard Baker, Meriel O'Dowd, Haydn Wheeler, Sheila Wiggins, Michelle Mackenzie, Antonia Squire, Sheila Marsh, Sue Strachan, Tom Cox, Virginia Astley, Louisa Adjoa Parker, Ed Roberts, Dickie Straker, Karen Lynch (aka The Folly Flaneuse), Tim and Sue Woolcott, Eileen

Baker, Margaret and John Heap, Alan and Eddie Baker. Museum staff everywhere were enthusiastic and helpful, as were guides at abbeys and churches, tolerant of my sometimes strange requests; special thanks are due to the team at The Dorset History Centre. Local libraries furnished many of the books I used; these vital services are under threat, more than ever, but The Manic Street Preachers were right. Give yourself some power, use a library.

Abridged versions of three pieces previously appeared in *The Guardian*: thanks to Andy Pietrasik for his support and kindness. The essay on Tarrant Rushton was published on the excellent website *Caught by the River*, run by the brilliant Jeff Barrett and Diva Harris of Heavenly Records. The gorgeous map at the front of this book was provided by Catherine Speakman, aka Tess of the Vale – Catherine/Tess knows far more about Dorset than I do – her website has walks and rides across the county combined with local and landscape history.

Lastly, heartfelt gratitude and boundless love to my wife, Helen. Bizarrely tolerant of her husband's Dorset obsession, she happily accompanied me on many of the trips (especially if a beach, a swim, ice cream or lunch might be included) but also was willing to read my words, give much needed guidance and to make appropriate use of the green ink where needed.

THE AUTHOR

Jon Woolcott is a writer and publisher, who has lived in Dorset for fourteen years, and grew up nearby in southern Wiltshire. He currently works for the acclaimed independent publisher, Little Toller, where he also edits *The Clearing*, the online journal for new writing about place and nature. He has been Communications Officer for Cranborne Chase AONB, (straddling Dorset, Wiltshire and Somerset), and held senior marketing and buying roles for Stanfords, Waterstones and Ottakar's. His writing, which often focuses on Dorset, has appeared widely, including for *The Guardian, Caught by the River, The Bookseller, Sightly Foxed, Echtrai Journal* and *History Press*.

INDEX

Other Titles in the series: